Real-Resumes for Teachers

Anne McKinney, Editor

PREP PUBLISHING

FAYETTEVILLE, NC

PREP Publishing
1110½ Hay Street
Fayetteville, NC 28305
(910) 483-6611

Copyright © 2012 by Anne McKinney

Cover design by Chris Pearl

Library of Congress Cataloging-in-Publication Data

Real-resumes for teachers : actual job-winning resumes and cover letters of teachers / Anne McKinney (editor).
      p. cm. -- (Real-resumes series)
   ISBN 978-1475094008; 1475094000
    1. Teachers--Employment 2. Resumes (Employment). 3. Cover letters. I. McKinney, Anne, 1948- II. Series.

  LB1780 .R43 2000
  808' .06665–dc21

                                  00-031384
                                       CIP

Printed in the United States of America

By PREP Publishing

Business and Career Series:

RESUMES AND COVER LETTERS THAT HAVE WORKED

RESUMES AND COVER LETTERS THAT HAVE WORKED FOR MILITARY PROFESSIONALS

GOVERNMENT JOB APPLICATIONS AND FEDERAL RESUMES

COVER LETTERS THAT BLOW DOORS OPEN

LETTERS FOR SPECIAL SITUATIONS

RESUMES AND COVER LETTERS FOR MANAGERS

REAL-RESUMES FOR TEACHERS

REAL-RESUMES FOR STUDENTS

REAL-RESUMES FOR CAREER CHANGERS

REAL-RESUMES FOR SALES

REAL ESSAYS FOR COLLEGE & GRADUATE SCHOOL

Judeo-Christian Ethics Series:

SECOND TIME AROUND

BACK IN TIME

WHAT THE BIBLE SAYS ABOUT...Words that can lead to success and happiness

A GENTLE BREEZE FROM GOSSAMER WINGS

BIBLE STORIES FROM THE OLD TESTAMENT

Fiction:

KIJABE...An African Historical Saga

Table of Contents

A WORD FROM THE EDITOR: ABOUT THE REAL-RESUMES SERIES

Welcome to the Real-Resumes Series. The Real-Resumes Series is a series of books which have been developed based on the experiences of real job hunters and which target specialized fields or types of resumes. As the editor of the series, I have carefully selected resumes and cover letters (with names and other key data disguised, of course) which have been used successfully in real job hunts. That's what we mean by "Real-Resumes." What you see in this book are *real* resumes and cover letters which helped real people get ahead in their careers.

The Real-Resumes Series is based on the work of the country's oldest resume-preparation company known as PREP Resumes. If you would like a free information packet describing the company's resume preparation services, call 910-483-6611 or write to PREP at 1110½ Hay Street, Fayetteville, NC 28305. If you have a job hunting experience you would like to share with our staff at the Real-Resumes Series, please contact us at preppub@aol.com or visit our website at http://www.prep-pub.com.

The resumes and cover letters in this book are designed to be of most value to people already in teaching, to people who want to be in a teaching career, and to people who have been in teaching but want to make a career change. If we could give you one word of advice about your career, here's what we would say: Manage your career and don't stumble from job to job in an incoherent pattern. Try to find work that interests you, and then identify prosperous industries which need work performed of the type you want to do. Learn early in your working life that a great resume and cover letter can blow doors open for you and help you maximize your salary.

This book is dedicated to the teachers who have the power to shape our beliefs and instill knowledge. It is hoped that this book will help you achieve your career goal, whether you want to stay in teaching, get noticed and get ahead in teaching, or get out of teaching.

Real-Resumes for Teachers may be the only book about resumes, cover letters, and job hunting which teachers will ever need. This book contains helpful advice for individuals launching a career in teaching, advancing in the teaching field, seeking a federal government teaching job, and finding a second career after some teaching experience.

"A Picture Is Worth a Thousand Words."
As a way of illustrating how important the cover letter can be, we have chosen to show you on the next two pages the cover letter and resume of a young person seeking her first job in the teaching field. If the employer received only her resume without a cover letter, this promising young teacher would look like a cook and restaurant worker! A busy principal would probably not be motivated to dial her telephone number to suggest an interview time. In her case, the cover letter is probably more important than the resume she has been asked to submit. What the cover letter allows her to do is to explain that she worked as a cook, closing manager, and cashier full time while going back to school to earn her college degree. This puts her work experience in a different perspective. The cover letter is the critical ingredient in a job hunt such as Marcia Vivero's because the cover letter allows her to say a lot of things that just don't "fit" on the resume. For example, she can emphasize her commitment to the teaching profession and stress her talent for teaching mathematics to people who find the subject difficult. One of the things that sets her apart from other new graduates in her field is that she is a mature professional who, at age 27, is accustomed to a demanding work schedule. She's no "old lady" but she is five years older and wiser than the typical 22-year-old college graduate. In the high-stress profession which high school teaching is often considered to be, many principals will perceive of her age and experience as a positive factor. Although the general rule is that women do not mention how many children they have in their resume and cover letter, there are exceptions to every rule, and Ms. Vivero breaks that rule for a good reason. She points out that she is a mother and would bring to the classroom an in-depth understanding of different learning styles. Finally, the cover letter gives her a chance to stress the outstanding character and personal values which she feels will be a positive influence on the high school students to whom she wishes to teach mathematics.

Get Your Resume and Cover Letter to the Principal.
Getting your resume and cover letter to the right person in a job hunt is a critical part of a successful job campaign. If you are like Ms. Vivero on the following pages, you need to submit your resume and cover letter to a central location, but you also need to send your resume and cover letter selectively to principals at the schools where you most would like to work. You will see on the next two pages that the cover letter gives you a chance to "get personal" with the person to whom you are writing whereas the resume is a more formal document. Even if a cover letter is not requested, we believe that it is *always* in your best interest to send a cover letter with your resume. The aim of this book is to show you examples of resumes and cover letters designed to blow doors open so that you can develop your own cover letters and increase the number of interviews you have and opportunities you create. In subsequent pages, you will read advice about formatting your cover letters.

Date

Exact Name of Principal
Exact Title
School Name
School Address
City, State Zip

**New graduate
seeking her first job
in the teaching field**

Although this cover
letter has a very
"personal" tone, it has
been written so that Ms.
Vivero can send it to
principals at all the high
schools in her area. If
there is a school where
she particularly wants
to work, she would be
wise to get the exact
name of the principal
so she can address the
letter to him or her by
name and title.
Otherwise, she can
duplicate this "Dear Sir
or Madam" letter, date
and sign it, and send it
to principals at the
schools where she
might want to seek
employment.

Dear Exact Name: (or Dear Principal if you don't know the Exact Name)

With the enclosed resume, I would like to introduce myself and initiate the process of being considered for a position as a Mathematics Teacher in your high school.

As you will see from my resume, I recently graduated from the University of Rhode Island with a B.S. degree in Mathematics which I earned **magna cum laude**. I am especially proud of graduating with honors since I was combining a rigorous academic curriculum with a demanding work schedule which involved handling a variety of managerial, accounting, and customer service responsibilities.

Although I graduated in May 2000 with my B.S. degree, I am 27 years old and offer considerable experience in working with children of all ages. Since I am a wife and mother, I would bring to the classroom much understanding of the varying learning styles of children. I feel I would be skilled in classroom behavior management, and I would offer a maturity which younger college graduates might not have. I am a responsible individual known for my well-organized work habits and disciplined style.

I am deeply committed to a career in the teaching profession, and I intend in my spare time to earn my Master's degree in Mathematics and then a Ph.D. I am a highly motivated hard worker, and I feel my own strong values could be an inspiration to high school students. Although I have earned my degree in Mathematics with high honors, I am fully aware of how difficult mathematics is for many people, and I excel in translating abstract concepts into understandable language.

If you can use a vibrant young teaching professional who could enhance the fine reputation of your school, I hope you will contact me to suggest a time when I could make myself available for a personal interview. I can provide outstanding personal and professional references.

Sincerely,

Marcia Vivero

MARCIA VIVERO

1110½ Hay Street, Providence, RI 28305 • (910) 483-6611 • preppub@aol.com

---

OBJECTIVE   To contribute to a high school that can use a dedicated mathematics teacher who is attuned to the varied learning abilities and styles which students bring to the classroom.

EDUCATION   Earned B.S. degree in **Mathematics,** University of Rhode Island, Providence, RI, May 2000.
- Graduated **Magna Cum Laude** with a GPA of 3.754.
- Received the Certificate of Excellence and was named to the Chancellor's List.
- Excelled academically while working part-time to finance my college education.

Graduated from Eastern Senior High School, Pawtucket, RI, 1992.
- Participated in track and intramural sports.

EXPERIENCE   **CLOSING MANAGER, COOK, CASHIER.** Chuck's Chicken & Barbecue, Providence, RI (1993-present).
- Was singled out to handle a variety of management responsibilities, and became known for my trustworthiness and cheerful disposition while simultaneously earning my college degree **with honors.**
- Refined my interpersonal skills working with all types of customers and with other employees.
- Trained other employees; assigned tasks to junior employees and supervised their work.
- Expertly operated a cash register, and was known for my accuracy in handling large amounts of cash; trained other employees to use the register.
- As Closing Manager, was responsible for closing the store at the end of the business day; accounted for financial transactions and oversaw end-of-the-day maintenance and security matters.
- Was frequently commended for my gracious style of dealing with the public and for my courteous approach to customer service.

COMPUTER OPERATOR/CLERICAL AIDE. Clear Lake Elementary School, Pawtucket, RI (summer 1992).
- In the summer after my high school graduation, excelled in an office position handling numerous responsibilities related to record keeping for students in summer school.
- Operated a computer in order to input data and maintain records.
- Filed and typed as needed.
- Was known for my attention to detail and accuracy when handling large volumes of work under tight deadlines.

PERSONAL   Have aspirations to earn my Master's degree in Mathematics, and believe I could be a great asset to the teaching profession. Can provide outstanding references. Have taught in Bible School Programs. Believe all students can learn, and am skilled at communicating difficult mathematics concepts to students who find math difficult.

Addressing the Cover Letter: Get the exact name of the person to whom you are writing. She could address the letter to all high school principals in her area.

First Paragraph: The first paragraph explains why you are writing.

Second Paragraph: Here you have a chance to talk about your most distinguishing feature.

Third Paragraph: In the third paragraph, you can bring up your next most distinguishing qualities. Sell yourself!

Fourth Paragraph: Here you have another opportunity to reveal qualities or achievements which will impress your future employer.

Final Paragraph: She asks the employer to contact her. Make sure your reader knows what the "next step" is.

Alternate Final Paragraph: It's more aggressive (but not too aggressive) to let the employer know that you will be calling him or her. Don't be afraid to be persistent. Employers are looking for people who know what they want to do.

Date

Exact Name of Person
Exact Title of Person
Company Name
Address
City, State Zip

Dear Sir or Madam:

   With the enclosed resume, I would like to make you aware of my strong desire to become a part of your elementary teaching staff. ·

   As you will see from my resume, I recently earned my Bachelor of Science in Education (B.S.E.) degree at the University of Georgia. Since it has always been my childhood dream to become a teacher, my college graduation was an especially meaningful event in my life.

   As you will see from my resume, I recently completed a teaching internship as a first grade student teacher, and I successfully assumed all the duties of a first grade teacher. During those two months, under the guidance of an experienced educator, I wrote and completed my own professional growth and development plan, and I also planned and implemented a classroom and behavior management program.

   In my previous two-month internship as a kindergarten student teacher, I performed with distinction in planning and implementing creative lessons, communicating with teaching professionals and parents, and working with the children. You will notice from my resume that I have expressed my true love for children through my summer and part-time jobs while in college. For four years, I was a nanny for a professional family and in that capacity I cared for three triplet newborns as well as two older children. It is an understatement to say that I refined my time management skills in that part-time job!

   If you can use a highly motivated young professional with unlimited personal initiative as well as strong personal qualities of dependability and trustworthiness, I hope you will contact me to suggest a time when we might meet to discuss your needs. I can provide excellent personal and professional references, and I am eager to apply my strong teaching skills and true love for children in an academic institution which emphasizes hard work and a commitment to the highest learning goals.

   Sincerely,

   Melanie Thompson

Alternate final paragraph:
   I hope you will welcome my call soon when I contact you to try to arrange a brief meeting to discuss your needs and how my talents might help you. I appreciate whatever time you could give me in the process of exploring your needs.

Date

Three blank spaces

Address

Salutation
One blank space

Body

One blank space

Signature

cc: Indicates you are
sending a copy of the
letter to someone

Exact Name of Person
Title or Position
Name of Company
Address (number and street)
Address (city, state, and zip)

Dear Exact Name of Person: (or Dear Sir or Madam if answering a blind ad)

I would appreciate an opportunity to talk with you soon about how I could contribute to your school through my outstanding communication skills as well as through my desire to make a significant contribution to the teaching profession.

You will see from my resume that I began working with Revco when I was 16 years old; I continued my employment with Revco while attending college and was promoted to Shift Manager while earning my Bachelor of Social Studies degree. Although the company strongly encouraged me to enter its management trainee program upon college graduation, I remain steadfastly loyal to my goal of becoming a teaching professional. Through my extensive work experience, I have developed highly refined time management skills which could be valuable in the process of managing a classroom and creating efficient lesson plans.

In my senior year, I worked in a Teaching Internship with the Frederick Douglass Middle School in Albany, NY. I earned the confidence of an experienced teacher who came to rely upon me for my initiative and creativity in handling student problems, implementing complex lesson plans, and interfacing with parents on her behalf when she was involved in staff development activities.

I have recently relocated permanently to the LaFayette area because I married and my husband owns and manages his own business in this area. I am eager to establish my teaching career in the LaFayette School System, and I am confident that I will be an asset to the teaching profession and to the community.

If you can use a self-starter who could rapidly become a valuable member of your teaching staff, I hope you will contact me to suggest a time when we might meet to discuss your needs and how I might serve them. I can provide excellent personal and professional references.

Sincerely,

Louise Patton

cc: Thomas Crane

HOW TO USE THIS BOOK
TO YOUR MAXIMUM ADVANTAGE

How to use this book...

By deliberate design, this book has been developed as a manageable size so that its reader will have time to look over all of the resumes and cover letters. Visit the Table of Contents and you will find teachers in varying career situations. But regardless of the type of position you hold or are seeking in the teaching field, you can learn something from every resume in this book.

- **Getting into teaching? Part One** will interest you if you are seeking to establish your first or second career in teaching. The resumes and cover letters on pages 7-27 will be of the most value.
- **Getting into federal teaching jobs or the civil service system? Part Two** on pages 28-35 which will show you how to prepare a specialized application called an OF 612 or a specialized resume for a federal government job.
- **Getting ahead--and getting noticed--in teaching?** You may be on the "fast track" in teaching and are seeking guidance on how to prepare specialized materials such as "Teacher of the Year" packets or essays for acceptance into a graduate school. **Part Three** on pages 36-67 will give you some ideas about how to answer challenging essay questions for purposes which range from applying to a Ph.D. or Master's program, to applying for special honors or awards which require you to present yourself in essay form.
- **Real-Resumes for teachers** begin on page 69, and **Part Four** is the main part of the book. You may find your "look-a-like" in this section if you are, for example, a teacher who is also a varsity coach, a counselor, an aspiring assistant principal, a superintendent, a military science instructor, a college professor, or many other types of educators.
- **Curriculum vitae?** Yes, in Part Four you can find curriculum vitae on pages 92-103.
- **Getting out of teaching?** In **Part Five** on pages 149-177 you will resumes and cover letters of individuals seeking a new career after some teaching experience.

Learn from other teachers...

In conclusion, read as many resumes and cover letters in this book as you can. You can learn something from every resume and cover letter in this book. And we sincerely hope you do.

In this section, you will find resumes and cover letters of people embarking on a first or second career in the teaching field.

Launching a career in teaching requires a resume that "sells" you.
This is not just a slogan in a book. If you are launching a career in a new field, your resume and cover letter must be more original and creative than the resume and cover letter of experienced professionals because you are selling "potential." Part One contains resumes and cover letters of individuals who have little or no teaching experience, except perhaps student teaching experience. All the resumes are one page, and all are accompanied by a cover letter. This section will be especially helpful to those who want to get into teaching.

Even in an employment market where there are numerous opportunities, launching a new career takes brainwork.

Getting Into Teaching

Exact Name of Person
Exact Title
Exact Name of Company
Address
City, State, Zip

Biology Teaching

Dear Exact Name of Person: (or Dear Sir or Madam if answering a blind ad):

A great cover letter helps someone "get to know you." Notice that this cover letter is personal and revealing. She helps the reader gain insight into why she chose Biology Teaching as a field, and she reveals some of her strong personal qualities. Remember this in a cover letter: You're not interviewing for the job yet, you're simply trying to come across as someone who would be nice to meet.

With the enclosed resume, I would like to make you aware of my interest in teaching biology at your school. I have earned my B.S. in Biology Teaching and recently completed a highly successful student teaching assignment at a high school in Wyeth, GA. I was commended by the teacher who supervised me for my exceptional creativity and for my willingness to tackle and follow through on difficult assignments.

My interest in teaching biology developed while I was serving my country in the U.S. Army, where I was trained as a Laboratory Technician. In order to gauge the depth of my interest in the field, I became a Volunteer with the Red Cross at an Army hospital. When I decided to leave military service and enter the civilian work force, I explored opportunities for earning my Biology Teaching degree and I chose Bainbridge College. You will notice from my resume that I worked nearly 30 hours a week in a demanding job throughout my college career.

Because I am slightly older than the average college graduate, I feel I have a degree of maturity which could be most beneficial in a high school classroom. Since I was myself the first person in my family to graduate from college, I am confident that I could be a powerful motivator to youth who are unsure of their goals in life. I am a highly motivated individual and I believe in leading by example.

If you can use a well-trained individual who offers outstanding communication skills along with a proven ability to work well with others, I hope you will contact me to suggest a time when we might meet to discuss your goals. I can provide outstanding references at the appropriate time.

Sincerely,

Janet McCue

JANET McCUE
1110½ Hay Street, Fayetteville, NC 28305 • preppub@aol.com • (910) 483-6611

OBJECTIVE
To offer my strong desire to teach and work with young people by applying my degree in the science field as well as my creativity, motivational skills, knowledge of computer operations, and practical experience with a variety of laboratory procedures.

EDUCATION
Bachelor of Science, Biology Teaching, Bainbridge College, Bainbridge, GA, 2000.
- Named to the Chancellor's List in recognition of academic achievements in maintaining a GPA of 3.8 or higher.
- Excelled in specialized coursework including:

methods of teaching	analytical chemistry	histology
anatomy and physiology	medical terminology	biochemistry
probability and statistics	human development	Spanish
computers in education — emphasis on Lotus 1-2-3, Word, Report Card		

- Held membership in the Science Club.

EXPERIENCE
STUDENT TEACHER. Georgia Board of Education, Wyeth, GA (2000). Instructed a diverse student population at Wyeth High School while teaching Biology I and Biology II to ninth through 12th grade students.
- Applied active learning techniques while motivating students to participate in class activities and open themselves to learning.
- Implemented positive classroom management strategies to encourage proper behavior and respect for others.
- Utilized planning and organizational skills in carrying out classroom support activities including completing interesting and thorough lesson plans as well as preparing test materials and monitoring testing.
- Earned the teacher's respect for my true concern for the students, willingness to tackle hard assignments, and ability to follow through on any project.
- Displayed creativity and initiative in the development of informative bulletin boards.

CASHIER. Taco Bell, Bainbridge, GA (1997-2000). Refined time management skills and displayed a high level of self-motivation while working 30 hours a week.
- Known for my dedication to providing high quality customer service, was entrusted with training new employees and setting an example for them to follow.

LABORATORY ASSISTANT. The American Red Cross, Germany (1995-96). As a volunteer in the chemistry department lab of a U.S. Army hospital in Germany, logged in and separated blood specimens and then ran them through the SMA-18 machine which analyzed specimens for 18 separate chemical tests.
- Assisted in drawing blood from patients and doing electrolyte testing.

Highlights of earlier experience as a LABORATORY TECHNICIAN, U.S. Army:
- Processed urine specimens for military personnel throughout the Pacific while screening for illegal substances including heroin, cocaine, barbiturates, and amphetamines.
- Conducted drug screening procedures at a facility which supported Army, Navy, and Air Force personnel based in the Philippines, Japan, Korea, and Hawaii.
- Assisted a doctor doing research on high blood pressure and the effects of high altitude.

PERSONAL
Am an open water-certified SCUBA diver; received Red Cross certification in CPR and life-saving techniques. Offer empathy for the problems and tough choices facing young people.

Getting Into Teaching

Date

Exact Name of Person
Exact Title
Exact Name of Company
Address
City, State, Zip

Communications Graduate

Dear Exact Name of Person: (or Dear Sir or Madam if answering a blind ad):

Communications Graduate

Throughout his life, this young fellow has imagined himself as a part of the teaching profession. He points out that he believes his strong interpersonal and communication skills would be a credit to teaching.

With the enclosed resume, I would like to make you aware of my desire to explore employment opportunities with your organization. I am completing my Bachelor of Science degree in Communications from Winona State University and feel I have much to offer your school system.

As you will see from my resume, I have worked up to 30 hours a week during college in jobs which provided me an opportunity to partially finance my college education. In one job as a Waiter I enjoyed working as a part of a small team committed to delivering top-notch customer service. I simultaneously worked in another job as a Sales Representative.

You will also notice from my resume that I worked every summer during college as a Counselor and then as Activities Manager for a church camp. I became a respected role model not only for young campers but also for other counselors and program staff. It was during those years that I developed a strong desire to become a part of the teaching profession because I feel I can be effective in training and molding youth.

I offer strong communication and interpersonal skills. In college, I utilized those skills while serving my fraternity in numerous capacities which involved acting as a spokesman and serving as an organizer and manager of special events. I possess a gift for motivating and leading others which I believe could be powerful assets in a classroom environment.

If you can use a dedicated young professional with a strong desire to excel in all I do, I hope you will contact me to suggest a time when we can meet to discuss your needs. I can provide excellent personal and professional references.

Sincerely,

James LaHaye

JAMES LaHAYE

1110½ Hay Street, Fayetteville, NC 28305 • preppub@aol.com • (910) 483-6611

OBJECTIVE   I want to contribute to an organization that can use an outgoing young professional who offers strong communication skills and proven classroom management potential along with a desire to instill in youth a love of learning and a desire to become productive citizens.

EDUCATION   **Bachelor of Science in Communications,** Winona State University, Winona, MN, 2000; major was in Applied Communications and minor was in General Business.
- Have been active as a campus leader and in intramural sports.
- Served as **Social Chairman,** Delta Zappa Fraternity, 1998-99; and as **Communications Chairman,** 1999-2000. Was selected by the President for these positions because of my outstanding organizational and management skills. Managed numerous projects which involved managing a budget and planning events for hundreds of people.
- Functioned as **Captain** of the intramural championship soccer team, 1999-2000.
- Was nominated as **Homecoming King** by Delta Zappa Fraternity, 2000.
- Was named Interfraternity Council (IFC) Representative, 1997-98.

Graduated from Winona High School, MN, 1996.
- On the varsity soccer team, lettered in the sport and was named **All-Conference.**
- Was named **Captain** of the varsity soccer team in my senior year.
- Lettered in baseball in my junior and senior years.

COMPUTERS   Windows operating systems and Microsoft Word, Works, Excel.

EXPERIENCE   **WAITER.** Winona Inn, Winona, MN (1999-present). Work up to 30 hours weekly in order to partially finance my college education while completing my Bachelor's degree.
- Have become known for my reliability and excellent customer service skills.
- Have learned to work effectively as part of a small team committed to delivering top-notch customer service and quality food service.
- Also work as a **Sales Representative** and **Landscape Assistant** for a landscaping company; have become known for my strong sales skills as well as my creativity in solving landscaping problems and implementing effective designs.

Was promoted in the following track record of advancement by Camp Knowles, Highstead, MN, during my summer employment over four consecutive summers: Summers, 1998 and 1999: ACTIVITIES MANAGER. Was promoted to this job as a member of the program staff; continuously developed and implemented ideas for new programs in order to stimulate campers while strengthening their social and physical skills.
- Became skilled in leading large groups of people and in developing programs which appealed to different age groups ranging from elementary, to junior high, to senior high.
- Planned the camp's daily sports program which included kickball, three ball, volleyball, soccer, and numerous "made-up" games.
- On my own initiative, built new soccer goals which greatly enhanced the enjoyment of this sport.
Summers, 1996 and 1997: COUNSELOR. Excelled in leading ten one-week sessions of camp for elementary school children, junior high campers, senior high campers, and handicapped campers; became a respected part of the counseling staff, and was a role model not only to young campers but also to other counselors.

PERSONAL   Am an effective communicator and naturally outgoing individual. References upon request.

Getting Into Teaching

Date

Exact Name of Person
Exact Title
Exact Name of Company
Address
City, State, Zip

Education Major

Dear Exact Name of Person (or Dear Sir or Madam if answering a blind ad):

This young professional emphasizes her excellent work in her recent student teaching assignment in order to interest principals in her potential for contributing to the teaching profession. Although the editor of this book personally likes resumes which contain an Objective section, here is a resume which does not have an Objective.

With this cover letter and enclosed resume, I would like to initiate the process of receiving consideration for a teaching position with your school.

You will see from the enclosed resume that I received my B.A. in Education from Ohio University, Athens, OH. An honor graduate, I maintained a GPA of 3.8 or higher while majoring in English. Specialized course work I completed included English literature and composition, public speaking, speech communications, adolescent developmental psychology, and adolescent education.

As a Student Teacher at the high school level, I instructed a diverse student population of ninth grade general and academically gifted students. During this learning period, I earned the respect of the regular classroom teacher for my true concern for the students and ability to stimulate interest in reading comprehension and literary analysis. I took the creative approach of correlating themes in classical poetry and drama with real and hypothetical contemporary situations which allowed the students to participate in lively classroom discussions.

If you can use an enthusiastic, articulate, and caring young professional who quickly masters new procedures and excels in passing that knowledge on to others, I hope you will call me soon. I can provide excellent professional and personal references at the appropriate time. I can assure you that I could quickly become a valuable part of your school's team and the efforts to provide a safe and caring atmosphere where students can grow and learn.

Sincerely,

Eleanor G. Powers

ELEANOR G. POWERS

1110½ Hay Street, Fayetteville, NC 28305   ·   preppub@aol.com   ·   (910) 483-6611

EDUCATION

Earned a ***Bachelor of Arts in Education***, Ohio University, Athens, OH, 2001; maintained a 3.38 GPA in major while majoring in English. Courses included:

English literature and composition   speech communications

public speaking   adolescent education

adolescent developmental psychology

Pratt High School, Columbus, OH.
Earned a diploma in June 1997 while accomplishing the following honors:
- Academic Advanced Placement in English and Calculus
- Academic Honors all terms
- Named Ohio Scholar
- Awarded State Scholar-Athlete honors
- Graduated third in class

TEACHING EXPERIENCE

Student Teacher.
Schneider High School, Columbus, OH. Fall 2000.
Taught ninth-grade general and academically gifted students. Stimulated interest in reading comprehension and literary analysis by correlating themes in classical poetry and drama with contemporary situations, both real and hypothetical.

EXPERIENCE

Wait Staff Manager. Red Lobster, Columbus, OH. August 1999-current.
Skilled in handling numerous responsibilities which include Wait Staff Manager (Assistant Front-of-the-House Manager). Supervise scheduling and training for new employees. Provide top-quality customer service and prepare nightly deposits for a high-volume restaurant.

Counselor. Americaworks, Zanesville, OH. Summer 2000.
Initiated job searching skills and strategies in alternative vocations for clients with job-related injuries and followed up with intense job coaching in successful placements.

Waitperson, Saloon Keeper, and Administrative Assistant. Max and Erma's, Newark, OH. Summers 1998-2000.
In a job simultaneous with the one above, greeted and served guests, maintained and recorded liquor and beer inventory, collected servers' sales, and prepared nightly deposits for this busy restaurant chain.

Nanny. Columbus, OH. Summer 1998.
Provided overnight and weekly basic care for a two-year-old toddler.

Summers 1996-97:
Various part-time positions in retail sales, clerical, data processing, and customer service.

SPECIAL SKILLS

Typing: 55 wpm
Word processing: 65 wpm
Computers: Lotus 1-2-3, Microsoft Word, Microsoft Excel, Windows, WordPerfect.

PERSONAL

Enjoy reading and jogging. Avid sports fan. Participate in charitable events including the local Heartwalk and Special Olympics. Excellent references.

Date

Rene Acosta
Principal
Central Middle School
1616 Ireland Drive
Port Huron, MI 48060

**English and Media
Journalism**

A background in sales
may not seem the best
for teaching, but this
young professional is
aware of the shortage
of teachers and has
developed a strong
desire to enter the
teaching profession.
She has been very
active in college, and
much of the Experience
section on her resume
showcases her
leadership ability and
involvements in
organizations.

Dear Sir or Madam:

With the enclosed resume, I would like to initiate the process of formally applying for a lateral-entry teaching position in your school system.

You will see from my resume that I hold a BA degree in English and Media Journalism and was named to the Dean's List for academic achievements. In a part-time job as a reporter with the *Times Herald*, I am utilizing my strong writing and editing skills but I feel I would be best suited to a situation in which I could teach skills and concepts in English, language arts, and journalism to middle school or high school students. As a means of partially financing my college education, I tutored students throughout my college career. I am a seasoned public speaker and offer a proven ability to enthusiastically and articulately present academic material in well-developed lesson plans.

Since my professional goal is now to embark upon public school teaching as a career, I would intend to pursue coursework which would lead to formal teaching certification.

As a high school student, I was known as one of the area's outstanding young leaders and was elected president of the Port Huron Northern High School student body. I was also active in student government when I went to college. I enjoy working with youth, and you will see from my resume that I have volunteered my time as a young adult to Big Sister programs, Special Olympics planning committees, and teen organizations. I am confident that I could become a strong positive role model for youth, and I am positive I could help youth grow in academic excellence, social maturity, professional skills, and emotional well being.

Please consider me for any lateral-teaching position you may have in the English, language arts, journalism, or social studies area, and I would be very happy to learn what would be the next step for me to take in formally pursuing a teaching position for the next calendar year.

Sincerely yours,

Sybil Dawes

SYBIL DAWES
1110½ Hay Street, Fayetteville, NC 28305 • preppub@aol.com • (910) 483-6611

OBJECTIVE	To contribute to an organization through my strong communication skills as well as through my creativity, intelligence, and interpersonal relations skills.
EDUCATION	Earned a **Bachelor of Arts (B.A.) degree in English and Media Journalism,** Austin College, Sherman, TX, 2001.

* Excelled in specialized course work such as:

Introduction to Public Relations	Editing and Writing
Writing for Radio and Television	Article and Feature Writing

* Was named to the Dean's List for my academic achievements.

EXPERIENCE

SALES ASSOCIATE. Belk Leggett, Sherman, TX (1998-present). In this part-time job used to finance my college education, gained a strong base of experience in retail sales and support activities for this major regional department store while also taking care of stocking and customer service.

* Selected to attend regular marketing department seminars, added practical knowledge of marketing techniques to expand on what I had learned in college.
* Applied my enthusiastic and energetic personality while contributing to the creation of a good working atmosphere among my colleagues as well as with the public.
* In a simultaneous part-time job as a **REPORTER** with the *Times Herald,* am refining my writing and editing skills.

Refined my time management skills attending college full time while participating in numerous community service and volunteer activities:

COMMITTEE MEMBER. Delta Sigma Theta Sorority, Inc., Sherman, TX (1999-present). Participate in activities designed to promote economic, educational, and political growth as well as international awareness and physical/mental health among community members.

* Played a key role in planning, organizing, and carrying out the first Special Olympics Games hosted by the university.

"BIG SISTER" PROGRAM VOLUNTEER. Project LIFE, Powell Elementary School, Sherman, TX (1997-99). Provided an 11-year-old girl with one-on-one attention and a positive role model by helping her learn better study habits and build confidence and self-esteem.

STUDENT GOVERNMENT MEMBER. Student Government Association, Austin College, Sherman, TX (1997-00). Represented the freshman class during activities which included organizing fund raising events, social events, and class trips while working as a team player within the student government association.

* Learned how to conduct contract negotiations following university policy.
* Was instrumental in planning the first freshman class trip in eight years.

Highlights of other experience: Earned several awards for community involvement and leadership in high school activities: received a $1,000 academic scholarship along with recognition by such groups as the Kiwanis Club and Parks and Recreation Department.

* Was Student Body President at Port Huron Northern High School, Port Huron, MI.

COMPUTERS	Am experienced in using MS Word for word processing applications.
PERSONAL	Am a creative individual with a positive attitude. Offer a high level of energy and enthusiasm.

Getting Into Teaching

Date

Exact Name of Person
Exact Title
Exact Name of Company
Address
City, State, Zip

English Degree

Don't worry about how a job like "driver" will look on your resume. Prospective employers know that it is honest work, and they admire an individual who had to work to put herself through school.

Dear Exact Name of Person: (or Dear Sir or Madam if answering a blind ad):

With the enclosed resume, I would like to introduce you to my educational background and versatile experience as well as to express my interest in receiving consideration for a teaching position in your school system.

As you will see from my resume, I received my B.A. in English from Alverno College in 2001. While attending college, I continued to refine my time management and organizational skills while also working and holding volunteer positions. Presently polishing my communication skills in a fast-paced food service environment, I have become known for my ability to deal with customers and co-workers while completing twice the normal number of deliveries in a shift.

One of my proudest accomplishments was a tutoring project involving a fourth grade student. The student had been diagnosed with Attention Deficit Disorder (ADD) and was struggling to maintain a D average in school. I provided him with the guidance and motivation which allowed him to increase two full letter grades to a B average. In addition to preparing lesson plans, I also oversaw him as he completed assigned schoolwork and helped him prepare for tests to be taken in his regular classroom.

While in college, I also served as a radio news reader providing services for the blind. I read selected news articles and other materials to the listening audience and was known for my ability to speak clearly and plainly so that listeners could understand what was being read on the air. I am confident that through my reputation as an articulate and intelligent young professional, I have refined the skills and knowledge which would allow me to be effective in the classroom. With a degree in English and my strong interest in reading literature, history, and philosophy, I believe I would be most effective as an English teacher at the secondary school level.

If you can use an adaptable young professional who can handle pressure and deadlines and who is known for high levels of drive and initiative, I hope you will welcome my call soon when I try to arrange a brief meeting to discuss your goals and how my background might serve your needs. I can provide outstanding references at the appropriate time.

Sincerely,

Robyn Smith

ROBYN SMITH

1110½ Hay Street, Fayetteville, NC 28305 • preppub@aol.com • (910) 483-6611

OBJECTIVE	To contribute to a school system that can use an articulate and mature young professional who can offer a background of experience in positions requiring keen analytical skills, planning and organizational abilities, and a talent for instructing and educating others.
EDUCATION	**Bachelor of Arts (B.A.) degree in English**, Alverno College, Milwaukee, WI, 2001. • Spent two summers abroad studying Literature.
COMPUTER KNOWLEDGE	Offer extensive knowledge of automated systems using Windows, Word, WordPerfect, and Lotus 1-2-3 using Macintosh and IBM-compatible PCs.
EXPERIENCE	*Developed excellent time management skills while attending college, volunteering, and working to help finance my education in jobs which have included the following:* **CUSTOMER SERVICE SPECIALIST** and **DRIVER.** Domino's Pizza, Milwaukee, WI (1998-present). Gained and am refining a variety of skills in dealing with the public and co-workers while becoming known for my ability to prioritize tasks and deal with pressure and deadlines in a fast-paced environment. • Completed twice the normal number of deliveries for the same time period through well-refined time management skills. • Am known for my ability to deal with customers in a helpful and pleasant manner while taking phone orders accurately on a multiline phone system. • Have become skilled in using computers and in handling large amounts of cash. **PRIVATE TUTOR.** Milwaukee, WI (1998). Took a fourth grade student who had been making Ds in all school subjects and, through intense personal attention to his abilities and limitations, helped bring his grades up two full letter grades to a B average. • Excelled in motivating a young child diagnosed with ADD (Attention Deficit Disorder) and in finding the methods for helping him learn how to focus and study so that his performance was greatly improved. • Emphasized the improvement of skills in basic reading and arithmetic. • Prepared lesson plans and assigned additional tasks designed to improve educational abilities as well as coping skills and ways to overcome his learning disabilities. **RADIO ON-AIR READER.** S.E.N.C. Radio Reading Service, Alverno College, Milwaukee, WI (1996-98). Provided radio reading services for the blind as a volunteer reading selected news articles and other materials on the air. • Was known for my ability to speak clearly and plainly so that radio listeners could understand the information which was being given to them on the air. • Gained a feeling of pride in my skills and in my ability to be of service to the community. **SALES AND CUSTOMER SERVICE REPRESENTATIVE.** Joe's Pawn Shop, Milwaukee, WI (1995-96). Was cited for my time management and organizational skills while handling multiple duties such as assisting customers with their purchases, completing sales, maintaining stock, and providing security for large amounts of cash. *Highlights of earlier experience:* Became recognized as a mature and skilled young professional while serving in the U.S. Navy.
PERSONAL	Feel that among my greatest strengths are my intelligence and adaptive reasoning skills.

Getting Into Teaching

Date

Exact Name of Person
Title or Position
Name of Company
Address (number and street)
Address (city, state, and zip)

Mathematics

Dear Exact Name of Person: (or Dear Sir or Madam if answering a blind ad.)

Although the job on his resume as Carpenter's Helper has nothing to do with his mathematics degree, school systems will take a positive view of a young man who has worked hard to earn his degree. Even jobs outside the mathematics field can help an individual gain excellent work habits, and the principals and administrators doing the hiring are aware of this as they peruse resumes to identify a pattern of reliability.

I would appreciate an opportunity to talk with you soon about how I could contribute to your school system through my strong desire to teach mathematics at the secondary school level.

You will see by my enclosed resume that, while earning my B.S. in Mathematics, I gained practical experience in summer and part-time positions which included Concrete Technician and Engineering Technician.

I offer well-developed communication skills partially as a result of my eight years of service in the U.S. Army where I was heavily involved in training and supervision of teams of up to nine well-trained people. I also refined my ability to communicate effectively during a period where I tutored students in mathematics at a college learning center where most of my students needed assistance in precalculus or calculus. It was during my military service that I developed a desire to become a member of the teaching profession.

My computer skills include familiarity with Windows and UNIX operating systems with some experience in programming in Pascal. I enjoy technical challenges and learning new theories and mechanics, and I feel confident I could instill a love of learning mathematics in others. From my tutoring experience I am aware that many people are intimidated by the study of mathematics, and I offer a knack for translating complex mathematical concepts into understandable language.

I hope you will welcome my call soon to arrange a brief meeting at your convenience to discuss your current and future needs and how I might serve them. Thank you in advance for your time.

Sincerely yours,

David Callahan

Alternate last paragraph:
I hope you will call or write me soon to suggest a time convenient for us to meet and discuss your current and future needs and how I might serve them. Thank you in advance for your time.

DAVID CALLAHAN

1110½ Hay Street, Fayetteville, NC 28305   •   preppub@aol.com   •   (910) 483-6611

OBJECTIVE   To offer my analytical and mathematical abilities to an organization that can use a technically oriented young professional with a reputation as a team player known for outstanding communication, problem-solving, and planning abilities.

EDUCATION   **Bachelor of Science degree in Mathematics,** Virginia Tech, Blacksburg, VA, 2000.
- Was inducted into Pi Mu Epsilon National Mathematics Honor Society as a math major with a 3.5 GPA.
- Earned departmental honors in mathematics in recognition of my high GPA and completion of a semester of directed study with a presentation made to department faculty.
- Became a member of the Mathematical Association of America (MAA), 1998.

TECHNICAL KNOWLEDGE   Familiar with the Windows and UNIX operating systems and use computer software such as Lotus 1-2-3, dBase, MS Word and WordPerfect; have experience with programming in Pascal.

LANGUAGE   Fluently speak, read, and write Spanish.
- Have traveled extensively throughout Central and South America.

EXPERIENCE   *Gained practical experience and refined my time management skills while juggling the demands of attending college full time and working to help finance my education:*
CARPENTER'S HELPER. Allton Construction, Blacksburg, VA (1999-2000). Earned a reputation as a dependable and trustworthy employee while learning commercial carpentry working on ceilings and dry walls; was rehired in 2000 based on my performance during the summer of 1999.

QUALITY ASSURANCE CLERK. Roadway Package System, Hartwood, VA (Summer, 1998). Polished customer service skills while involved in activities including redirecting packages which had been improperly routed, processing damaged parcels, maintaining various types of records and documentation, and responding to customer complaints and problems.
- Was cited as the driving force behind providing satisfactory quality assurance operations for the first time since the terminal was built.

MATHEMATICS TUTOR. Germanna Community College, Blacksburg, VA (Summer and Fall 1998). Applied my well-developed communication skills and mathematical abilities while helping students experiencing difficulties in subjects such as precalculus and calculus.
- Became adept at explaining technical subject matter concisely and clearly.
- Refined customer service skills while assisting in resource center operations.

ENGINEERING TECHNICIAN. Geowave Materials Testing, Inc., Blacksburg, VA (Summer, 1997). Further enhanced my knowledge of concrete testing and learned soil testing techniques while preparing reports prior to collecting samples.

MILITARY EXPERIENCE: Served my country in the U.S. Army for eight years and was promoted ahead of my peers to management; supervised teams of up to nine people.

PERSONAL   Working knowledge of German. Enjoy reading scientific/technical books on subjects such as quantum mechanics. Like technical challenges and learning new theories .

Getting Into Teaching

Exact Name of Person
Exact Title
Exact Name of Company
Address
City, State, Zip

Music Education Major

This young music teacher emphasizes her musical expertise as well as her work-study experience in college. **Tip:** Here's a tip about when to put your GPA on your resume. Show it off if it is 3.5 or higher. Omit giving your GPA if lower than 3.5.

Dear Exact Name of Person (or Dear Sir or Madam if answering a blind ad):

With the enclosed resume, I would like to make you aware of my background as an educated professional with a degree in Music Education who offers exceptional communication, organizational, and motivational skills.

As you will see, I recently completed my Bachelor of Science program in Music Education, graduating **cum laude** from Florida Southern College. I maintained a cumulative GPA of 3.64 while working part-time and maintaining a heavy schedule of ensemble performances and recitals throughout my collegiate career.

Recently I served as a Student Teacher at Markham Elementary School in Lakeland, Florida, where I excelled at providing instruction to beginning band students in their primary instruments in grades 4-6. In addition, I assisted in a fundraising campaign that generated several thousand dollars to pay for a band trip to New York City, where students performed before the Music Educator's National Conference (MENC) annual convention. I conducted fifth and sixth grade students in the concert band as well as coordinating and preparing students for district band auditions. Prior to this position, I was a Student Teacher at Price Junior/ Senior High School, developing and implementing creative lesson plans for band and general music students which increased the students' knowledge of basic music theory.

In earlier work-study positions, I demonstrated the communication, organizational, planning, and motivational skills that would later serve me well as a student teacher. As a Residence Hall Office Manager for the Office of Housing and Residence Life, I supervised and trained as many as 15 employees while ensuring that exemplary administrative support was provided. Further responsibilities included managing labor hours, writing schedules for office personnel, and maintaining accurate payroll reports for all office staff.

If you can use an enthusiastic young educator with a strong work ethic and a sincere desire to motivate young people through my genuine love of music, I hope you will contact me soon. I can assure you that I have an excellent reputation and would quickly become an asset to your school.

Sincerely,

Brenda S. Engel

BRENDA S. ENGEL

1110½ Hay Street, Fayetteville, NC 28305 • preppub@aol.com • 910-483-6611

OBJECTIVE

To benefit an organization that can use an enthusiastic young educator with excellent communication, organizational, and motivational skills who offers a degree in Music Education.

EDUCATION

Earned **Bachelor of Science** degree in **Music Education**, Florida Southern College, Lakeland, FL, 2001.
- Graduated **cum laude**, maintaining a 3.64 QPA while working up to 20 hours a week to finance my education and performing in numerous concerts and recitals.
- Named to the **Dean's List** five out of nine semesters.

Graduated from West Heights Senior High School, Clearwater, FL, 1996.

CERTIFICATIONS

Florida State Teaching Certificate, Music K-12.

AFFILIATIONS

Member, Music Educator's National Conference (MENC).
- Serve on the Advertising Committee.

Member, Florida State Educator's Association.

Member, Florida Music Educator's Association.

EXPERIENCE

While excelling in a demanding Music Education degree program, honed teaching skills serving as a student teacher at local primary and secondary schools:

STUDENT TEACHER. Markham Elementary, Lakeland, FL (2001). Provided instruction to beginning band students in their primary instruments in grades 4-6 as well as general music classes to first, second, and fourth grade students.
- Conducted fifth and sixth grade students in the concert band and coordinated auditions for sixth grade students who wanted to try out for district band.
- Taught general music to as many as 25 elementary students; used handbells and rhythm sticks to teach the rudiments of harmony, melody, and rhythm.
- Created and maintained an interactive bulletin board which aided students in learning to read music by allowing them to place musical notes in their correct positions on the staff.

STUDENT TEACHER. Price Jr./Sr. High School, Lakeland, FL (2000). Taught concert band and general music classes, gaining valuable teaching experience while assisting the band director at this local school.
- Effectively managed and motivated students in class sizes ranging from 25 to 45.
- Developed and implemented lesson plans designed to increase students' knowledge of basic music theory while increasing their proficiency in their primary instruments as well as their interest in playing and practicing.
- Directed two concert bands while providing music instruction in their primary instruments to band students in grades 7-12.

RESEARCHER. Mower Industries, Tallahassee, FL (1999). Contacted manufacturers of microprocessor-based systems and software, conducting vital research into potential loss of data or damage to systems due to the inability of some systems to generate correct dates after 1999.

ACTIVITIES

Played flute and percussion in a number of different ensembles, including:

Lucas County Community Band, Florida Southern College Symphony Band, Florida Southern College Marching Band, and Florida Southern College Flute Ensemble.

Getting Into Teaching

Date

Exact Name of Person
Exact Title
Exact Name of Company
Address
City, State, Zip

Natural Sciences

Dear Exact Name of Person (or Dear Sir or Madam if answering a blind ad):

With the enclosed resume, I would like to make you aware of my strong educational background in science and medicine, my highly developed analytical and problem-solving skills, and my extensive laboratory experience.

Although this young woman could utilize her technical and scientific knowledge in the business world, she has decided she would like to make a career in teaching. This professional has the typical background of a student; she has worked in many jobs unrelated to her chosen field. Nevertheless, any work experience helps you acquire work habits which could be useful to potential employers.

As you will see, I am currently completing a Bachelor of Science degree in Natural Sciences with a concentration in Biology from Wright State University. In addition to the rigorous course load of my degree program and my teaching responsibilities, I have taken courses from the biotechnology program which have provided an opportunity to develop cutting edge knowledge and learn to operate state-of-the-art laboratory equipment. While learning the fundamentals of DNA manipulation, I have used micropipettes, centrifuges, thermocyclers, and gel electrophorens apparatuses. I have studied techniques of DNA cloning, restriction digestion, transformation, plasmid isolation, bacterial culturing, and gel electrophorese. During a one-year project, I assisted on work involving the cloning of microbial resistant genes.

Although I could use my scientific knowledge in a profit-making environment, I have decided that I wish to be involved in educating young minds and training promising young scientific professionals.

If you can use a dedicated young professional with highly developed analytical and technical skills who offers a strong background in laboratory testing, I hope you will contact me soon to suggest a time when we might meet to discuss your needs. I can assure you in advance that I have an excellent reputation and would rapidly become a valuable addition to your school system.

Sincerely,

Elka Westervelt

ELKA WESTERVELT

1110½ Hay Street, Fayetteville, NC 28305 • preppub@aol.com • (910) 483-6611

OBJECTIVE   To benefit an organization that can use an articulate and intelligent young professional with exceptional technical and analytical skills who offers a strong educational background related to the natural sciences along with a strong desire to use my knowledge as a teacher.

EDUCATION   Completing a **Bachelor of Science degree in Natural Sciences**, with a concentration in Biology, Wright State University, Dayton, OH; degree to be awarded May, 2001.
Have studied a wide range of difficult courses related to science and medicine, including:

Cellular and Molecular Biology	Techniques in Microbiology	Genetics
Radiation Biology	Comparative Anatomy	Chemistry I
Integrated Zoology	Calculus w/Analytic Geometry	Chemistry II
General Physics I, II, & III	Anatomy & Physiology I & II	Botany
Ecology and Evolution	Elementary Statistics	Spanish I & II
Animal Development	Intro To Computer Science	
Vertebrate Physiology	Special Problems (lab assignments)	

Completed 52 hours of **field experience teaching science** to local high school students.

TECHNICAL SKILLS   Excelled in a number of additional courses from the biotechnology program, developing skills in the following areas:
- Fundamentals of DNA manipulation using state-of-the-art equipment such as micropipettes, centrifuges, thermocyclers, and gel electrophorens apparati.
- Techniques of DNA cloning, restriction digestion, transformation, plasmid isolation, bacterial culturing, and gel electrophorens.
- Spent a year on work involving the cloning of microbial resistant genes.

EXPERIENCE   **TELEMARKETER.** Big Starr Telemarketing, Dayton, OH (Summers 1998, 1999, 2000). During summer breaks, demonstrated my exceptional verbal communication and listening skills while excelling in this fast-paced telephone direct sales environment.
- Quickly developed a rapport with customers, uncovered their objections, and used product knowledge and persuasion to close the sale.
- Provided direct marketing sales and support, presenting customers with the benefits and advantages of various products offered by the company.

CUSTODIAN. North High School, Dayton, OH (1997). In a part-time job while in college, performed general maintenance, cleaning, and landscaping services in order to beautify and prepare the school's interior, exterior, and grounds for the fall enrollment.

SEWING MACHINE OPERATOR. D& D Jeans, Dayton, OH (1996-1997). Worked in this commission-based position in a busy clothing production plant.

COOK and **CASHIER.** Burger King, Dayton, OH (1995-1996). While in high school, honed my skills in teamwork and time management while cooking and providing customer service for this local branch of the large national fast food chain.
- Was frequently called upon to accept the additional responsibility of training new employees due to my patience and exceptional communication skills.
- Provided customer service, taking food orders and operating a cash register.

PERSONAL   Excellent personal and professional references are available upon request.

Getting Into Teaching

Date

Exact Name of Person
Exact Title
Exact Name of Company
Address
City, State, Zip

Sociology

A versatile job hunt is what Ms. Pratt has in mind. She is primarily oriented toward teaching, but she would take a counseling position in the social services field if a suitable teaching post is not available in the small town to which she has relocated with her husband.

Dear Exact Name of Person (or Dear Sir or Madam if answering a blind ad):

With the enclosed resume, I would like to offer my services to a school system that can make use of a confident and highly motivated professional with strong organizational and communication skills and a firm commitment to making a difference in the lives of others.

As you will see, I have recently completed my Bachelor of Arts in Sociology. While pursuing my degree, I worked as a student teacher and attended extracurricular seminars in order to further prepare myself. Being a mother of two, I have acquired insights into the varying learning styles of children as I have wrestled with choosing age-appropriate materials for my own children.

In previous positions, I have shown myself to be a versatile and results-oriented team player who works well with little or no supervision. For example, I quickly learned the spreadsheet program used by First Union to access and modify account information and I also compiled and published the bank's monthly newsletter. I am known for my strong oral and written communication skills.

If you can use an enthusiastic and knowledgeable counselor or teacher, I hope you will contact me to suggest a time when we might meet to discuss your present and future needs. I can assure you in advance that I could rapidly become an asset to your organization.

Sincerely,

Edith Pratt

EDITH PRATT

1110½ Hay Street, Fayetteville, NC 28305 • preppub@aol.com • (910) 483-6611

OBJECTIVE   To benefit an organization that can use a confident and highly motivated individual with strong organizational and communication skills along with a firm commitment to making a difference in the lives of others.

EDUCATION   **Bachelor of Arts in Sociology,** Albion College, Albion, MI, 2001.
Attended numerous seminars to supplement my degree program, including modules on good parenting, the difficult child, homework skills, and abuse issues.

COMPUTERS   Proficient with numerous popular software programs including Word.

EXPERIENCE   **COLLEGE STUDENT.** Albion College, Albion, MI (1997-2001). Completed my Bachelor of Arts degree in Sociology.

KINDERGARTEN STUDENT TEACHER. Roosevelt Elementary School, Albion, MI (2001). Was a Student Teacher Assistant while completing my Bachelor's degree.
- Planned and executed various activities, such as reading to the students, developing arts and crafts activities, and coordinating music education.
- Supported the regular classroom teacher in the implementation of lesson plans.
- Developed excellent rapport with the children under my care; assisted those having difficulty with reading, spelling, and math.

ADMINISTRATIVE ASSISTANT, LOAN DEPARTMENT. First Union Bank, Albion, MI (1998-2000). In a part-time job, prepared consumer loan paperwork and entered it into a database; compiled and published the bank's monthly newsletter.
- Entered consumer loan information into a computer; utilized the software to retrieve and modify existing files.
- Utilized computers to check account balances and payment status of existing loans.
- Prepared financial documents and maintained the filing system.

POSTAL WORKER/MAIL HANDLER. U.S. Post Office, Jacsonille, FL (1997). Excelled in this physically strenuous environment, performing a variety of different tasks; as an Equipment Operator, operated mail processing machines, binding machines, automated labeling equipment, embossing and addressing machines, bundle belt, return-to-sender machines, as well as machines for casing, stacking, lifting, and loading.

MICROFILMING TECHNICIAN. State Board of Health, Jacksonville, FL (Summer, 1996). Transferred official documents from hard copy to microfilm; prepared/sealed documents to be microfilmed; produced microfilm of birth certificates, marriage certificates, and adoption papers; once the documents were transferred to microfilm, packed original paper copies for long-term storage.

Other experience: **TUTOR** and **SUPERVISOR**. Albion Urban League, Albion, MT. Excelled in summer jobs for two summers. In the first summer, worked as a Tutor for young children; in the second summer, supervised 25 young tutors aged 16-20 in tutoring children aged K-5 in reading and writing.

PERSONAL   Excellent personal and professional references on request.

Getting Into Teaching

Exact Name of Person
Exact Title
Exact Name of Company
Address
City, State, Zip

Social Studies Teaching Certification, Degree in History

Most people have three distinctly different careers in their working lifetimes. This mature professional has had a successful first career as a military professional, and he has decided to establish his second career in the teaching field.

Dear Exact Name of Person (or Dear Sir or Madam if answering a blind ad):

With the enclosed resume, I would like to make you aware of my background, degree, and leadership abilities as well as of my strong interest in education.

As you will see, I have recently graduated from Castleton State College in Castleton, VT, where I earned my B.S. in History with teacher certification in Social Studies. I was named to the National Dean's List and inducted into Kappa Delta Pi, a national honor society for education majors. While maintaining a GPA of 3.5, I completed my student teaching at E.E. Cummings High School in April with a 400-hour block of practical classroom experience. I had previously completed 40-hour practicums at three area high schools.

My work experience includes distinguished service in the U.S. Air Force where I advanced in rank ahead of my peers and earned a reputation as a dynamic motivator and superior training chief. I was consistently described as an enthusiastic and results-oriented professional who could be counted on to find ways to increase productivity and efficiency while eliminating waste and excess. I have controlled multimillion-dollar inventories, prepared budgets, and built new operations from the ground up while training and motivating personnel.

The recipient of numerous medals and awards for exceptional performance, I was often singled out as an exceptional teacher and trainer. I have always enjoyed the opportunity to mentor others and feel that I am highly effective in accomplishing this goal. If you can use a mature professional with an enthusiastic and energetic style, I hope you will contact me to suggest a time when we might meet to discuss your needs. I can assure you in advance that I could rapidly become an asset to your organization.

Sincerely,

Martin Caverley

MARTIN CAVERLEY

1110½ Hay Street, Fayetteville, NC 28305 • preppub@aol.com • (910) 483-6611

OBJECTIVE   To contribute to a school system that can use a mature professional with outstanding communication and interpersonal skills along with a reputation as a powerful motivator.

EDUCATION   **Bachelor of Science** in **History with Teacher Certification in Social Studies,** Castleton State College, Castleton, VT, 2001. Named to the **National Dean's List** and inducted into **Kappa Delta Pi**, a national honor society for education majors; GPA 3.5.
- Completed a concentrated 400-hour block as a Student Teacher at E.E. Cummings High School, Castleton, VT, 2000.
- Completed three 40 hour semesters of field experience at area high schools in 1999-2000.

Associate of Arts in **Management**, Community College of the Air Force, 1997.

COMPUTERS   Proficient with many of the most popular computer operating systems and software including Windows, Microsoft Word, Excel, and PowerPoint; E-mail; and the Internet.

EXPERIENCE   **STUDENT TEACHER.** E.E. Cummings High School, Castleton, VT (2001). Assisted the teacher with homeroom and taught one class of World History and two classes of Politics, Economics, and Law to as many as 27 ninth through 12th grade students; assembled course materials, prepared lesson plans, issued assignments, and administered quizzes.

Advanced in rank ahead of my peers and held managerial roles in the U.S. Air Force:
CHIEF OF SUPPLY AND LOGISTICS SUPPORT. Ft. Campbell, KY (1996-1997). As a key member of the Group Commander's staff, was described as a "dynamic" and "superior performer" and credited with developing and implementing improvements to policies and procedures for one of the Air Force's largest fighter groups, consisting of 51 aircraft, an operations section, and a maintenance department.
- Managed and wrote the Operating Instructions for a $26 million aviation petroleum, oils, and lubricants (POL) program.

TRAINING CHIEF. Bristol AFB, TX (1995-96). Recognized for single-handedly improving numerous key programs through my initiative, enthusiasm, and the application of expert knowledge of aviation logistics support actions.
- Converted an aviation POL program from a manual to an automated system.

SUPPLY AND MAINTENANCE SUPPORT MANAGER. Korea (1994-95). Supervised eight employees, establishing and controlling procedures which allowed 285 organizations with 2,400 vehicles and 58 aircraft to respond within 15 minutes to requests for flight services.
- Provided the leadership which allowed the unit to achieve fully operational status above 90% and pre-packaged spare parts kits requests to be filled 95% of the time.

SPECIAL INVENTORY MANAGER. Beale AFB, CA (1992-94). Supervised a staff of 22 personnel and controlled a $14 million inventory of high-priority and readiness spare parts kits.
- Handpicked to build an operation in the United Kingdom from the ground up, managed a $4 million supply account and served as resource advisor for a $320,000 budget.

PERSONAL   Honored with two prestigious Meritorious Service and three Air Force Commendation Medals in recognition of "distinguished service" and exceptional accomplishments. Have acquired a reputation as a leader who believes in "leadership by example."

You may be interested in teaching in the federal government system. If so, you will need to submit specialized paperwork which is different from the paperwork you normally provide to a school system for a "civilian" job. Usually you will submit either a 612 *or* a two-page resume in application for a federal government job. Please be aware that the federal government is constantly changing its forms and requirements, so consult appropriate officials to verify what you need.

The Optional Form 612

The Optional Form 612 can be obtained from any Civilian Personnel Office (CPO) or you may download the form from http://www.OPM.gov or http://www.fedjobs.com. The form looks simple, but it is to your advantage to complete the form by using "continuation sheets" such as those shown on the next few pages so that you can show your background in extensive detail. In other words, don't just type your experience in the space in the boxes provided on the form; use continuation sheets. Your 612 actually gets a numerical score which will determine your ranking among your competitors, so you want to make sure your 612 is comprehensive and detailed. Always type or word process your 612. Never submit a handwritten 612. You need to present your background in reverse chronological order, beginning with what you have been doing most recently so that those reading your 612 can see your skills, abilities, and knowledge.

The "Civil Service" Resume

Instead of preparing a 612, you may opt to submit a "civil-service" resume. The resume you submit for federal jobs is usually longer and more detailed than the resume you submit for "civilian" teaching positions. In addition, the resume you submit for federal positions contains salary information, names of supervisors, and other data (such as your social security number and citizenship status) which are usually not included on a "regular resume."

Position Vacancy Announcements

If you are wondering how you can find out about the requirements for teaching positions, you can visit the websites identified above and probably numerous other websites which will acquaint you with current federal openings. If your job hunt is geographical in nature, you may want to visit the appropriate hiring authorities to find out their suggested methods of applying for federal teaching positions. Most jobs available in the federal system are described by a "position vacancy announcement" which will tell you the qualifications and skills sought as well as where and how to send your resume.

The OF-612 can be used to apply for federal teaching positions.

HOLLY M. BROOKS

SSN: 000-00-0000

CONTINUATION SHEET FOR 612 ITEM 8 (1)

Job Title: Kindergarten Teacher
From (MM/YY): 09/99
To (MM/YY): Present
Salary: $28,568 per year
Hours per week: 40
Employer's name and address: Camden County Board of Education, Hay Street, St. Louis, MO 28305
Supervisor's name and phone number: Mr. Francis Sweeney, (910) 483-6611

Classroom emphasis on building self respect, fostering positive relationships, rewarding individual achievement, and encouraging creativity:
Am applying all early childhood theories and principles within my classroom while also using my creativity and training in curriculum development to create innovative new tools for use in this kindergarten classroom.

- Designed and created an age-appropriate learning environment for kindergarten which encourages active exploration and which teaches behavior patterns allowing optimal interaction among children in order to accentuate language development.
- Use my imagination and my training to create a learning environment in which children are continuously developed while their self-concept is enhanced through the mastery of skills which foster self-reliance and self-respect.
- Instill in children by all my actions and words the concept that their physical environment at school is a friendly space designed for their personal growth and enrichment while requiring good manners and cooperation toward others.
- Emphasize the sharing of good values as we strive for an environment which rewards both positive teamwork as well as individual achievement.
- Am teaching children to listen to their natural curiosity and to respond in positive ways to their feelings; also instill in children the value of self control.
- Throughout the class day, assure the optimal usage of the materials, space, time, and equipment in order to develop a "learning rhythm" which children react to with enthusiasm and interest.
- Incorporate learning centers throughout my K classroom for continuous learning.

Active utilization of many tools and methods in teaching:
While encouraging activities which promote mastery learning of various skills, utilize a variety of tools. For example, creatively utilize mediums including painting and clay modeling in order to promote the development of fine and gross motor skills while enhancing self-expression within a creative context. Am known for my highly creative use of dry erase boards and bulletin boards to spark the children's interest and ignite their creative energy. Personally design and create all the bulletin boards in my classroom, and pay special attention to making sure the classroom is creatively decorated so that it is a welcoming yet stimulating "home away from home" for each child. Believe that the layout of existing furniture can greatly enhance the learning process and personally design the layout of my classroom in order to integrate furniture, fixtures, and materials in the most effective manner. Have become proficient in using the Camden Learning Resources Center to construct educational manipulatives and learning tools.

**Continuation Sheet
For 612 Item 8 (1)**

This is a 612 of a teacher who wants to work for the federal system in a staff development role. Accordingly you will notice that her skills related to relationship-building are emphasized more than her classroom-teaching abilities.

This 612 reveals a lot about her philosophy of teaching.

Page Two of Continuation Sheet For 612 Item 8 (1)

The space provided on the 612 form itself was only the size of a paragraph and would not have done justice to this individual's career and teaching experience. Notice that she has used two continuation sheets to describe her current job.

You will see this person's personality expressed in her job descriptions.

Integrating reading and math into daily life:

Subtly introduce reading and counting concepts by developing a routine in which children learn to print the names of (and label) the hundreds of items in our physical classroom environment. Introduce counting/math skills by having the children acquire the habit of counting (in addition to labeling) many of the items in our classroom. Promote reading readiness skills by making time available for children to look at picture books and listen to many of those books read out loud to them.

- With a strong belief that the development of strong communication skills is fundamental to success in most careers, stress the early acquisition of these skills. Each student keeps a creative writing journal and makes entries in it on a daily basis.

Continuing education:

Attended staff development workshops on special services and intervention, child abuse/HIV, copyright laws, and curriculum development. Also have examined new mathematics teaching kits, and have incorporated several of the ideas in those teaching kits into classroom use. Am continually refining my ability to develop exciting lesson plans which promote mastery while holding the attention span of young children. Have familiarized myself with the state and local learning curriculum objectives and goals. Have acquired advanced skills in assessing motor development—both large and small—through observation. Have refined my skills in conducting developmental screening.

The creation of lesson plans—that essential building block of education:

With a belief that quality lesson plans lead to quality teaching and quality learning, am continuously refining the long-term lesson plans which I prepare. Create short- and long-term goals for each student after an assessment of their educational goals, and tailor the overall class lesson plans to the goals we have established for student development. Utilize various teaching methods including units of study, learning centers, and skills groups as I attempt to teach an integrated curriculum instead of "separate subjects." Implement "whole language" reading and writing with thematic science and social studies units.

The focus is on the child in my classroom:

Provide a variety of activities for my assessment of the whole child and attempt to connect somehow to each child's home environment. Promote home-school relations through newsletters, positive phone calls and messages, parent involvement in the classroom, Parent-Teacher open houses, parent conferences, and special communication about upcoming events. Believe that my goal is to gain the parent's/guardian's trust and to form a partnership between home and school.

HOLLY M. BROOKS

SSN: 000-00-0000

CONTINUATION SHEET FOR 612 ITEM 8 (2)

Job Title: First Grade Teacher
From (MM/YY): 09/95
To (MM/YY): 05/99
Salary: $18,950 per year
Hours per week: 40
Employer's name and address: Camden County Schools, Hay St., St. Louis, MO 28305
Supervisor's name and phone number: Dr. F. Sweeney, (910) 483-6611

Selection as Staff Development Trainer:

After excelling as a first-grade teacher, was selected as a Staff Development Trainer from 1996-97 and became an Early Childhood Curriculum Training Specialist. Presented staff development workshops once a month throughout the county, and workshops which I presented included topics such as:

- Integrating creative language activities into curricula
- Choosing age-appropriate equipment for physical play
- Sharing ideas for early intervention pertaining to at-risk children
- Innovative topics related to curriculum development and reform
- Detecting child abuse and neglect
- Applying Federal laws including American Disabilities Act and Vocational Rehabilitation Act in educational environments
- Involving parents in their children's education

Highlights of activities as an Early Childhood Training Specialist:

Planned, coordinated, and directed staff development in Developmentally Appropriate Practices to approximately 100 childhood teachers in the Camden County School System. Formulated training sessions, programs, and scheduled independently and with a training unit of eight trainers. Selected appropriate instructional procedures and methods such as large and small group instruction, self study, lectures, demonstrations, and role play. Trained early childhood teachers in developmentally appropriate procedures and in effective management of the developmentally appropriate program; developed and conducted training sessions and varied my training techniques in each presentation to accommodate the different styles of learners. Evaluated training packages which contained reference materials, reference articles, course outline, training text, and handouts.

- Utilized reference materials published by the National Association for the Education of Young Children.
- Presented staff development sessions in the following specific areas:
  History of Developmentally Appropriate Practices (DAP), Rationale, and the school system's Implementation Plan
  National Perspective on DAP and National Organizations devoted to DAP
  The Definition of DAP
  Myths concerning DAP
  The 12 Principles of DAP
  Characteristics of Young Children

Continuation Sheet For 612 Item 8 (2)

Staff Development Trainer is the position she is trying to obtain in federal service. So she is emphasizing a subsidiary role she held as "Staff Development Trainer" rather than her classroom duties, which consumed most of her time.

HOLLY M. BROOKS
SSN: 000-00-0000
CONTINUATION SHEET FOR 612 ITEM 13

Continuation Sheet
For 612 Item 13
The OF 612 has a Question 13 which asks you to provide information about your "Other Qualifications." This means your training courses, job-related skills, job-related certificates and licenses, job-related honors, memberships in professional societies, and so forth.

There's no way she could show all this information in the small space provided on the form 612. A continuation sheet provides her with the space to present all her "other qualifications" and she knows that what she *doesn't* include, she *doesn't* get credit for.

Job-Related Training Courses:

"New Teacher Orientation," 2000

"The Society for Developmental Education Seminars," 2000

"School Improvement," 2000

"Introduction to the 4Mat System: Teaching to Learn Styles With Right/Left Mode Techniques," 1999

"School Improvement," 1999

"Lions Quest—Skills for Growing," 1999

"Characteristics of Developmentally Appropriate Programs,"

"Learning Environment as a 3-D Textbook," 1997

"Continuous Progress and Multi-aged Programs," 1997

"Assessment/Portfolios," 1997

"New Assessment for the First and Second Grades," 1996

"Planning and Organizing for Developmentally Appropriate Learning in Early Childhood Education," 1996

"Principles of Child Development: How Children Learn," 1996

"Developmentally Appropriate Curriculum Related to Physical, Social, and Cognitive Needs (K-3)," 1996

"Communicating DAP with Parents and Others," 1995

"Assessment: Recordkeeping Strategies Consistent with Developmentally Appropriate Practices in Early Childhood Education," 1995

"Quality Schools: Critical Components," 1995

"The Study and Implementation of Elements of Instruction," 1995

"Instructional Alignment of the Curriculum," 1994

"Effective Instruction," 1994

"Mastery Learning," 1993

"Effective Teacher Training," 1993

"Mathematics for Education," 1993

"Cooperative Learning," 1993

"Curriculum Alignment of the Communication Skills," 1993

"Manipulative Instructional Techniques," 1992

"Computer Technology," 1992

Public Speaking:

· Frequently spoke to large groups (approximately 100) and small groups (approximately 20) of early childhood teachers during monthly staff development sessions during the school year.

· As Coordinator of Assembly Programs throughout the school year, I presented awards, certificates, and bumper stickers to approximately 250 students, teachers, and parents.

· Presented a speech to my high school faculty consisting of 25-30 teachers prior to being chosen as the Daughters of the Revolutionary War Good Citizenship Student.

Publications:

Edited and narrated the manuscript and text of a video production by the Camden County Schools System explaining the developmental; educational practices which were being promoted and implemented in the primary and elementary schools; the video is available to all the early childhood educators throughout Camden County schools.

Membership:
- National Association for the Education of Young Children (NAEYC); a member-supported organization of people committed to fostering the growth and development of children birth through age 8.
- National Education Association
- Missouri Education Association
- Missouri Association for Childhood Education (past membership)
- Phi Mu Fraternity

Page Two of
Continuation Sheet
For 612 Item 13

Computers:
- Utilize Macintosh, IBM, and Apple computers with software for word processing and statistical analysis.

Certifications:
- Successfully completed CPR and First Aid instruction (not certified)
- Certificate in Creative Floor Work and Conditioning
- Certificate in Choreography Clinic
- Former Lifeguard (not currently certified)

Continuation sheets allow you to show much detail. She provides a two-page response to the Question 13 about "Other Qualifications."

Music Training:
- Took singing lessons for 10 years
- Participated in church choirs preschool through youth; had a role in the school musical "Bye Bye Birdie."

Languages:
Took high school courses in Spanish and French.

Honors and Awards:
- Won an award in high school from the Daughters of the American Revolution (DAR) for good citizenship called "DAR Citizenship Girl." Selected by committee to honor one senior girl and one senior boy for activities, attitude, and speech.

Travel:
- Use my travel experience in promoting multicultural education; spent 10 days touring the country of Italy.

Personal Library:
- Have created an extensive collection of books and manuals related to Developmentally Appropriate Practices (DAP) and guides which now constitutes a library of resources related to DAP.

This is a 2-page resume used to apply for a federal government teaching position.

CATHERINE WARREN

Until 7/30/2001: 1110 Hay Street, Fayetteville, NC 28305
Home: (910) 483-6611
After 7/30/2001: P.O. Box 66, Silas, TX 77834
Home: (777) 555-1212
SSN: 000-99-0000

Geographic preference: Germany
Citizen of: U.S.
Veteran's preference: NA

Position, Title, Series, Grade: _____
Announcement Number: _____

This young teacher is relocating with her husband, who is a military professional being reassigned to Germany. She could have used either this **two-page "civil service" resume** or an OF 612, shown on the preceding pages, in order to apply for a federal teaching position. Notice that a "federal resume" or "civil service resume" contains some information, such as salary history, not usually provided on "civilian resumes."

EDUCATION & TRAINING

B.S., Elementary Education, Atlanta State University, Atlanta, GA May 1990; minor concentration in Early Childhood Education.
- Excelled academically and maintained a 3.64 GPA.

Completed Professional Teacher Development Courses, Wilson Bench Technical Community College, NC:
- Phonics, 2001
- Teaching Children with Special Needs, 2000
- Humor in the Classroom, 2000
- Computing in Today's World, 2000
- Creating for Innovative Teaching: A Make and Take Workshop for Elementary Educators, 1999
- How to Teach Eureka! (Math), 1998
- Smart Teachers/Smart Students, 1997
- Winning with Difficult Personalities, 1997
- Effective Listening and Speaking, 1997
- First Aid and CPR, 1997
- Graduated from Silas High School, Silas, TX, 1986

EXPERIENCE

THIRD GRADE TEACHER. Hazelwood Academy, 1100 Hay Street, Franklin, SC 28305 (8/96-present). Salary: $19,200. Supervisor: Mr. Pat Mack (910) 483-6611. Have taught for four years at a private school with 500 students from pre-kindergarten through 12th grade, am one of three third grade teachers.
- Teach all subjects—reading, math, language, spelling, history, science, and Bible—to 14 students.
- Implemented a reading program utilizing the Book-It Program which resulted in rewards such as a pizza party.
- Offered trophies as incentives for mastering multiplication and division and enhanced the study of history by creating informative pictorial bulletin boards.
- Ensured each student received individual attention by providing one-on-one attention and tutoring as well as through a student-of-the-week program.
- Maintained daily contact with parents to keep each of them informed of their child's progress.
- Emphasized the need for taking responsibility for one's own actions by assigning homework and insisting on neatness and pride in work completed.

She could have used a 612 *or* this "federal resume" to apply for a federal teaching post.

- Was known for using positive reinforcement of good behavior and moral character and for my firm but fair methods of discipline.
- Represented the school as a Delegate for the Association of Teacher's Convention, 2000, 1999, 1998, and 1997.

DATA PROCESSING CLERK. Dr. Frances Sweeney, Napierville, IL 73535 (2/96-6/96). Salary: $6.50 per hour. 20 hours per week. Supervisor: Dr. Sweeney (910) 483-6611. Carried out a wide range of office support activities: entered patient charges, processed insurance forms for payment, and prepared daily and monthly reports.

MEDICAL RECORDS CLERK. Calgary Hospital, Calgary, CA 99842 (9/93-1/96). Salary: $5.75 per hour. 40 hours per week. Supervisor: Marylou Kennedy (910) 933-7523. Worked directly with physicians in the doctors' "dictation and incomplete room."
- Demonstrated an eye for detail while analyzing charts, inputting data, tracking deficiencies, locating charts for filing, and compiling lists of incomplete charts.

RECORDS CLERK. Nationwide Medical, Dallas, TX 86542 (6/93-9/93). Salary: $5.75 per hour. 40 hours per week. Supervisor: Penelope Long (910) 483-7523. Received and processed requests for medical records while providing patients with assistance on matters concerning their records; prepared daily and monthly reports.

CLIENT CONTACT SPECIALIST. Blue Cross & Blue Shield, Houston, TX 76542 (3/93-6/93). Salary: $500 per month. 40 hours per week. Supervisor: Grace Black, (910) 988-4559. Called existing and prospective clients to set up meetings with an agent concerning sales and services for a financial planning company.
- Provided support for regular seminars to include generating rosters, identifying people who would be attending, and preparing correspondence.

BUYER and **SECRETARY.** Dynatec Corporation, Mount Helen, WA 89995 (8/92-11/92). Salary: $5.50 per hour. 40+ hours per week. Supervisor: various senior personnel (phone unknown). As a Buyer, handled purchase requisitions and verified the quantity, costs, and type of materials received. As a Secretary, entered and reviewed receipts, also coordinated travel arrangements for staff members.
- Utilized automated systems to generate charts and graphs for use in seminars.

SIXTH GRADE TEACHER. Holy Name School, 406 Willow Street, Coffeyville, KS 67337 (8/90-5/91). Salary: $16,500. 40 hours per week. Supervisor: Sister Janice Roberts (516) 251-0480. Taught all subject material to a class of 23 students in a Catholic school while providing a challenging environment through the selection of appropriate instructional material.
- Selected, organized, and introduced curriculum in all subject areas including reading, spelling, math, language, science, social studies, art, physical education, and religion.
- Refined time management and organizational skills while planning lessons and coordinating classroom and school events.
- Earned respect for my firm yet fair style of discipline and ability to create a positive learning atmosphere for all students.

HONORS Certificates of Appreciation, 2000, 1999, 1998 (two awards), and 1995 that were given in recognition of my service as a volunteer with the Urban League.

AFFILIATIONS Member, Conners United Methodist Church

PERSONAL Enjoy volunteering my time to help others. Proficient in using Microsoft Word.

Part Three
Getting Ahead--and Getting Noticed--in Teaching

In Part Three, you will find "resumes" of a different sort. This section is primarily for people who want to "get ahead" in teaching. Getting ahead involves "getting noticed" and that is why we call this section Getting Ahead—and Getting Noticed—in Teaching.

Applying for Teacher of the Year?
Teacher of the Year packets often need to be assembled by teachers who are getting ahead in their careers. In this section you will find responses of talented teachers to the essays required for "Teacher of the Year."

Applying for graduate school?
If you are a teacher applying for a graduate program or a Ph.D. program, you will also have to answer essay questions which are essentially resumes of a different sort. In this section, you will find examples of responses given to essay questions on real applications for graduate schools and professional schools.

Essays in this section
Here are essay questions and responses which you will find in this section:
"Describe the most significant influencing factors in your life and discuss your greatest contribution."
"Describe your commitment to community."
"Tell us about your personal beliefs."
"Describe your personal teaching style."
"What do you think are the major issues facing public education?"
"How would you improve the teaching profession?"
"What do you feel is the best form of accountability?"
"Personal Statement of Kathryn Diangelo."
"What are your teaching philosophies and beliefs?"
"What are the key issues facing public education?"
"Describe your teaching philosophy."
"If you were elected teacher of theyear, what would your message be?"
"Describe your work and accomplishments in a program of significance with public schools. An Exciting New Approach: Combined Education."
"Why do you want to pursue a doctorate?"
"Essay describing my purpose in pursuing a doctorate."
"If you believe your standardized test results or your undergraduate GPA are not an accurate reflection of your ability to be successful in graduate school, please explain."
"What special project in education have you completed?"
"Describe your leadership style in 30 words or less."
"Describe how relationships between community and school affect education."
"Describe what your philosophy and practices would be as an education administrator."
"Describe how you resolve specific administrative problems in education."
"How would you improve student achievement?"
"Provide any information not previously provided to the selection committee."
Cover letter and resume to accompany application for Ph.D. program
Cover letter and resume accompanying application for a fellowship

DESCRIBE THE MOST SIGNIFICANT INFLUENCING FACTORS IN YOUR LIFE AND DISCUSS YOUR GREATEST CONTRIBUTIONS.

It is my belief that positive role models and an innate desire to work with children were the primary forces that influenced me to choose teaching as a career.

I was very fortunate to have had supportive, caring, talented, and devoted teachers as role models when I was a child. The manner in which they presented themselves and their obvious love for teaching inspired me to want to be a teacher.

My innate desire to work with children was another influencing factor. This gift has been reflected in aptitude tests throughout my school career. I have always had a good rapport with children, even from an early age. As a child, I loved to "play school" and "teach" the neighborhood children. Furthermore, I wrote short plays and "directed" my siblings and friends in neighborhood productions. I had a yearning for sharing knowledge with my peers. This passion manifested itself, and I knew that, when it came time to declare my major in college, it would be education.

The greatest contributions I have made in education are those that are not tangible to the touch, but to the minds and hearts of my students. By presenting myself as a positive role model each day in class, I feel I am making an impression that will last a lifetime with these young boys and girls. Kind words, understanding, fairness, and patience have been motivating and contributing factors to success in school for my students.

The giving of my time, talents, and knowledge are also contributions I have made to education. Imparting those essentials to students, parents, and co-workers has contributed to positive growth and learning experiences.

I feel very honored by being selected *Teacher of the Year* by the members of my faculty. It is an accomplishment equated to the "icing on the cake." Being recognized for that which you love to do is truly special and rewarding.

Another specific accomplishment that comes to mind is my being a part of an Inclusion Program last year. Three high-functioning autistic students were "included" in my class. Making these students part of a regular classroom and having them achieve success was a heart-warming accomplishment.

Chairing, organizing, and implementing a behavior management plan for students last year was another accomplishment. Students that consistently followed school rules were allowed to attend "Wonderful Wednesdays" during which they were treated to special entertainment. Those students who needed to work on their behavior were sent to "It's Your Choice" to participate in cooperative lessons to reinforce positive behavior.

Finally, strengthening my abilities by earning a master's degree and reading certification are accomplishments that will enhance my performance in the classroom.

Essay for a Teacher Seeking to Advance in a Teacher of the Year Competition

This teacher has been honored by selection as Teacher of the Year by the faculty at her school. Now she is answering a series of questions which will be used by a committee to select regional, state, and national winners.

Getting Ahead--and Getting Noticed--in Teaching

DESCRIBE YOUR COMMITMENT TO COMMUNITY.

Commitment to my community first lies in giving the students with whom I work the best education available. Secondly, I am committed to the families of my students. Last Christmas, I, along with representatives of several local corporations, provided clothes for one of my students and his siblings. When there is a need such as this, I cannot help but respond.

Describe your commitment to community and Tell us about your personal beliefs: essay questions for a Teacher of the Year competition

Often an essay is an opportunity to share one's philosophy or some personal event in your life which helped shaped someone else's life.

I am deeply committed to my church, the Calvary United Methodist Church, having taught Sunday School for many years there before becoming an active member of the adult choir. As an active member of the church, I feel a genuine concern and responsibility for our youth. During 1998, I served on the Administrative Board and was the Chairperson for the Council of Children's Ministries, coordinating all children's programs for the year. One of the most successful programs offered was our Wednesday Evening Fellowship; the program included various community service persons from the Red Cross, the local museum, the arts council, the county library, and several area utility companies. I was nominated in 2000 for a three-year term as Chairman of the church's Education Committee and, in that capacity, we have instituted a "Reading is Fun" Program with a nearby elementary school in which children are paired up after school, one day a week, to read with a church volunteer. The aim of this program is to increase the reading competency of at-risk elementary school children. The elementary school with which we are working says it is a tremendously popular program for which there is a waiting list of children anxious to be selected, and we are pleased that it has not been tainted with a reputation as a program for "slow learners."

TELL US ABOUT YOUR PERSONAL BELIEFS.

I believe that teaching is one of the most rewarding and demanding jobs in our nation. As a teacher, you possess the seeds of knowledge for the future. How you choose to sow those seeds determines famine or plenty.

There have been many changes in my philosophy of teaching since my entering the field 19 years ago. I have prided myself in being flexible and creative enough to try different teaching styles. **It appears to me that no matter what style you use, the key to student success is motivation.**

It is known that it is much easier to chase a child than to drag him. This is a philosophy that I support. By showing students respect, giving them choices, and making them feel that they belong, you create an environment that provides important elements for motivation. Motivate a child and you will be well along the way to school success.

One factor which I feel makes me an outstanding teacher is that I accept all children as they come to me in their own unique packages. Physical impairments or learning disabilities do not influence my expectations of each student. I emphatically impress upon my students that they need to strive to do their best always and to meet each challenge with a positive frame of mind.

The rewards I receive from teaching come through everyday experiences:
- the smile on a child's face when he finally learns the multiplication tables;
- the excitement in a child's eyes when she learns how to form a word in cursive;

- the pat on the back from a co-worker for help you rendered;
- the former student who drops by to let you know how much he liked your class;
- the parent who calls to express appreciation for all you did to help his or her child.

DESCRIBE YOUR PERSONAL TEACHING STYLE.

My beliefs about teaching are reflected each day through my personal teaching style. **I am an advocate of cooperative learning and incorporate cooperative lessons in everyday planning.** As previously mentioned, my philosophy centers around motivation as the key to success. I use cooperative lessons to motivate students in my class. Learning is not a solitary activity, and hands-on experiences and the sharing of ideas instill confidence in children. Through cooperative learning, students are able to make choices, share thoughts, and have positive interactions among themselves.

Teaching, rather than telling, is another part of my personal teaching style. The incorporation of the SCIS Program is an effective tool in supporting this philosophy. Rather than giving all the answers, the children are able to explore with me to find the answers. It is a pleasure to chase my students rather than drag them!

WHAT DO YOU THINK ARE THE MAJOR ISSUES FACING PUBLIC EDUCATION?

Violence, teacher accountability, inclusion, testing, and illiteracy are what I consider to be the major public education issues of today. Violence is what I look upon as the most serious problem facing our schools in the new millennium. The spread of violence is on the rise. Its causes are numerous and its effects are devastating.

Unfortunately, more and more children are being abused or exposed to abusive situations in the home. Research has proven that abused children become abusive themselves as they grow older. These children do not know how to deal with their emotions and react impulsively, often causing harm to others.

A wrong message is being sent to our youth through the airwaves. Violence is being portrayed as funny in certain children's cartoons and television programs. Our youth see violence as brave and macho in today's movies. Teens listen to violent lyrics in music. Popular music channels celebrate violence toward women and others.

Our schools are being exposed to more violence because of the formation of gangs. Gangs encourage youth to steal, intimidate, carry and use weapons, become involved in drugs, fight, and sometimes kill.

The effects of violence are being carried over into our schools at an alarming rate. More and more children are coming to school with low self-esteem and psychological problems as a result. Another result of violence is that we are losing more and more youth at the hands of others or because of suicide. How it saddens me to hear that a young life has been so needlessly destroyed.

There is no one clear-cut way to resolve the problem of violence. I do believe there are steps and measures that can be taken to begin the process of turning this problem around.

Describe your personal teaching style: An essay question prepared for a Teacher of the Year application packet

These essays are intended to make this individual come across not just as a competent teacher but as a unique, caring, thinking individual who cares deeply about her work and the impact it has on those whom she teaches.

Getting Ahead--and Getting Noticed--in Teaching

First, we must have better psychological counseling in our schools for victims of violence. We cannot count on parents to provide the proper mental health care for their children.

Next, as educators, parents, or concerned members of society, we can write television companies, movie studios, and recording artists to express our concerns about violence and the effects their medium has on our youth.

What do you think are the major issues facing public education? This is a question in an applicant packet for Teacher of the Year.

In questions such as these, there is usually not one "correct" response. Committees evaluating your essay responses want to see how you think and feel about creative and social issues facing society and the profession.

We can provide afterschool programs for our youth to encourage them to stay off the streets and out of trouble. I envision a joint effort with the community in establishing programs in sports, homemaking, art, music, dance, and a multitude of other disciplines that would enrich the lives of our youth rather than take their lives. Through my chairmanship of my church's Education Committee, I have seen how partnerships between neighborhood churches and schools can bear fruit, as demonstrated through the "Reading is Fun" program for 50 at-risk children sponsored by our church and a local elementary school. I also celebrate the efforts of our police chief in teaching martial arts classes to youth who are seeking physical expression of their aggressions.

I believe that it is short-sighted not to include the building of gymnasiums when money is raised through bond issues for the building of new schools or the renovation of existing schools. I would love to see the local school gymnasium become the "hangout" for children after school. I have never seen a child who enjoyed anything more than throwing, kicking, or playing with a ball. Gymnasiums at our schools could do much to keep children off the street. Children need inexpensive physical outlets for their considerable youthful energies.

Finally, the continuation of programs such as D.A.R.E. and the proliferation of other enrichment programs are a must. We need more programs like this in our schools to properly educate youth concerning the consequences of drug involvement and acts of violence.

HOW WOULD YOU IMPROVE THE TEACHING PROFESSION?

I feel that one of the best ways I can strengthen and improve the teaching profession is **to strengthen and improve myself** both professionally and personally. Presenting myself as a professional and positive role model to the public exhibits success and strength.

Continuing education through staff development, workshops, conventions, and professional magazines keeps me informed and updated with key issues and new trends in education. It has always been a habit of mine to share information, ideas, and materials with my co-workers. Through this type of sharing, we can gain strength and grow professionally. Teachers are, by definition, mentors for other teachers.

Participating in professional organizations is another way to improve and strengthen the teaching profession. These organizations provide educators many opportunities to promote education in the community and have a say in the decision-making process within the profession. I believe I am doing my part to strengthen the profession through my role as building representative for two professional organizations.

Serving as mentors to student teachers and beginning teachers is a major way in which we can strengthen our profession. In this complex and fast-paced age in which technological advances place a strain on all of us just to "keep up," I think it is imperative that we all find opportunities to share our knowledge and discoveries with others.

One thing I like about teaching is that it is cooperative rather than competitive. If we were in the business world, our peers might well be our competitors and we would be well advised to safeguard our insights and our knowledge. I enjoy working in an environment in which I can share my knowledge.

WHAT DO YOU FEEL IS THE BEST FORM OF ACCOUNTABILITY?

It is sad, but true, that most of the public views standardized test scores as the basis for teacher accountability. I do not accept this viewpoint and take issue with those who feel that one test at the end of the school year measures all that has been taught. Furthermore, a test score is not always a true indicator of what a child has or has not attained.

In my opinion, **teachers should be accountable for student success.** Realistically, however, we know that some children will never score well on tests; therefore, I believe we need to reassess the tool or tools we use to measure success.

Student portfolios may be better indicators of what has been achieved throughout the year and give a more accurate representation of student growth. Portfolios would reveal documentation of the day-by-day achievements of the students and help the teacher better assess students' needs. Teachers should then be held accountable for ensuring that students achieve success at their own developmental level.

What do you feel is the best form of accountability?

In writing an essay such as this one, it's important to "be yourself" but you might also have to do some research into accountability methods used at other schools. There's usually not one right answer to a question like this one, but you might want to be on your guard to be "politically correct" in your response. For example, if a new accountability method is being proposed and hotly debated in your school system, you may want to think carefully before you take an aggressive stand.

Getting Ahead--and Getting Noticed--in Teaching

PERSONAL STATEMENT OF KATHRYN DIANGELO

PERSONAL STATEMENT AS PART OF AN APPLICATION TO GRADUATE SCHOOL IN PURSUIT OF A MASTER'S DEGREE

An essay is an opportunity to provide an intensely personal glimpse into who you are, where you've been, why you've done some of the things you've done, and what goals you envision for the future.

I was born in New York, New York, to working class parents. My father worked at a factory and my mother stayed home to raise us. I took for granted the fact that she picked up me and my two sisters from school in the afternoons, stood over us as we did our homework at the kitchen table, and was involved in our school activities. I believe I have been "called" into the teaching profession, and I believe that God has given me abilities and talents that make me special as a teacher, but I did not realize that I wanted to be a teacher until I was working in a well paid job after college graduation.

In 1996 I graduated from Michigan State University with a B.S. in Biology and a minor in Chemistry. While in college, I was known as a campus leader and was appointed administrative aide of my 50-resident dorm. I was also elected Freshman Class Treasurer. Although I came from a family that loves me, I never had any encouragement from my family to attend college, and I am the only one of my sisters to this date who has graduated from college. I have always known that I wanted to "make something of myself," and I figured out that a college degree would help me do that. I met my husband, John, when I was a sophomore at MSU, and I found in him a "soul mate" who also wanted to achieve things in life. John was from a broken home but he had the attitude that "you are what you make of yourself." His confidence in himself and his confidence in me has been a major motivating force in my life.

After we graduated from Michigan State University, I found that there were many employers who wanted to hire young people with degrees in science. My B.S. degree in Biology with a minor in Chemistry helped me land a job at Parker Laboratories for $37,000 a year. I happily accepted the job and thought I was "set."

Although I excelled in my job at Parker Laboratories and was told I had a bright future with the company, something was missing. I couldn't quite put my finger on what was missing, but when I began to analyze what I wanted professionally, I began to realize that I am happiest when I am around children. I had worked with children in a work-study program at the Child Care Center at MSU while earning my college degree, and I had thoroughly enjoyed feeling needed and feeling that I was making a difference in the lives of sensitive, fragile young people. Knowing that a career move to teaching would require a cut in salary as well as other adjustments, I cautiously discussed my feelings with my husband, and he wholeheartedly encouraged me to "follow my heart" and give teaching a chance. In January of 1998 I was hired as a 6th grade teacher at Fallworth Elementary School as a lateral-entry teacher, and I taught all subjects in a self-contained classroom. In my second year at Fallworth, I was singled out by the principal for the Professional Development Award, and that honor signified to me that someone else besides me could see that I had gifts and talents that were well suited to teaching! That honor gave me the encouragement I needed to complete my teacher certification courses, and I became certified to teach math and science in 1999.

Since receiving that first award recognizing my teaching accomplishments, I have added the Dedicated Educator Award, the PTA Appreciation Award, and the Teacher of the Year Award. I am humbled and gratified by these honors, and I am even more convinced now that I have been called to teach middle school children.

My greatest contributions and accomplishments in education are the lives I have helped to shape and the minds I have taught. I believe that I cannot teach a mind unless I first shape an attitude—so I always approach teaching with the attitude that I must first communicate to my students that I respect them and that I want their respect in return. I do demand excellence in all things, but I am a role model for the excellence I ask them to strive for, and they can always see me working hard and "practicing what I preach."

I have learned that middle school children are LOUD because they want to be listened to, so I bring a respectful, listening style of teaching into my classroom. I am a self-disciplined person who believes that, without discipline, one cannot accomplish much in life, so I strive to instill in my students the desire to set high goals and be disciplined in achieving them.

One example of the effectiveness of my style is a teaching assignment I had recently at Caison Middle School. The principal asked me to take over a class of "troublemakers" which had lost two teachers in rapid succession. I agreed. Within a few months, I had built a relationship with those 7th graders, and students previously branded as troublemakers were setting high goals and achieving them. I take a very hands-on approach to the teaching of science, and middle school students love doing things and working with their hands rather than just studying theories from books.

I believe the best teachers are also cheerfully involved in activities outside the classroom. At Caison Middle School, I am very involved with the Junior Beta Club, which is essentially a junior honor society. We have bake sales and other events that help us sponsor the Academic Banquet each year which honors scholastic excellence.

I have been extensively involved, also, in community activities. I was Chairperson for the Committee to Elect Tom Smith for Commissioner of the town of Battle Creek. This was his first campaign for political election, and I was honored that he chose me to head his campaign. We performed extensive telemarketing, encouraged people to register to vote, helped transport people to the polls, conducted numerous educational events to explain the issues and explore voter concerns, and developed informational mailings. I was personally thrilled to see Tom elected for a variety of reasons, not the least of which is that he cares deeply about education and will aggressively support any initiatives which place priority on our children's educations and on their future.

I am also active in my church. As an active adult volunteer with the Youth Department at Kensington Baptist Church, I am constantly interacting with youth of all ages, from middle school up to high school. I coordinate a number of youth activities ranging from Bible studies to banquets, and I organize youth for church activities including reading Bible verses and helping with the choir. I also serve as a **church deaconess** and am extensively involved with the church's **missionary activities,** both in our own country and abroad. I have also played a key role in the **tutorial program** sponsored by the church in conjunction with Battle Creek County Schools. The program takes a different form and caters to different age groups each year, but this year the tutorial program is serving up to 45 children who are brought to the church after school one day a week for one hour after school. Through the program, volunteers are provided who assist the students in small groups in math, reading, and writing. I personally tutor the children involved in this program, and I have seen what a difference it can make in a child's life to know that "someone cares."

Getting Ahead--and Getting Noticed--in Teaching

What are your teaching philosophies and beliefs?

This is the kind of question you will need to answer in essays that you prepare for graduate school or Ph.D. programs.

On numerous occasions, and without pay, I have tutored high school students in chemistry. I serve as **Executive Secretary** and also as a **Lady Attendant** for Michener's Funeral Home, and I derive satisfaction from helping the bereaved to cope with their loss and find some peace. I have extensively volunteered my time to **Girl Scout Troop 92** working with cadets and helping young girls develop high moral standards.

In summary, I can only say that I believe that teaching is a lifestyle, not just a job. I am proud that people look at me and think "teacher." I hope my greatest accomplishment is that the students I have taught have genuinely felt the love and respect which I had for them. **I believe great teaching starts with an attitude, just as I believe that all learning must begin with a good attitude.** It is the attitude which I try to shape and influence before I attempt to transmit content, and children always feel that I *want* to be in the classroom with them. Education cannot be separated from love and respect.

WHAT ARE YOUR TEACHING PHILOSOPHIES AND BELIEFS?

I have five main teaching beliefs.

1. **Respect the student.** I take the view that I cannot teach the brain until I break through the child's attitude. I have learned in teaching that an outwardly belligerent child is often using unruly behavior as a mask for his feelings of insecurity, so I respect the fact that the troublemakers are often experiencing problems and troubles both in and out of school. I use humor, warmth, eye contact, and listening to "get through" to students who are accustomed to "turning off" other teachers through their antagonistic behavior. On numerous occasions, I have seen students respond to the respect I show them by "chilling out" and calming down in my class. It is not uncommon for many middle school children to behave like ladies and gentlemen in my class and then go down the hall to another class and become a troublemaker. While respecting the student, I always create an environment in which the process of learning is itself respected by both teacher and students.

2. **Have fun in the learning process.** My students accuse me sometimes of "getting crazy" because they know I am open to field trips, science experiments, and many other types of experiences that bring concepts "to life." Middle school children are extremely physical creatures, and I try to channel their tactile behavior and physical aggression into hands-on learning experiences that will help them acquire a love for learning and "see" concepts in a different way.

3. **Be positive.** I try never to fall into the trap of responding to negative behavior with negative reactions myself. This is not always easy, especially when middle school children try to "act up." But I feel I often talk loudest through my actions, and I try to return negativism with a positive response. Children are often amazed by this response, but they do notice. A positive attitude is infectious, and I try to spread a positive attitude.

4. **Respect the learning environment (i.e., maintain discipline).** Learning cannot be accomplished in an uncontrolled environment, so one thing I communicate aggressively but positively to my students is that we will respect the learning environment. I communicate clearly my expectations of high performance standards and good manners to each other in the classroom, but I communicate my expectations in a positive,

enthusiastic manner without being condescending to students and without putting them down.

5. **Be enthusiastic.** Ask any student, and he or she will tell you the difference between a "good" teacher and a "bad" teacher: The good teacher wants to be in the classroom, and the good teacher is enthusiastic about his subject area.

My rewards in teaching

I chose teaching as a profession and made a career change from a job that paid me better in money. However, I enjoy the "pay" I receive through teaching when I see a child's eyes light up because he or she has learned, or when I see an antagonistic or indifferent attitude in a child become ruled by a positive, enthusiastic attitude. I left a well-paid job in industry for a teaching career, and I haven't looked back once and regretted my decision. I love teaching, and I feel well compensated in many areas. I abandoned a career in which I would have focused on corporate profitability for a career which gives me an opportunity to make a lasting difference in people's lives. I take very seriously the fact that how I treat a child may impact significantly on his or her ability to lead a productive and satisfying life. When I am entrusted with a child's mind, I am not only attempting to fill that mind with a certain amount of math and science knowledge. I am also attempting to help a sensitive and fragile human being develop an attitude of respect for learning and a love of learning so that my student will literally "fall in love" with learning and its rewards. Many students whom I have taught call me frequently because they know that I am approachable, that I am their friend, and that I care about them.

My beliefs are reflected in my teaching style.

My teaching style reflects my belief that, you must first influence the attitude before you can teach the mind. Many children whom I have taught have been transformed from outcasts into high achievers because their attitudes changed! I have seen that behavior problems are frequently a mask for fear and insecurity, and I have become even bolder in my philosophy that I must first influence the attitude and then teach the brain. Children must feel self confident before they can set high goals for themselves. So many children in today's society have no leadership or guidance in the home. Often they are in single parent homes, where frequently the older siblings care for the younger ones, and it is not uncommon for many children in our region to go home to empty houses and then have parents who work at night. When they come to school, they are seeking love and affection and affirmation as much as anything else, and I am ready and willing to give them that love and affirmation! Of all the products that I could be associated with in the scientific community, I cannot think of one that would give me the joy that I receive from the opportunity to train a young mind and influence a young person in the development of his moral and ethical standards. I am proud to be a teacher and, on a daily basis, I try to be worthy of this high calling which I consider teaching to be! In an era of so much cynicism and indifference, I feel fortunate indeed to have found my "calling" in life—to be a teacher.

These essays may not show you what to say in your own essays, but they can get you thinking about your own philosophies.

Getting Ahead--and Getting Noticed--in Teaching

WHAT ARE THE KEY ISSUES FACING PUBLIC EDUCATION?

There are many major public education issues today about which I feel strongly including:

What are the key issues facing public education?

Here you see an essay written as part of an application for a Ph.D. program.

1. **Accountability is lacking.** There is need for strong accountability in teaching and education, which I feel the ABC plan is addressing adequately.

2. **Support for education is lacking.** There is a lack of support for education and a lack of emphasis on education given to the children of lower-economic families.

3. **Parents are often lacking.** The fact is that many children in our society are latch-key children and are almost literally raising themselves, with parents working nearly all the time and unable to spend much time with their children. Since I myself am an African-American, I hope I will be perceived as objective when I say that I have especially noticed that the classes of "troublemakers" I have taught have been composed of African-American children. As a member of that race and culture, I feel I could do much to speak to that community and to reach out to that community's churches, families, and network to try to motivate them to help their children acquire strong personal values and an attitude of self-discipline.

4. **Unfortunately, violence is not lacking.** The sad fact is that so many children choose violence and fighting as a way of resolving their problems, and that truth is that our schools are not as safe as they should be.

While there are many issues affecting public education about which I feel strongly, I would choose the issue of safety in schools as the issue I would like to address in depth.

Our schools need to be a safe place!

It is vital to the educational process that we ensure a safe and orderly environment in order for quality teaching and learning to occur. It is no secret that many teachers, students, and parents are concerned that the school environment is not safe enough. We need a shared vision of a safe and effective school that would serve as a beginning point for planning. All schools should strive to increase or improve the order, discipline, and safety of the school environment, which will result in a more positive school climate or culture. I realize there may be different kinds of safety problems in elementary, middle, and high schools, so I would urge that a study group be convened at each school made up of students and teachers who could study the unique safety problems at that school.

My basic approach in choosing safety as a major public education issue is that I feel safety is as much an attitude and a value as it is anything else. It is a respect for safety and the non-violent handling of problems that I feel should receive greater emphasis in our schools. The particular approach I would like to see taken in emphasizing safety is to use safety as way of promoting non-violence and non-aggression. The type of "Safety First" program I have in mind is a way of teaching children values and helping them acquire a more disciplined approach to solving their problems than hitting someone or lashing out in anger.

Safety at elementary schools. I feel an emphasis on safety at the elementary school level would promote character development in young children by stressing that fighting and physical assaults will not be tolerated. I would also like to see safety stressed in all school-related activities such as fund raisers, since there have been a few instances when children crossing busy highways to sell fundraiser products have been killed. Safety First is as much a program to teach young children to handle their problems non-aggressively as it is a program about fire or building safety.

Safety at middle schools. In middle schools, there are major problems related to violence and intimidation, so the safety emphasis in middle schools would include a major emphasis on no fighting. Again, the emphasis on safety and on finding non-violent and non-physical avenues of solving problems is a way of helping middle school children learn values of self-discipline and self-control. I believe we must be firm in disciplining children who fight and who assault other children, but I believe the standard "detention" should be married up with educational programs—perhaps in video form— to help children understand concepts related to self control and anger control.

Safety in high schools. Hopefully a safety program at the middle school level would have acquainted youth with concepts related to self discipline and anger control, but safety violations may have to be dealt with more aggressively at the high school level. Our court systems use community service instead of jail time as a way of punishing/rehabilitating violent offenders in some situations, and I believe we could require our high school students who use violence and fighting to perform some community service as a form of retribution for their crimes. I do not think anyone "wins" when high school students do not graduate from high school, so I would use permanent expulsion as the totally last resort with our high school students who use violence and physical aggression against their peers.

In summary, I believe greater emphasis on safety in our schools is really a way of championing strong personal values of non-aggression and non-violence as a means of solving problems.

Strengthening and improving the teaching profession

I came to teaching from the scientific community, where research and development are paramount and where "finding a better way of doing things" is always of utmost importance. In teaching as well, I strongly believe in "R & D" and in continuously reaching out to find new approaches. I have learned much from the staff development training I have taken, and I believe continuous training is a vital part of strengthening and improving the teaching profession.

I would, however, like to see some more funding provided for teachers who wish to participate in extensive training programs. If teachers could have access to a wider range of grants and fellowships in their pursuit of teaching excellence, I believe more teachers would take advantage of opportunities during the summers to improve their teaching techniques and subject knowledge. I would also like to see teachers rewarded for their initiatives in pursuing teacher training opportunities outside the classroom.

I believe I can personally strengthen and improve the teaching profession by my dedication and personal example. **I am a firm believer in the fact that a great deal can be accomplished by single individuals full of passion and purpose.** I am honored to be a part of the teaching profession and I am excited about making a difference in the lives of others in the future.

This essay is intended to convey her passion for and commitment to her field. She has been asked to take one issue and discuss it at length in this essay. Such an essay gives an admissions committee a chance to see how she thinks and how she articulates her point of view.

Getting Ahead--and Getting Noticed--in Teaching

DESCRIBE YOUR TEACHING PHILOSOPHY.

Teachers are the professionals in our society who are most likely to influence the values, morals, and attitudes of the next generation. I take very seriously this privilege and this responsibility, and I believe I can strengthen and improve the teaching profession through my emphasis on "the whole child" and my belief that teachers must interact each day with the "whole child"—not just the child's brain but his or her emotions, insecurities, values or lack of them, and attitude. My approach is to educate the "whole child" and I believe I can make a significant contribution to the teaching profession by helping junior teaching professionals understand this concept and learn how to implement the proven techniques in the classroom I have found successful.

Accountability in the teaching profession: I support the ABC model.

I wholeheartedly endorse the ABC school-based accountability model which has been introduced to improve accountability in the teaching profession. Good teachers want to be accountable, and I believe the ABC model is a viable approach that will strengthen teaching. Here are three reasons why I support the ABC model.

1. Student performance on end-of-grade tests is measured.

The **"A" stands for Achievement Levels,** and the ABC model identifies performance levels ranging from insufficient mastery to superior mastery, based on student performance on end-of-grade tests. It is vital that we identify where each student is in the learning process so that we can develop a suitable plan for raising performance.

2. Learning the basics of reading, writing, and arithmetic is measured.

The ABC Plan emphasizes **"The Basics,"** **which is what the "B" stands for,** and I believe the model is correct in emphasizing the key skill areas of reading, writing, and mathematics. I personally look forward to the day when each student will master a foreign language before graduating from college, but we cannot get to that level of performance until students master the basics.

3. Each school's performance is measured.

Finally, the ABC plan provides a **Composite Score,** **which is what the "C" stands for,** so that each school can measure its aggregate performance and compare its performance to sister schools. I believe it is vital that each school knows how it is doing as a unit in order for teacher and student performance to improve.

The ABC Plan works.

After some experience with the ABC plan, I believe it provides methods for establishing standards and using accountability measures in the classroom that can facilitate and strengthen learning. I have personally been a major advocate behind the scenes of this new accountability system, and I have observed that many teachers who were resistant to this approach have come to see its value. This ABC plan was piloted in 10 school systems during the recent school year, and experiences in those schools influenced the model. I have observed that the ABC plan as implemented in our school has provided the teaching staff with key areas to target.

I would like to see a strong ABC Committee at each school made up of teachers, administrators, and PTA officers who would meet at least quarterly to review the requirements of the ABC plan and find resourceful ways to administer it. For example, such a committee might decide that more tutoring of at-risk students would be beneficial, so the PTA could assist in locating the needed volunteer resources. Parents are certainly needed to proctor the End-of-Grade tests, so again the committee could assist in finding volunteers who could assist with implementation of the ABC Plan. In summary, I would like to see the ABC plan recently introduced into our school system embraced and strengthened by both parents and teachers alike who share a common belief that quality education and mastery learning is our goal.

IF YOU WERE ELECTED TEACHER OF THE YEAR, WHAT WOULD YOUR MESSAGE BE?

It is difficult for me to choose the main message I would communicate as Teacher of the Year, because I feel passionate about both (1) the issue of accountability in the teaching profession and (2) the issue of school safety. I believe I could do much good communicating with teachers about the value of the ABC and about my own positive experiences with it. The ABC plan is in its infancy and is in need of enthusiastic advocates, and I believe I could be a major spokesperson for the benefits of this accountability model. Teachers need to view the ABC plan in a positive light, and I am positive I could "sell" the ABC plan to veteran teachers.

However, I also feel very strongly about the issue of school safety, and since I must identify the **one** issue I would choose as my main message, I wish to choose school safety.

One thing all parents, teachers, and students can agree on is that our schools are not safe environments. It is inappropriate that students ever have to experience fear in a school environment, and I wish to be a powerful spokesperson for improving school safety. I have a three-point plan which I would recommend to all schools. My motto would be, "My Choice: Non-Violence!"

First, I would advocate the establishment of a committee at each school made up of students, parents, and educators who would be called the School Safety Committee. This committee would meet monthly during the school year, and students would be elected to serve on it. General safety issues would be discussed, and a subcommittee of this School Committee would function as a Disciplinary Court which would provide a "court of last resort" for students who are threatened with severe disciplinary action or expulsion. I believe many of the answers to school violence problems will be provided by the students, and this committee would get students involved in solving the problem.

Second, during my year as Teacher of the Year I would encourage schools to choose suitable methods of emphasizing non-violent methods of dispute resolution. From the student altercations I have seen, violence is used as a primitive method of solving a problem, so I would ask teachers to help students refine their problem-solving skills by learning techniques of mediation, negotiation, and arbitration. I would hope I could seek the assistance of the American Arbitration Association in sponsoring workshops and perhaps essay contests which celebrate non-violent problem solving. I would choose Martin Luther King Day as a special opportunity to celebrate non-violence in dispute resolution, and I believe Dr. King would heartily approve.

Third, I would emphasize to all communities and to parents the importance of their involvement in students' lives. The whole village must be involved in educating a child and in supporting the main themes espoused in the school environment.

If you choose to write about a common issue such as school safety, make sure you try to discuss the issue in a detailed and original fashion.

Getting Ahead--and Getting Noticed--in Teaching

DESCRIBE YOUR WORK AND ACCOMPLISHMENTS IN A PROGRAM OF SIGNIFICANCE WITH PUBLIC SCHOOLS

AN EXCITING NEW APPROACH—COMBINED EDUCATION

I had the pleasure of working as a change agent implementing a new educational approach within the Webster County School System, and that experience gave me new insight into my ability to formulate and implement change of a significant nature within the public school system.

Historically, students with moderate to severe disabilities have been educated in settings separate from non-handicapped peers.

During the past several years, parents and educators have advocated including students with moderate to severe disabilities in general education classrooms within their neighborhood schools. This concept is known as **combined education** and is being addressed nationally in public schools. **Combined education** is not a mandate but is an attempt to further meet the mandate of educating handicapped students to the maximum extent appropriate with non-handicapped peers.

From 1996-2000, I was involved in the committee that would study and implement **combined education** in the county schools. We realized that inclusion would require thoughtful planning and much staff development for all educational personnel and parents. We recognized that changing attitudes would be the first hurdle.

The first step--choosing a model.
The first step was to determine a model to follow. After researching various models, our committee selected the Murphy Teaching Model which we had observed being implemented in Maine schools. The Murphy Teaching Model is "an educational approach in which general and special educators work to jointly teach heterogeneous groups of students in general education classrooms. Both teachers are simultaneously involved in instruction.

The second step--selecting an expert.
We chose an expert to direct us through this change process. Dr. Howard Jennings, Associate Professor at Columbia University, was selected to be the lead consultant and to train our teachers. He is nationally recognized in the field of special education and combined classrooms.

The next step in implementing change was to sponsor top-quality staff development, and our process was to begin with a small number of "voluntary" schools. We had two high schools, two junior high schools, and two elementary schools during the first year of implementing the change.

The principals were designated as the first professionals to have staff development. As the instructional leaders of their schools, they had to be supportive of combined education if it was to be successful.

Staff development was then provided to teams of regular education and special education teachers.

Describe your work and accomplishments in a program of significance with public schools.
This was an essay which accompanied an application for graduate school.

After staff development, the model was implemented within the schools. The students with mild to moderate disabilities were selected to participate. These students were receiving special education from a traditional "pull-out" model—one to three hours daily, rather than the more severely handicapped students who received most of their special education in a separate special education classroom. These were the students who would most likely obtain high school diplomas and would greatly benefit from instruction in a general education setting.

There were two options available to the teachers:

(1) Team teaching: The regular education teacher and the special education teacher jointly plan and teach the academic subject content to all students.

(2) Complementary instruction: The general education teacher maintains primary responsibility for teaching subject content and the special education teacher provides instruction in specific strategies to students who might benefit.

The school had the flexibility of selecting the option that would best meet their students' needs. Most of the schools initially used the team teaching option, primarily because the special education teachers wanted to be actively involved in instruction. Their greatest fear was that they would become "assistants."

Results and conclusions

Informal data was collected at the end of that year so that results could be measured.

Result 1: We discovered that grades and test scores increased while attendance and discipline problems decreased!

Result 2: We found that at-risk students and non-handicapped students had benefited as well as the handicapped students.

Result 3: The most positive findings were reports from the students of increased self-esteem. They liked remaining in the classroom; being "pulled out" made them feel different.

Result 4: Students also liked achieving at grade level curriculum and they liked having two teachers, because there was always a teacher to answer questions and assist them.

Result 5: Although some parents had been hesitant initially, parent reports were very positive at the end of the year.

These "pilot" sites were used for other schools in the school system to visit. The county teaching model was expanded into most of the schools over the next few years. This county has become a model site for other school systems to visit.

At the present time, many of the moderate-needs students are receiving their special education through the Murphy Teaching Model. However, there are students whose needs were not met in this setting, and those students are provided their special education needs through the traditional "pull-out" program.

Getting Ahead--and Getting Noticed--in Teaching

WHY DO YOU WANT TO PURSUE A DOCTORATE?

"Why do you want to pursue a doctorate?

If you were a member of an admissions committee, wouldn't you want to know the answer to that question?

My desire to obtain a doctorate is not new. Indeed, pursuing a doctorate has been my goal since earning my M.A. in Elementary Education. Now, I feel the timing is right, and, furthermore, it would be a great honor to earn the terminal degree in my field from an institution where I earned both my B.S. (magna cum laude) and my M.A.. My commitment to education is well illustrated in my career. After earning my B.S. degree (major Psychology, minor English), I excelled as part of the Adult Basic Education and Human Resources Development Instructor with Adirondack Community College. Subsequently I taught sixth grade at Carter Elementary School. From 1990-97, I taught fourth grade at Edison Elementary School. From 1997-present, I have served as Assistant Principal at Liberty Elementary School, and I have made major contributions through my administrative ability, creativity, and true love for children. I am especially proud of two programs: we have implemented a Success-Only Math Lab which has improved mathematics skills, and we have pioneered a unique In-School Suspension Program aimed at lessening negative and inappropriate behaviors.

My goal after receiving the doctoral degree is to apply my administrative skills and teaching ability in leadership positions at local, county, or state levels. After earning the doctorate, I would seek a position in which I could play a significant role in helping children (and teachers) by designing and implementing educational policy. I would seek to serve in positions such as Principal, Superintendent of Schools, as well as in policy-making roles at the state and federal levels. I believe my diverse experience outside the academic world would help me in refining our public educational systems after I receive my doctorate, and I also believe that I could enrich a doctoral program through my experience in teaching and other areas. For example, I have been a member of the Youth Services Advisory Board (an appointed position by the county commissioners) and was a co-chair of the Student Service Team for four years. As I believe my extensive memberships and affiliations demonstrate, I have always reached out to serve on community organizations which aim to help children both inside and outside the classroom. These memberships and involvements have equipped me with rich insights which I believe could make me a vital and valuable part of the doctoral program. I am a strong believer in involving as many community agencies as possible in the educational process, and I generously devote my time to serving on such committees as a member and leader.

I love education, and I am proud to be dedicating my life to this great field. For that reason, I am always very proud and deeply honored when I earn the respect of my colleagues, as I did when I was named "Teacher of the Year" at Carter Elementary School.

If accepted into the doctoral program, I would consider it a great honor which would permit me to imagine, discover, and conceptualize creative concepts in education and student services which could be implemented in this century. I believe that the success of our nation depends upon high standards of educational excellence. I support high standards for student behavior and achievement; excellence in teaching; a positive school environment; and vigorous parental involvement. I believe teaching is a social as well as an academic process and cannot be separated from the total character and tasks of society. The more a student feels that school is an institution in which he can grow and work in connection with the natural tasks such as life requires, the happier and more productive he/she will be, and the more our society as a whole will benefit.

It is my deep desire to be of service to our state and nation that motivates me to seek the doctoral degree. There is nothing that thrills me more than to see our public schools graduate students who are ready for employment and who are equipped with the self confidence to face life enthusiastically.

I am confident that I could enthusiastically, intelligently, and resourcefully contribute to the goals of public education, and I believe the world could be a better place for us all if I were equipped with the doctorate and with the additional knowledge and tools it would give me so that I can work at the highest levels of professional activity for the benefit of our schools and the students we educate.

When admissions committees evaluate essays, they are trying to find the people who could contribute the most to the profession and they are trying to discover the individuals who will become renowned members of the profession. If you have an idea that you will one day be a credit to the institution to which you are applying, say so!

Getting Ahead--and Getting Noticed--in Teaching

ESSAY DESCRIBING MY PURPOSE IN PURSUING A DOCTORATE

Pursuing a doctorate has been my goal since earning my M.ED. in Special Education. I had an opportunity in 1998 to attend a workshop at Adrian University and was impressed with the positive atmosphere and open learning environment. After investigating the credentials and background of the faculty, I became convinced that Adrian University was the perfect place for me to pursue my doctoral studies.

Compare this essay to the one on the previous page so that you can assess for yourself the difference in style and subject chosen to write about.

If accepted into the doctoral program, I am planning on taking leave from my current job as Director of Exceptional Children's Programs with Baldwin County Schools where I currently supervise 85 teachers, teacher assistants, speech pathologists, and psychologists while also writing federal grants and developing innovative new training opportunities for educators. While earning my doctorate, I plan on completing a textbook on special education strategies for parents which I have been writing for more than seven years. Two publishers have already indicated their interest in reading the manuscript. My credentials in the special education arena are top-notch, and it is my desire to strengthen my knowledge and skills related to special education through my pursuit of a doctorate.

My goal after receiving the doctoral degree is to apply my knowledge in a staff or managerial policy-making position at the national level. While specializing in the field of exceptional children's programs, I have acquired an ability to adapt quickly to the fast pace of change in the way exceptional children's needs are met within school systems and by individual teachers in classrooms. I offer considerable experience as a "change agent" within public school systems. I believe my expert knowledge of exceptional children's programs and needs could be a valuable addition to your doctoral program and could provide enriching insights for the other doctoral candidates.

If you look at my vitae, I believe you will see that your doctoral program is the obvious next step in my professional life so that I can contribute to an even greater extent to public school education in our state and nation. As a doctoral candidate, I would offer a "track record" of committed service to education along with expert knowledge of the area of exceptional children's programs administration. I began my teaching career as a teacher of 3rd and 4th grade students in Maine and, in that first teaching position, I encountered the problem of having students who were non-readers. That experience in my "rookie" year of teaching caused me to make a commitment to gain more specialization as a teacher so that I could help children who were not learning. After obtaining my M.ED in Special Education, I taught in exceptional children's programs and have been involved in the supervision of exceptional children's programs in Baldwin County Schools and Caldwell County Schools.

As we embark upon the challenges of the 21st century, I foresee greater and greater cultural and educational diversity in our classrooms. This is already happening! With a reputation statewide as an expert in the field of exceptional children's programs, I am intimately acquainted with the increasing tendency toward more inclusion of handicapped children in regular classrooms. That reality means, very simply, that teachers cannot teach a heterogeneous student population in the same way that they would teach a homogeneous population.

I have a sincere desire to help teachers figure out the best way to teach as they find themselves working in these increasingly complex and diversified classroom environments.

It is my strong professional belief that teacher preparatory programs will eventually be moving away from training teachers as **either** regular teachers **or** special education teachers. As more and more children with special needs are being included in regular classrooms, I believe teacher preparatory programs at the college and university level eventually will be training teachers to work with diverse populations—at-risk, handicapped, multi-cultural, and other specialized groups. While this trend in combined education will eventually dramatically impact university teacher preparatory programs, the changes caused by combined education will even more immediately require sensitive and capable administrators who have the vision and knowledge to help teachers, students, and parents respond to the new challenges of combined classrooms.

In summary, it is my deep desire to be of service to our nation that motivates me to seek the doctoral degree. There is nothing that thrills me more than to see our public schools graduate students who are ready for employment and who are equipped with the self confidence to face life enthusiastically—both of which can be produced by a quality public school education. As a practical person with 15 years of experience in teaching and administration, I believe the doctoral program will enhance my skills as a practitioner and enable me to continue to manage growth and change within the highly exciting and fast-paced world of public education.

Getting Ahead--and Getting Noticed--in Teaching

"IF YOU BELIEVE THAT YOUR STANDARDIZED TEST RESULTS OR YOUR UNDERGRADUATE GRADE POINT AVERAGE ARE NOT AN ACCURATE REFLECTION OF YOUR ABILITY TO BE SUCCESSFUL IN GRADUATE SCHOOL, PLEASE EXPLAIN IN SOME DETAIL."

A question such as this one can give you an opportunity to explain a weakness or a reckless or lackluster period in your history. This question is frequently asked and permits you to explain any shortcomings in your background. Notice how cleverly this person approaches this question. Not only does this individual use this essay as an opportunity to answer the question asked, but also he uses the question as an opportunity to showcase his unique background since the days in which he earned the mediocre GPA.

I do not believe that GPA or standardized tests are always an accurate reflection of an individual's ability. If GPA and standardized test scores were accurate barometers of ability, then my scorings in undergraduate school would hardly predict the successful and rewarding career I have enjoyed since graduation. As a young student, it is often difficult to see the applicability of many aspects of classroom learning to real-world environment. I struggled with this throughout college as reflected by my GPA.

My undergraduate were filled with a misplaced certainty that I was wasting time before getting my hands dirty in the real-world. I wanted to "do," not study. I am now filled with the humility and insight that I must glean every kernel of knowledge offered by the best and the brightest at your university. Experience has brought maturity and a sense of mission to my life. After extensive real-world experience, I see the functionality of conceptual classroom study. I see clearly now that "street smarts" and "book learning" are companion tools for problem solving in life.

Since my undergraduate days, I have been out in the real world and have gotten my hands dirty. I have found that I enjoy working in the trenches with at-risk youth. But I have learned that I still have a lot to learn about how to help them, and it is that realization that has brought me to the doorstep of your institution, application in hand. I strongly desire to become one of the 12 handpicked doctoral candidates for your Ph.D. program. I know I can be a credit to the program. My extensive work with at-risk children in homes for youth offenders will enable me to provide insights as a Ph.D. candidate which other doctoral candidates might not have, and I am confident that my experience will enrich the doctoral program at your university.

I believe that the ingredients for success in graduate school include excellent analytical and problem-solving abilities, superior written and public speaking skills, and relentless persistence to succeed in spite of all obstacles. I also believe that a professional in any field pursuing a doctoral degree must possess the highest ethical and moral standards and be someone in whom the public can place absolute confidence. I am an individual who lives by high personal principles and strong moral values, and I also possess the strong analytical and communication skills required by your rigorous program.

My innovative approach to problem-solving has been apparent in my chosen career since my graduation from undergraduate school. I have excelled in troubled youth intervention and treatment in an area where many fail. After military discipline programs failed with hard-core gang members, I tried art. One young man who was facing hard prison time graduated from my program and is now a successful artist in Houston. If art failed, I have tried gardening and animal care. Through determined love, I have shown these children how to care about something in a world that they had previously felt was beyond caring for them. This determination to succeed, no matter what, is what I feel will make me a successful doctoral candidate.

I have seen how effective intervention programs can be, and I am now frustrated that I cannot implement more far-reaching programs. Without a doctoral degree I can go no farther in the current infrastructure of intervention programs. I have a passion for my work and will work tirelessly to succeed in your program. I have seen firsthand that each youth who does not find himself in an effective intervention program is a youth lost to the system. That I find unacceptable. By accepting my application to graduate school, the board is not only investing in me as an individual but in some of tomorrow's most troubled youth.

I would like to make you aware that attending graduate school is an exceedingly difficult choice for me. It means that I must leave to others the administration of the programs which I have developed. It also means that fewer youth will be helped than would be helped if I remained in my current position because, due to budget constraints, my position will not be replaced until my graduation from the doctoral program. I must give up the day-to-day rewards of working side-by-side with kids who have the potential to be tomorrow's leaders or tomorrow's "most wanted." The choice I have made, however, is the strategic one. I must help the many even if it sacrifices a few due to my absence.

Armed with the doctoral degree, I feel that I could help develop a nationwide network of intervention programs that will be much more effective and far-reaching than those currently in place. I have received grant aid for this network conditional to my graduation from your doctoral program. My passion to help our nation's children will undoubtedly prove to be an excellent motivating factor throughout your program, and I humbly ask the admissions committee to favorably review my application for admission.

Getting Ahead--and Getting Noticed--in Teaching

WHAT SPECIAL PROJECT IN EDUCATION HAVE YOU COMPLETED?

One of the most successful projects in our school was "Give me a book and I'll read it." This was a project which I conceived of, planned, and implemented which was designed to increase the entire student body's interest in literacy. While applying my skills as a writer of grant proposals, we were able to utilize grant money to purchase two book titles for each grade level. The books were used to teach reading and writing using an integrated approach according to the goals and objectives of the Arkansas Standard Course of Study and End-of-Grade tests.

Teacher of the Year essay questions

Questions such as these help admissions committees, and Teacher of the Year committees, distinguish between you and other talented teaching professionals. Your goal is to make yourself come across as unique. Sometimes committees test your ability to say a lot in few words, such as the question on this page which must be answered in "30 words or less."

A primary objective of the project was for each child to have two books, one of which was left at school and the other sent home. The purpose of this objective was to enable each child to establish or add to his/her own personal library. By accomplishing this goal of helping the child start or add to a personal book collection, we hope the child will be inspired to develop a love of reading and to see books as a daily companion.

As a result of this project, we have motivated our parents to become actively involved with our "We're a Family of Readers!" Program. In this family reading program, parents establish and maintain the habit/discipline of reading at least fifteen minutes each night with their children and the reading time is documented on a reading log form which is turned in to the child's teacher. In evaluating the program, we have found that children who have a "reading buddy" at home enjoy the one-on-one attention they receive during the special reading time. The time spent reading with the child seems to be a form of "leadership by example" in which the child sees clearly that reading is viewed as an important activity by an adult whose behavior is noticed and often gets copied by the child. We have often discovered that shared reading time enhances the self-esteem of children because they feel special that this reading time is set aside by the parent. The child seems to feel important because the parent makes the time to read alone with the child each day.

DESCRIBE YOUR LEADERSHIP STYLE IN 30 WORDS OR LESS.

A believer in leadership by example, I excel in utilizing encouragement and praise to motivate teachers. I create an atmosphere which encourages creativity, teamwork as well as personal accountability, and a striving for excellent results. I emphasize the cultivation of personal qualities that include self respect and respect for others.

DESCRIBE HOW RELATIONSHIPS BETWEEN COMMUNITY AND SCHOOLS AFFECT EDUCATION.

It is my belief that the purpose of education is to provide the best education possible for all students. In order for teachers and administrators to do an excellent job in educating children, we must not only let the community know our school's mission but also inform the community about specific ways in which it can be a part of that mission. As the principal of Seven Hills Elementary School, I make an assertive effort to share all the school's activities with the community.

As a guest speaker, I have communicated the school's mission to the Duquenes Kiwanis Club, many churches in the community and surrounding areas, Boy Scout troops, Business and Women's Clubs, the Kiwanis Community Center, and several groups at local universities. Frequent speaking engagements in the community give me an opportunity to personalize the school while discussing in detail our goals, objectives, philosophies, and purposes. I ardently believe in "getting the word out" to various community groups about the extent to which our teachers and assistants are involved with students' learning and the positive results we are getting. In each speech I give, I always provide specific examples of how the community can get involved in order to help individual children while assuring that excellent educational standards are maintained for the benefit of local employers and the community at large.

One way I encourage the community to get involved is through our Mentor-Tutor Program, which is the highlight of our school's volunteer program. This program is comprised of parents, grandparents, professors, and students from Northwestern University (Education Department, Computer Department, Law School, Medical School, and The Student Union). We use our volunteers to provide one-on-one instruction for the students. Presently we have nearly 50 volunteers participating in this program, and they have volunteered hundreds of hours since the program began.

Our Adopt-a-School Partners are members of the greater community, as well as our parents. They sponsor student incentive programs such as Terrific Kids, Students of the Week, Students of the Month, Writers of the Month, Perfect Attendance, and Honor Rolls. All of these programs inspire our students to have high expectations and achieve recognitions in areas that promote student interest and emphasize their purpose for being in school. As principal, I emphasize to my teaching staff the idea that children learn by example and that children learn more from what we do than from what we say. Therefore, I believe it is imperative for parents and other caring community people to be visibly involved in school activities, and we are delighted at the excellent participation of the community in our Adopt-a-School Partners Program.

Our students are caring and responsible students who want to help our less fortunate citizens. Our student body as a whole has participated in local service projects and national service projects. For example, the fifth grade students have organized food drives at Thanksgiving for the Department of Social Services in Brighton County. They have also sponsored a non-perishable items' drive for victims of Hurricane Andrew in Florida. Grades three through five participate in the Children's Hospital Math-a-Thon each year. Our students have raised approximately $2,500 for the past three years for the Children's Hospital Project.

In summary, we are very fortunate to have excellent parental support and involvement in all facets of our school: tutors, volunteers, service projects, fund raisers, family reading program, Fall Carnival, Heritage Day, award assemblies, and other programs. The parents' high level of participation allowed us to receive the Golden Key Award for Parental Involvement in my first year as principal at Seven Hills Elementary School. I can say without overstating anything that "Seven Hills is truly a community school."

Getting Ahead--and Getting Noticed--in Teaching

DESCRIBE WHAT YOUR PHILOSOPHY AND PRACTICES WOULD BE AS AN EDUCATION ADMINISTRATOR.

It was the spring, and I had just finished my masters program. Our staff at that time had received notice from the Central Office that we would be transferred to Dark Mouth Elementary School in the fall. The transfer added more staff members and an assistant principal position. Until that point in time, I earnestly believed that my mission in life was to be the very best teacher I could be for the boys and girls in my class.

At that point in my life, when I and other teachers were anticipating a transfer to Dark Mouth Elementary School, my principal came to me and shared a vision that he said he and my peers had for me: becoming an assistant principal. He told me that it was the unanimous feeling of my peers that I should take my respected teaching expertise to an even higher level of education—to the job of assistant principal— where I could combine my teaching background with my leadership and management skills in order to make a major impact on students, staff, and other teachers. I was overwhelmed and touched by the reality that my principal and peers had such high regard for me and shared this vision of where I should be professionally so that I could "make a difference" in education for all of us. I humbly agreed to take the job of assistant principal.

My mission in life now is to positively impact the lives of students, staff, and parents through my job as a principal. All of my efforts as a principal I appreciatively dedicate to my former principal and to the former staff and teachers at Mason Heights Elementary School who placed their faith in me. Without their expression of faith in me, I might not have taken that step toward assistant principal and principal. This is what we do as teachers, too: we encourage, embolden, motivate, inspire, and help people to see and achieve their potential. I thank God that I am a teacher and I thank teachers for just being teachers.

I regard the job of principal as one in which I am constantly solving problems and finding new opportunities to positively impact the lives of students, teachers, and parents. As principal, I am privileged to have an opportunity to share my commitment to education with others; I communicate to teachers and other staff the philosophy that we are all accountable because we share as a team the same vision and goals.

As an offshoot of my belief that we are all accountable for our results, I continuously seek to find practical ways of measuring our successes as well as our shortcomings. I believe strongly that teaching professionals will be more likely to work to achieve goals that they themselves have helped to establish, so I assume a "hands-on" management style as teacher and foster an atmosphere in which teachers' opinions are listened to and respected. Together, we set goals that are ambitious and achievable, and then we develop the specific plans to achieve our goals. Once we achieve our goals, I believe in publicizing our success stories, so we are a marketing-oriented school that aggressively seeks to communicate to parents, students, and the community the strides we are making in helping students develop to their fullest academic, physical, and mental capacity.

One of my main jobs as principal is to listen. I believe that listening is often the "forgotten part" of the communication process, and I make an effort to make myself

Describe what your philosophy and practices would be as an education administrator.
This principal must answer some probing questions in order to reveal whether he is the best candidate for a position which would place him in charge of a school system.

available to listen to students, teachers, parents, and community members. Some of my best ideas for new programs and for modifications of existing programs have come about because I have taken the time to listen. **The contribution I would like to make in this field is to be an instructional leader who loves to select, develop, and empower outstanding teachers and assistants who can ensure accountability.** I believe this will be best accomplished by utilizing strategies and techniques in teaching designed to improve student outcomes which have been developed through teamwork.

DESCRIBE HOW YOU RESOLVE SPECIFIC ADMINISTRATIVE PROBLEMS IN EDUCATION.

Our school is in a small community and everyone knows almost everyone else in the school. I try to avoid changing a student to another teacher's class once the rosters are posted, unless there is a situation where the child's year will be impacted in a negative way unless this is accomplished. For example, one day the parents of one student asked me to change their child from one teacher's class to another because of personality differences which were affecting the child in an adversely emotional manner. I listened to the parents, empathized with them about their perceived differences in the classrooms, and discussed my reasons for not making it a general rule to change classroom assignments. However, I told them that I would make the change based on the students' emotional distress, which was documented by a doctor's note.

In the situation which I am describing, it was not only important to make the right decision, but it was also important to implement the decision in a sensitive manner. I told the parents that I must first inform the teachers and share some things with them because our job is to provide opportunities for the best possible education for each child. I held private sessions with each teacher involved, and I communicated to each one in a tactful, sensitive manner so that no one's feelings were hurt and no professional pride diminished. The teachers involved both understood that they had my complete confidence and full support, and they were both supportive of making a change that seemed in the child's best interests.

The rules of confidentiality were observed, and I have carefully monitored the situation since the change in classroom was made. All parties seem happy, and I believe this change was necessary. This was a situation in which it would have been wrong, in my opinion, to "stick by the rules" and refuse to adjust a situation which was becoming dysfunctional. I feel strongly that I made the right decision and implemented the decision correctly, and I would not alter in any way the way I handled this particular problem.

Getting Ahead--and Getting Noticed--in Teaching

HOW WOULD YOU IMPROVE STUDENT ACHIEVEMENT?

One of the major issues facing educators today is accountability for principals and teachers for improved test scores on End-of-Grade tests. I have used my position as an instructional leader at New York Elementary School to inform teachers, students, parents, and the community about students' progress in the following ways:

1. Reviewed the goals and objectives of the New York Standard Course of Study by grade level.

How would you improve student achievement?

The purpose of an essay question is to "see how you think," not to see if you can guess the "right answer."

2. Reviewed the benchmarks and proficiencies for each grade level in reading, writing, and mathematics.

3. Analyzed test data to determine our strengths and weaknesses on grade level.

4. Implemented strategies to maintain strengths and to improve weaknesses of skills in the curriculum.

5. Evaluated our gains from year to year for each grade level.

6. Targeted students in grades K-2 that are at-risk in language development skills. Targeted students in grades 3-6 that made a level 1 or level 2 on End-of-Grade tests.

7. Implemented a whole language reading program for kindergartners, "Early Opportunities to Read," to improve language development before entering first grade.

8. Utilized the services of an education consultant to assist teachers with writing across the curriculum, to develop curriculum maps that centered on themes for each grade level to help children connect learning across the curriculum, to teach the philosophies of mastery learning and learning styles. Strategies from these activities helped teachers to adjust their teaching techniques to meet the needs of all students.

9. Utilized grant money to purchase trade books and novels to teach reading and writing skills across the curriculum.

10. Utilized teacher assistants, parent volunteers, and students from New York University to work with at-risk students individually or in small groups.

11. Provided daily exposure and practices to concepts, materials, and terminology relevant to End-of-Grade tests.

12. Involved parents in a well-publicized home reading program to improve students' reading interest and reading level. It also provides an opportunity for parents to become more involved with their children's school work. Research shows that when parents are actively involved with students' learning, it increases their test scores, graduation rates, and college enrollment.

13. Provided an atmosphere that is nurturing and caring for all.

The above strategies provide opportunities for teachers to teach a comprehensive reading, writing, and mathematics program that will inspire each child to excel to his or her greatest potential.

PROVIDE ANY INFORMATION NOT PREVIOUSLY PROVIDED TO THE SELECTION COMMITTEE.

If I were to take over the leadership of the Bellweather School System, I would see myself as a team leader. The progress of children in any school is positive and successful when certain factors and beliefs exist among the team members responsible for improvements in student learning. Our team consists of our teachers, staff, parents, students, and members of our community. Our goals and purposes are the same. We want to inspire our students in such a way that each of them will have a zest for life-long learning.

We are dedicated to the improvement of children. Therefore, we believe that what is best for children must be our highest priority at all times. Through our partnership and shared vision, we must provide for children a sense of love, hope, fair play, respect for others, and a positive self-image.

The achievements of our children are part of a comprehensive process which does not focus on End-of-Grade tests only, but on the overall improvement of all school components including parental involvement, community involvement, staff development, accountability, positive work climate, and a common belief system. In my current position as principal at Drayton Hall School System, we have focused on the above components to enhance skills in our curriculum. We now have a better sense of sharing, coaching, and mentoring. The knowledge gained from working as a team has enabled us to analyze our progress and map out strategies for future goals and objectives. We realize that true school improvement starts at the school level, but it takes the whole team to make positive outcomes with our children.

I feel privileged that destiny has positioned me as the team leader of this vibrant educational process, and I delight every day in the challenges and opportunities that being a principal offers me as I humbly try to be a positive force in the life of each and every student, teacher, parent, staff person, and community member with whom I come into contact.

This is an essay for an individual who seeks to lead a school system, and he has been given an opportunity to answer this open-ended question. This type of essay question should be viewed as an opportunity to express his views in a persuasive manner and to articulate his unique style.

Getting Ahead--and Getting Noticed--in Teaching

Date

Cover Letter to Accompany Application a Resume and Other Materials Used to Apply for a Ph.D. Program

On this and the opposite page, you will see the cover letter and resume which accompanied an application for a Ph.D. Program. You might want to look at the essay question on pages 50 and 51 to which this letter refers. This is the type of cover letter and resume which would accompany an application to a graduate school or Ph.D. program.

Dear Dr.:

With the enclosed materials, I am making formal application to the Ed.D. in Educational Leadership Program at University of Nevada.

You will see from my enclosed resume that I have an M.ED in Special Education and have gained a statewide reputation as an expert in the field of exceptional children's programs. In my current job with Webster County Schools, I supervise 95 teachers, teacher assistants, speech pathologists, and psychologists while directing the day-to-day operations of programs for special populations of children.

I was quite excited to see a question on the application related to my work in a program of significance with public schools, and I have written about my experience as a change agent implementing a new educational approach called Combined Education within the Webster County Schools.

I am committed to spending the rest of my life involved in the design and implementation of programs which will be "user-friendly" to teachers and students in the public schools, and I offer a "track record" of contributions to educational development within Nevada. I have been active in developing programs for transition from school to work for handicapped students, and I strongly believe the handicapped can be prepared and trained to become productive employees.

I would be delighted to make myself available to you for a personal interview, if you feel this is desirable or necessary. I am confident that I could become a distinguished alumnus of the doctoral program at UN, and I feel certain that my experience in teaching and administration would enrich the learning environment of the other doctoral students. Thank you in advance for giving my application every consideration.

Sincerely yours,

Nancy J. Vetstein

NANCY J. VETSTEIN

1110 1/2 Hay Street, Fayetteville, NC 28305 • preppub@aol.com • 910-483-6611

OBJECTIVE
To apply to the Doctoral Program (Ed.D.) in Educational Leadership in order to gain insight and knowledge that will enable me to continue, at even higher levels of leadership, my "track record" of contributions to educational development within Nevada and the nation.

EDUCATION
Certificate in Educational Administration and Supervision, University of Nevada, 1986.
M.ED. in Special Education, University of Nevada, Reno, NV, SC, 1974.
B.A. in History and Art, University of Nevada, 1971.
Extensive continuing education in areas related to Combined Education, Strategies for Teaching SLD Students, Mastery Learning, and other areas.

AFFILIATIONS & COMMUNITY LEADERSHIP
- Member, Liaison Committee, Kibler Mental Health Agency
- Active supporter, CARE Center, Muscular Dystrophy Association
- Advisory Board Member, NV Partnership Training System, University of Nevada
- Member for 20 years, national and state Council for Exceptional Children

EXPERIENCE
DIRECTOR OF EXCEPTIONAL CHILDREN'S PROGRAMS. Webster County Schools, Reno, NV (1994-present). Was promoted from Supervisor to Director, and now manage 95 teachers, teacher assistants, speech pathologists, and psychologists while directing the day-to-day operations of programs for handicapped children.
- Developed innovative new workshops and training opportunities for teachers on writing IEPs and transition education; gained considerable experience in writing federal grants.
- Worked closely with the Office of Civil Rights in collecting data related to transportation.

SUPERVISOR, EXCEPTIONAL CHILDREN'S PROGRAMS. Webster County Schools, Reno, NV (1988-94). Became knowledgeable about laws governing Exceptional Children's Programs while coordinating staff development workshops, chairing the Administrative Placement Committee, supervising Educational Diagnostic Centers, and overseeing services provided through the Homebound/Hospital and Vision Impaired Programs.

INSTRUCTIONAL SPECIALIST. Webster County Schools, Reno, NV (1982-88). Supervised the Behavioral Emotionally Handicapped Programs which included training teachers in writing and implementing behavior management plans.
- Authored the Behavior Management System currently in use in Webster County.

COLLEGE INSTRUCTOR. University of Nevada, Reno, NV (1979-80). On a part-time basis, taught the Introduction to Special Education Course, the Testing & Measurement Course, and the Gifted & Talented Course.

TEACHER, EXCEPTIONAL CHILDREN'S (EC) PROGRAMS. Webster County Schools Reno, NV (1971-79). At three different elementary schools, taught students with severe learning and behavioral problems; developed individual education programs for academic and behavioral instruction while completing diagnostic evaluations on each student.
- Saw first-hand that students ranked "at the bottom" can learn and grow with consistent expectations and genuine respect; later saw many of these students graduate from high school and become employed in the community.

PERSONAL
Outstanding references upon request. Proven ability to work in harmony with others.

Getting Ahead--and Getting Noticed--in Teaching

Date

Exact Name of Person
Exact Title
Exact Name of Company
Address
City, State, Zip

Dear Exact Name of Person (or Dear Sir or Madam if answering a blind ad):

With this letter and the enclosed resume, I would like to initiate the process of applying for a fellowship with your organization and to acquaint you with my outstanding professional knowledge and skills.

As you will see from the resume, I am a well-educated and self-motivated professional with a background of community service and effectiveness in leadership roles both in professional settings and in community action environments. My educational background includes two master's degrees: most recently a Master of Library Science and an earlier Master of Adult Education along with a B.S. in Business Administration, all earned at the University of Washington in Seattle.

My background as a Media Specialist at area elementary schools led to my acceptance for this position at the high school level. At Easterling High School I have been selected for numerous additional duties including School Grants Coordinator and School Technology Specialist. In the former role I have become highly familiar with researching and writing grant applications while in the latter I apply my knowledge of the latest technology utilized in libraries to instruct other faculty members and conduct staff development workshops. In addition to serving the school as Audio-visual and Reference Librarian, I also was chosen as ACT Test Center Administrator to hire and train staff as well as making preparations for testing.

If you can use an articulate and mature professional with a wide range of abilities and knowledge, I hope you will call me soon for a brief discussion of how I could apply for fellowship opportunities within your organization. I will provide excellent professional and personal references at the appropriate time.

Sincerely,

Bonnie L. Bertolaet

BONNIE L. BERTOLAET

1110½ Hay Street, Fayetteville, NC 28305 • preppub@aol.com • (910) 483-6611

OBJECTIVE

I am seeking a fellowship based on my outstanding professional skills, proven leadership ability, and desire to make significant contributions in my field.

EDUCATION

Master of Library Science, University of Washington, Seattle, WA, 1990.
Master of Adult Education, University of Washington, Seattle, WA, 1982.
Bachelor of Science in Business Administration, University of Washington, Seattle, WA, 1980.

EXPERIENCE

MEDIA SPECIALIST (AV/Reference Librarian). Easterling High School, Seattle, WA (1993-present). Since August 1995-present, have served as the **ACT Test Center Administrator**; hired and trained staff to administer the ACT Assessment Test; prepared facilities and materials for test day.
- Instructed students in the use of reference books, library materials and electronic information sources.
- Purchased books, computer software, and equipment for the media center.
- Supervised student library assistants; co-sponsored library club.
- Cataloged and processed library materials.
- Conducted fundraisers.
- In an additional duty as **School Grants Coordinator,** compile and disseminate information about grants; assist with the application process; and plan grant writing workshops.
- As **School Technology Specialist,** instruct faculty in the use of technology; conduct staff development workshops.

MEDIA SPECIALIST. Dudley Elementary School, Seattle, WA (1991-93). Instructed students in the use of the media center and information skills; purchased books and equipment for the media center; planned activities to promote reading.

LIBRARY ASSISTANT & GRADUATE ASSISTANT. University of Washington, Seattle, WA (1989-90). As a Library Assistant, handled general circulation desk responsibilities and serial maintenance while answering reference questions, processing new books, and assisting students in the computer lab; as a Graduate Assistant, assisted with the bibliographic conversion for the library automation project.

Highlights of other experience:
GRADUATE ASSISTANT. University of Washington, School of Education, Seattle, WA. While obtaining my Master of Adult Education, assisted professors in the Department of Educational Administration and Supervision; performed typing, filing, and other clerical tasks; assisted in the preparation of seminars for principals and school administrators.
- Conducted research for Assistant Dean of the School of Education.

RESIDENT ADVISOR. University of Washington, Seattle, WA. While working toward my Master of Adult Education degree, supervised students in Telford Dormitory.

PERSONAL

Known for strong personal qualities: **Congenial:** Work well with others; **Conscientious:** Committed to excellence in any job I take on; **Resourceful:** Take the initiative when I see a task which needs to be accomplished; **Ambitious:** Willing to take on extra assignments; **Organized:** Have a talent for organizing things in an orderly way; **Open-minded:** Able to accept ideas contrary to my own. Flexible and adaptable.

PART FOUR: REAL-RESUMES FOR TEACHERS "ON THE MOVE" IN TEACHING!

The section you are about to enter is the heart of the book. In this section you will see resumes and cover letters of teachers, counselors, media specialists, varsity coaches, assistant principals, principals, and superintendents. You can learn something from every resume and cover letter in this book.

Getting your resume and cover letter to the right person

If you are looking for a teaching position, you have an easier job hunt than many people in private industry or business. You usually need to make sure that your resume gets to a central office so that you are "on file." But you also should send a copy of your resume and cover directly to the principals at the schools where you want to teach. Even if you are a high school teacher seeking a job in nearby communities, you probably can develop a "preferred list" of schools based on factors like commuting distance, reputation of the high school, curricula, etc. Write directly to the principal with cover letters such as the ones you will see in this section. Convey in the cover letter your strong desire to become a part of that school's teaching faculty. This kind of personal approach is what will open many doors for you.

Interviewing for the job

Because you are a teacher or a part of the teaching profession, you are "ahead of the game" in terms of interviewing for jobs. Because you teach, you have communication skills which you utilize daily, so having a conversation with a principal will probably not seem intimidating to you. Nevertheless, be sure to give a warm and firm handshake when you meet with interviewers, and don't forget that research shows that people who smile at interviews are perceived of as more intelligent than people who do not smile. (We're not sure why, but it's what the research shows.)

Aspiring Assistant Principal

Date

Assistant Principal

Dear Superintendent:

You might try this particular layout if you have had the same job title and performed the same functions at different schools.

With this letter of intent and the enclosed resume, I would like to express my interest in receiving your consideration for a position as principal of Davidson Elementary School.

Prior to taking on my current position as Assistant Principal at Davidson Road Elementary, I received my Certification in Educational Administration and Supervision from The University of Washington at Seattle in 1996. I also earned my M.A. in Elementary Education and B.S. in Education from the same institution. I have completed training at the Assistant Principal's Academy in 1998 and 1999, and I have been undergoing extensive Montessori training at the National Center for Montessori Teacher Education.

Prior to becoming an Assistant Principal, I earned a reputation as a skilled and concerned teacher, trainer, and mentor firmly committed to the value of education and the importance of the teaching profession. After approximately five years as a Classroom Teacher in the challenging environment of multi-age classrooms, I made a change into administrative roles where my leadership, administrative skills, and ability to communicate effectively have been of value.

With a reputation as an innovative "doer," I have played a key role in establishing Davidson Road Elementary as the first Montessori School in Davidson County. I co-authored the grants which resulted in the initial funding to start the project, and we are proud of the primary Montessori program we have in place for children 3-6 years old. The program serving children 6-9 years old will be implemented in 2000-2001.

It would be my honor to serve a school in need of a bright, energetic, and enthusiastic instructional professional.

Sincerely,

Janet Louise Klein

JANET LOUISE KLEIN

1110½ Hay Street, Fayetteville, NC 28305 • preppub@aol.com • (910) 483-6611

OBJECTIVE   To benefit the Jefferson County Schools as a principal through a combination of effective communication skills, an open and inquisitive mind, and a strong desire to maximize the learning opportunities of children.

EDUCATION   **Certification in Educational Administration and Supervision**, The University of Washington (UW), Seattle, WA, 1996.
Master of Arts in Elementary Education, UW, 1994.
Bachelor of Science in Education (K-6), UW, 1992.
- Named to "Who's Who Among Students in American Colleges and Universities," 1992.

EXPERIENCE   **ASSISTANT PRINCIPAL.** Davidson Road Elementary School, Seattle, WA (1997-present). Played a key role in establishing this school as the first Montessori School in Jefferson County, and am completing training provided by the University of Washington Center for Montessori Education.
- Co-authored the grants that resulted in the initial funding to start the project.
- Currently we have a primary Montessori program in place for children 3-6 years old; the program for children ages 6-9 years will be implemented in 2000-2001.

As a Classroom Teacher, excelled in providing a creative, productive, and accepting environment for elementary students in the Jefferson County Schools, Seattle, WA: Crawford Ellis Elementary School. (1996-97). For a combined third/fourth grade multi-age classroom, provided the discipline, attention, and love of learning which allowed students to work in harmony in an environment with age and learning differences.
- Served as a mentor for IC personnel and earned high praise for my ability to pass my ideas of effective instructional and administrative techniques on to teachers who were forming their own philosophy and methods of education.
- Was selected to represent the school as chairman of a SACS reaccreditation committee.

Highland Falls Elementary School. (1992-96). For two different multi-age classrooms, one a second/third grade and the other a third/fourth grade, displayed a high level of creativity and versatility by applying a variety of teaching methods which satisfied the different learning abilities of my students.
- Served as Cooperative Learning Trainer for the Jefferson County Schools.
- Was cited by other teachers (and administrators) for my emphasis on individual learning by using frequent praise and a concerned manner and by involving families in their child's educational successes and problems.
- Selected as the school's **Teacher of the Year** for 1995-96.

HIGHLIGHTS OF TRAINING

1999-00	Montessori Training, Washington Center for Montessori Teacher Education
1999	Assistant Principal's Academy
1998	Assistant Principal's Academy
1998	Technology Staff Development
1997	Multiple Intelligence and AIMS
1996	Thinking Maps, Identifying AG Students, and A Place Called School
1995	Character Education Training of Trainers, the Aspiring Principal
1994	TESA, School as a Home for the Mind, Staff Development, 4MAT, Peer Media

PERSONAL   Volunteer activities include Sunday School Teacher, officer in a homeowner's association, and participation in the March of Dimes Walk-a-Thon.

Assistant Principal

Compare the resume of this young educator with the resume on the previous page. Then you will see that there is not just one way to create a resume for an assistant principal! This is a good resume if you want to see how honors and memberships can be shown on a resume.

Date

Dear:

With the enclosed materials, I am indicating my interest in a position as Assistant Principal with your school system.

You will see from my enclosed resume that I have an M.A. in Elementary Education and am currently serving as Assistant Principal at Edmond Meany Elementary School, where I have played a key role in implementing innovative programs. We have implemented a Failure-Free Reading Lab which has improved language arts skills, and we have pioneered a unique In-School Suspension Program aimed at lessening negative and inappropriate behaviors. In a prior teaching position at Prenner Elementary School, I was named Teacher of the Year.

I believe strongly that educating children is a partnership of numerous organizations in the community, and for that reason I have generously devoted my time to serving on boards, organizations, and groups which take an interest in helping children. I have been a member of the Sullivan County Youth Services Advisory Board (an appointed position by the county commissioners), and I was a co-chair of the Student Team for four years.

I am committed to spending the rest of my life involved in the design and implementation of creative and resourceful programs which will be "user-friendly" to both teachers and students in the next century. I would be delighted to make myself available to you for a personal interview. Thank you in advance for giving my application every consideration.

Sincerely yours,

Linda M. Thoren

LINDA M. THOREN

1110½ Hay Street, Fayetteville, NC 28305   •   preppub@aol.com   •   (910) 483-6611

OBJECTIVE
To contribute to an academic institution as an Assistant Principal.

EDUCATION
Certificate: **Aspiring Principals' Academy,** Schenectady County Schools, Schenectady, NY, June 1996.
Certificate: **Educational Administration and Supervision,** St. Lawrence University, Schenectady, NY, May 1995.
M.A., St. Lawrence University, Schenectady, NY, May 1989.
Majors: **Elementary Education** (4-6) and **Math** (6-9).
B.S., Magna Cum Laude, St. Lawrence University, Schenectady, NY, May 1981.
Major: **Psychology;** Minor: **English.**

EMPLOYMENT
ASSISTANT PRINCIPAL. *Edmond Meany Elementary School,* New York, NY (September 1997-present). At a K-2 elementary school, have made major contributions through my administrative ability, creativity, and true love for children.
* Played a key role in implementing a Failure-Free Reading Lab which has improved language arts skills.
* Pioneered a unique In-School Suspension Program aimed at lessening negative and inappropriate behaviors.

ELEMENTARY TEACHER. *Prenner Elementary School.* New York, NY (1990-97). Taught fourth grade and implementing exciting lessons in Language Arts; Mathematics, Social Studies, Science/Health, and Computer Skills.

MIDDLE SCHOOL TEACHER. *Perry Ridge Elementary School.* New York, NY (1989-90). Taught sixth grade subjects including language arts, mathematics, social Studies, science/health and computer skills).

ADULT BASIC EDUCATION & HUMAN RESOURCES DEVELOPMENT INSTRUCTOR. St. Lawrence University. Schenectedy, NY. Taught as an adjunct professor (part-time) in a university setting in these two different roles.
* **A.B.E. Instructor.** (1981-1988). Diploma Program (English; Mathematics; Spelling; Reading; Writing and Consumer Skills)
* **H.R.D. Instructor.** (1981-1988). Taught job seeking skills and interviewing techniques and counseled students with various training and degrees in career choices.

MENTAL HEALTH COUNSELOR. Powers Psychiatric Hospital. Schenectedy, NY (1985-88). Provided care to patients in a therapeutic environment. Assisted with admission, discharge, and transfer of patients. Documented patient observations and nursing care.

HONORS
Nominated for **Outstanding Educator of the Year,** 1999-2000.
Nominated for Presidential Awards for Excellence in Teaching Mathematics, 1994-95.

MEMBERSHIPS
St. Lawrence University Youth Motivation Task Force
St. Lawrence University National Alumni Association
New York Bail Bondsmen Association
New York Notary Public Association
Sullivan County Association of Educators (Executive Board Member)
New York Association of Educators
National Association of Educators

Certified Nanny and Governess

Exact Name of Person
Exact Title
Exact Name of Company
Address
City, State, Zip

Certified Nanny and Governess

This young professional nanny is seeking a teaching position in a private home environment.

Dear Exact Name of Person (or Dear Sir or Madam if answering a blind ad):

With the enclosed resume, I would like to make you aware of a loving and caring young professional who truly enjoys active involvement with children and being a stable force in their growth and development.

As you will see from my enclosed resume, I am a graduate of the English Nanny & Governess School., Inc., in Rochester, NY. With practical experience as a Certified Professional Nanny (CPN), I have provided two professional families with in-home care for their children. For one family with two boys and another family with three young children, I oversaw the physical needs of the children by providing meals and transportation to their various activities as well as while changing diapers and assisting with toilet training. My responsibilities also were to provide a safe, fun, and educational environment where the children and their friends could play and spend time together.

With certification in infant-through-adult CPR, AAA Defensive Driving, and Red Cross Standard First Aid, I excelled in training which covered such subject matter as nutrition, health, hygiene, welfare, and safety. Other course work emphasized culturally enriching subjects such as literature, art, languages, music, and creative play. I feel that this training combines naturally with my own wide-ranging interests and hobbies to allow me to relate to others in many areas which include photography, art, plays and musicals, reading, and pottery as well as outdoor activities including horseback riding, baseball, and hiking.

If you can use an enthusiastic, articulate, and caring young professional who will meet the challenges of caring for your children in your home while ensuring that they are thriving in a safe, fun, and intellectually challenging environment, I hope you will call me soon. I can provide excellent professional and personal references at the appropriate time and can assure you that I could quickly become a valuable part of your family's efforts to provide the best for your children.

Sincerely,

Lelia Ann Schwerin

LELIA ANN SCHWERIN

1110½ Hay Street, Fayetteville, NC 28305 · preppub@aol.com · (910) 483-6611

OBJECTIVE To actively participate in supplying children with a stable and loving environment while seeing that children in my care have fun while enjoying intellectually stimulating activities.

EDUCATION Graduated from the English Nanny & Governess School, Inc., Rochester, NY, 1998.
- Completed three months in-house and a six-month internship in the Child Growth and Development course of study.
- Specialized course work included nutrition, health, hygiene, welfare, and safety as well as courses emphasizing cultural enrichment, language, literature, music, art, and creative play.
- Earned *certifications* in infant-through-adult CPR, AAA Defensive Driving, and Red Cross Standard First Aid.
- Completed a Field Practicum during which I provided in-home care for four children for the Walton family – a four month old, an 18 month old, a 4 year old, and a six year old.

Working toward a **B.S. in Child Psychology** in my spare time, Onondaga Community College, Onondaga, NY; completed specialized course work in English and psychology.

Graduated from Gregory High School, Buffalo, NY, 1996.
- Completed college preparatory curriculum which included courses in child development, psychology, and nutrition.

EXPERIENCE **CERTIFIED PROFESSIONAL NANNY (CPN).** Joseph and Phillys Cale, Buffalo, NY (1998-00). Cared for seven-year-old Tommy and six-year-old Travis with duties including preparing meals, providing transportation to and from various activities, and providing companionship and care for indoor and outdoor activities.
- Supervised two young boys and helped them with their homework; supervised activities while their friends were in the home to play and volunteered in their classrooms.

CHILD CARE PROVIDER. Newton Day Care Center, Buffalo, NY (1996-98). Handled child care from changing diapers, to preparing lunches, to feeding baby food and bottles, to toilet training, to art activities, to singing and rhyming reading, to outdoor activities.

CHILD CARE PROVIDER. Beth and Jim Calloway, Buffalo, NY (1993-98). Took care of three children–Aaron who is now 10, Matthew who is seven, and Emilee who is three.
- Handled daily care including changing diapers, feeding, toilet training, meal preparation, and play and learning activities; did light housekeeping such as laundry and dishes.

CHURCH NURSERY WORKER. St. Peter's Church, Buffalo, NY (1991-93). Cared for children ranging from infants though eight years of age during Sunday morning services.

INTERESTS Through my wide-ranging interests and hobbies, can communicate and relate to others in many areas: photography, art, pottery and ceramics, plays and musicals, reading, hiking and climbing, horseback riding, camping, traveling, and baseball.

PERSONAL Experienced with children of all ages, am energetic, honest, and compassionate with a good sense of humor. Am a self-starter who is willing to try new things, getting involved in children's activities and interests. A firm believer in positive reinforcement, communicate with children at their level. Excellent references are enclosed for your consideration.

Child Care Provider

Date

Exact Name of Person
Exact Title
Exact Name of Company
Address
City, State, Zip

Child Care Provider

Teaching in a day care
environment is the goal
of this young
professional. She uses
the cover letter to
accentuate her skills in
program development.
Use the cover letter to
identify skills and
accomplishments which
set you apart from
others in your field.

Dear Exact Name of Person (or Dear Sir or Madam if answering a blind ad):

With the enclosed resume, I would like to make you aware of my strong mentoring, planning, training, and leadership skills as well as my desire to work with children while providing a safe and stimulating learning environment.

You will see from my enclosed resume that I am experienced in educational program development and am known for my ability to develop and implement workable, age-appropriate lesson plans and activities for young children. With a background as the lead teacher for an after-school program for 25 children, I also supervise a junior teacher in a center which cares for an average of 200 children. I also advanced rapidly in another center where I provided training and supervision for three junior teachers in a center which cared for approximately 90 children from birth to six years of age.

In each child care center where I worked, I earned high ratings in periodic evaluations of all aspects of performance from teaching style, to classroom management, to parent interaction, to communication and work habits. I have been singled out for praise by supervisors for my ability to handle stress and described as a role model for the children under my care as well as for my peers.

With American Red Cross certification in CPR and First Aid, I also completed extensive training through workshops and seminars as well as on-the-job training in child care procedures with an emphasis on health, safety, and the development of the children's socialization and educational skills.

If you can use an enthusiastic, articulate, and caring young professional who quickly masters new procedures and who excels in passing knowledge on to others, I hope you will contact me. I can provide excellent professional and personal references at the appropriate time. I can assure you that I could quickly become a valuable part of your school's team and the efforts to provide a safe and caring atmosphere where children can grow and learn.

Sincerely,

Janet P. Townsend

JANET P. TOWNSEND

1110½ Hay Street, Fayetteville, NC 28305 • preppub@aol.com • (910) 483-6611

OBJECTIVE

I want to contribute to an organization that can use a hard-working young professional with a reputation as a fast learner who works well with others and is known for strong mentoring, planning, training, and leadership skills.

TRAINING

Completed extensive training by attending numerous workshops and seminars as well as receiving on-the-job training in child care procedures with an emphasis on health, safety, and skills development.

CERTIFICATIONS & SKILLS

Am American Red Cross certified in CPR and First Aid, updated 2000.
Have a home computer and am knowledgeable of Windows.
Am proficient in the operation of most standard office equipment.

EXPERIENCE

LEAD TEACHER. Cave Dweller Day Care, Louisville, KY (1999-present). Supervise one junior teacher while overseeing the After-School Program for an average of 25 children per day who range in age from four to seven.

- Apply my skills in a center which cares for approximately 200 children on an average day and am known for my caring and nurturing manner.
- Display adaptability working in other areas to support staff members in the Infant, Toddler, and Preschool Room.
- Implement activities which include games and outdoor play while also supervising children doing their homework.

EDUCATIONAL TECHNICIAN. Wilkins Child Development Center, Rothguard, Germany (1995-98). Earned rapid promotion and was given ever-increasing levels of responsibility in a center which cared for approximately 90 children from birth to six years of age.

- Designed and implemented stimulating, age-appropriate lesson plans and activities.
- Was cited for my time and efforts in providing training and supervision for three junior teachers.
- Contributed knowledge which allowed the center to earn accreditation.
- Earned excellent ratings in all areas during periodic performance evaluations of general work habits, communication and team building, technical competence, teaching style, classroom environment, parent interaction, and professionalism.

PROGRAM ASSISTANT. Zamore Child Development Center, Ft. Campbell, KY (1993-94). Assisted a Lead Teacher in the hourly-care program working with six to 12-year-old children while providing oversight which ensured a safe and healthy environment.

- Cited as a professional who worked well under stress; was described as a role model for the children under my care and for my peers.
- Kept attendance records, went on field trips, and prepared lesson plans.

PROGRAM ASSISTANT. Wright Child Development Center, Wright, Germany (1991-92). Completed extensive training while providing nurturing and age-appropriate activities for an average of six toddlers each day.

- Was evaluated as "possessing a rare talent … for maintaining a very happy and serene environment" through my "positive approach" and extensive knowledge.
- Was offered this job after a year of providing care in my home for six children.

PERSONAL

Have earned recognition for my ability to quickly learn new procedures and pass my knowledge on to others. Handle stress and pressure calmly and with control.

Developmentally Delayed & Troubled Youth Teaching Specialist

Date

Developmentally Delayed and Troubled Youth Teaching Specialist

There are some things you can learn from this cover letter and resume. When you read the cover letter, you will see that this young woman is emphasizing her experience in different environments in which she has encountered troubled youth and developmentally delayed populations. Here's the rule on whether to put Education or Experience first on the resume: put first the one that distinguishes you the most.

Exact Name of Person
Exact Title
Exact Name of Company
Address
City, State, Zip

Dear Exact Name of Person (or Dear Sir or Madam if answering a blind ad):

With the enclosed resume, I would like to make you aware of my background in teaching and curriculum development as well as my experience in working with troubled youth and with the developmentally delayed.

As you will see from my resume, I am currently a teacher in a legal facility housing children who are not allowed by the court system to attend public school. I teach all subjects to boys and girls aged 11 to 16, and I prepare the older students to take the GED. While serving as a go-between with agencies including mental health and social services, I handle extensive public speaking duties with organizations such as Lions Club, fraternities, and others in order to educate the community on the concept of a multi-purpose juvenile home.

In my previous job I excelled as a Teacher with the Public Schools of Moore County, where I taught the second, third, and fourth grades. Among the students I taught were the developmentally delayed, and I am experienced in developing lesson plans according to the needs of special populations.

You will also notice that I have worked as a Curriculum Specialist for a learning center which served 80 children aged birth through five years old. In that capacity I developed all curricula for all age groups for that newly started learning center, where I worked full-time for two years managing the second shift at that facility and working in the classrooms. Although I now work full-time at the multi-purpose juvenile home, I am continuing in a part-time capacity as Curriculum Specialist for that learning center.

With a degree in History as well as a degree in Education, I am certified to teach Elementary K-6 and History to 9-12.

If my considerable talents and skills interest you, I hope you will contact me to suggest a time when we might meet to discuss your needs and how I might serve them. I am committed to providing the highest quality learning tools and resources for the individuals I teach, and I am confident I could become a valuable addition to your team. Thank you in advance for your time and professional courtesies.

Yours sincerely,

Angela Davis

ANGELA DAVIS

1110½ Hay Street, Fayetteville, NC 28305   •   preppub@aol.com   •   (910) 483-6611

OBJECTIVE

I want to contribute to an organization that can use a teacher with experience in public school teaching and curriculum development who also offers a background in providing educational services for troubled youth as well as developmentally delayed children.

EXPERIENCE

TEACHER. Moore County Multi-Purpose Juvenile Home, Buffalo, NY (1998-present). Work as a teacher in this legal facility housing eight children who are not allowed to attend public school; teach boys and girls aged 11 to 16 in all subject areas, and prepare the older children for the GED.
- Facilitate learning while planning weekly lessons, handling extensive record keeping required by the legal and educational systems, and maintaining discipline.
- Am highly skilled in employing a wide variety of teaching methods and styles to fit the need of the student and his or her educational level.
- Provide needs assessment for each student; serve as liaison between parents and MHC and between the public schools and MHC while teaching all subject areas.
- Serve as a go-between for mental health, health department, and social services.
- Handle extensive public speaking as I am a popular speaker at organizations including churches, Lions Clubs, and fraternities; educate the public on multi-purpose juvenile homes.
- Work part-time as **Curriculum Specialist** for Lear's Learning Center in Buffalo.

TEACHER. Public Schools of Moore County, Buffalo, NY (1992-98). Taught the second, third and fourth grades in the public schools and became known as a highly articulate teaching professional with a sensitivity for the learning abilities of all students.
- Worked with developmentally delayed children and mainstream classroom children.
- Planned lesson plans and creatively implemented them, adjusting written plans as necessary depending upon the learning environment and needs of the children.

ADULT BASIC EDUCATION TEACHER (Full-Time Summer Job). Schwartz Community College, Buffalo, NY (July 1997-August 1997). At this community college, facilitated learning for students 18 and older while evaluating educational levels, testing students for knowledge and abilities, and developing individual lesson plans for students.
- Recruited students for the ABE program and handled record keeping.

CURRICULUM SPECIALIST (Full-Time Second Job). Lear's Learning Center, Buffalo, NY (1994-96). For this facility which served 80 children aged birth through five years old and which maintained operating hours of 6 AM to midnight, I managed the second shift in a full-time "second job" while also excelling as a teacher in the public schools.
- Tested children for physical and mental abilities; served as liaison with resource personnel including with special needs educators and medical personnel.

TUTOR FOR K-12. (Self-Employed). Buffalo, NY (1990-97). As a tutor for grades K-12, taught all subjects, evaluated student learning levels and styles, provided needs assessment for each student I tutored, and planned lessons.

EDUCATION

B.A. degree in History, Buffalo State College, Buffalo, NY, 1992.
B.A. degree in Education, Buffalo State College, Buffalo, NY, 1992.

CERTIFICATIONS

Certified to teach Elementary K-6 and History to 9-12.

PERSONAL

Enjoy contributing my time in my community as my schedule allows. Outstanding references.

Clinical Educator

Clinical Educator

This professional seeks a teaching position in a medical environment.

Date

Exact Name of Person
Exact Title
Exact Name of Company
Address
City, State, Zip

Dear Exact Name of Person (or Dear Sir or Madam if answering a blind ad):

With the enclosed resume, I would like to make you aware of my exceptional abilities in instructing, teaching, and training personnel in medical environments.

As you will see from my enclosed resume, I offer an extensive and versatile background in providing instruction in settings which have included a university medical/surgical clinic program, an in-service program for nurses and nursing assistants, and a hospital patient education program. I have carried out educational programs at the junior college level, for hospitals, for a home health care organization, and now in my current job, at the university level.

With Master of Science in Education and Bachelor of Science in Nursing degrees from Kent State University in Ohio, I also hold American Heart Association certification as a Cardiopulmonary Resuscitation Instructor.

In addition to my primary responsibilities as an educator, I also offer experience in administrative activities such as scheduling, evaluating and counseling students on their performance, documenting activities, and certifying students in various professional skills and abilities. For example, in my present job as a Clinical Instructor I serve as the liaison to the clinical unit and its managers for the Associate Degree Nursing II program, and earlier as a Regional In-service Educator served on the Nurse Advisory Board for the area health education center.

Through my knowledge and administrative skills, I have developed quality assurance programs, an education program for patients with diabetes mellitus, and one junior college's in-service training program for medical/surgical topics.

If your school or organization can use an enthusiastic, articulate, and mature educator with dynamic program development and administrative skills, I hope you will call me soon. I can provide excellent professional and personal references at the appropriate time.

Sincerely,

Davida Somerville

DAVIDA SOMERVILLE

1110½ Hay Street, Fayetteville, NC 28305   •   preppub@aol.com   •   (910) 483-6611

OBJECTIVE   To offer my background in program development, education, and administration to a dynamic and progressive organization or school.

EDUCATION   **Master of Science in Education,** Kent State University, Kent, OH, 1992.
Bachelor of Science in Nursing, Kent State University, Kent, OH, 1983.

TRAINING   Cardiopulmonary Resuscitation Instructor, American Heart Association (1990-present).

EXPERIENCE   **CLINICAL EDUCATOR, ASSOCIATE DEGREE NURSING II.** Kent State University, Columbus and Kent, OH, & Columbus, OH (1996-present). Clinical Instructor for five to ten students for rotations in medical-surgical clinical area.
- Assigned students to patient care; instructed students in clinical practice.
- Evaluated and counseled students' performance.
- Liaison to clinical unit and its managers for ADN II program.

REGIONAL IN-SERVICE EDUCATOR. Home Health Care, Columbus and Kent, OH (1993-95). Handled responsibilities related to training nurses, nursing assistants (NAs), and all other employees in bi-weekly orientation sessions; verified skills of nurses and NAs, implemented company policy and procedures; and evaluated and developed in-service training for up to five regional offices.
- Acted as liaison for the corporate education office to the regional offices.
- Conducted CPR classes each month; gave mandatory NA in-service classes.
- Developed a needs assessment survey; member of the KAHEC Nurse Advisory Board.

PATIENT EDUCATOR. Sarka Hospital, Kent, OH (1991-92). Developed several important new programs including the following: the first patient education program for patients with diabetes mellitus, reestablished the ADA in the city of Abilene by establishing a board of directors, served as the patient educator on the board.
- Developed a quality assurance program for the education department.
- Conducted bi-weekly employee orientation programs and regular weekly CPR classes.
- Developed in-service training for different wards; Completed ACLS certification.

CLINICAL COORDINATOR. Koch Junior College School of Nursing, Columbus, OH (1989-91). Developed the first LPN clinical rotation at a local trauma center and acted as liaison between the college and medical/nursing staff while coordinating the rotation.
- Developed and presented in-service training on medical/surgical topics.
- Certified students in CPR as well as testing and evaluating their performance.

STAFF NURSE/TEAM LEADER. Koch Hospital, Columbus, OH (1988-89). Administered direct nursing care to five to 20 patients each day and supervised team members in their nursing duties; made assignments; evaluated staff performance and patient care.
- Documented assignments on medical records and reported my observations to team members and the head nurse.

STAFF NURSE/CHARGE NURSE. Veterans Administration Medical Center, Kent, OH (1987-88). Delivered care to patients in the respiratory unit while supervising from four to six nursing staff per shift.

PERSONAL   Ohio license available upon request. High integrity ... flexible ... assertive ... goal oriented.

College Instructor

College Instructor

This teaching professional could seek positions teaching K-12 in school systems, but she is trying to establish her career in college teaching. Therefore, this cover letter is oriented exclusively toward colleges. She used another cover letter to explore teaching opportunities in school systems. Notice how she emphasizes her high GPA and academic excellence.

Dear Sir or Madam:

I am writing to express my strong interest in the position of Psychology Instructor at the University of Southeast Virginia recently advertised in the Richmond Times. With the enclosed resume, I would like to make you aware of my background as an articulate communicator and enthusiastic teacher whose exceptional skills in classroom instruction and counseling have been proven.

As you will see from my resume, I have excelled throughout my academic career, maintaining a **3.88 cumulative GPA** en route to completing my Masters of Education degree at the University of Virginia. I graduated **magna cum laude** while earning a Bachelor of Science in Psychology from the University of Virginia, where I was named to the Dean's List each semester for three years and was voted Most Distinguished Student by the faculty in recognition of my academic excellence and community involvement.

In my most recent position, I provided classroom instruction to 35 college students while teaching Psychology at University of Virginia. I presented course materials through oral presentations, written material, role playing, and other methods as well as composing and preparing lesson plans, projects, reports, and assignments. Through formal examination and personal observation, I evaluated individual performance and offered assistance to students who were having difficulty with the course materials.

If you can use an articulate communicator and skilled educator, I hope you will write or call me soon to suggest a time when we might meet to discuss your needs and goals and how my background might serve them. I can provide outstanding references and letters of recommendation at the appropriate time.

Sincerely,

Madeline Ruff

MADELINE RUFF

1110½ Hay Street, Fayetteville, NC 28305 • preppub@aol.com • (910) 483-6611

OBJECTIVE

To benefit an organization that can use a motivated, articulate human services professional who offers a strong background in classroom instruction as well as in individual and group counseling of diverse populations in public school, veteran's, and long-term care environments.

EDUCATION

Masters of Education in **Counseling**, University of Virginia, Charlottesville, VA, 1998; graduated with a **3.88 cumulative GPA.**
Bachelor of Arts in **Psychology**, University of Virginia, Charlottesville, VA, 1996; graduated **magna cum laude**, with a **cumulative GPA** of **3.68 overall, 4.0 in my major.**
- Named to the **Dean's List** each semester from 1993-1995.
- Honored by the faculty members with the **Most Distinguished Student** award for my academic excellence and commitment to community involvement.

AFFILIATIONS

Member, American Counseling Association
Student Member, American Psychological Association
Member, Psychology Association
Elected Treasurer of the University of Virginia chapter of the Psychology Association

EXPERIENCE

PSYCHOLOGY INSTRUCTOR. University of Virginia, Charlottesville, VA (1999-present). Taught psychology to 35 students at this university; presented course materials through oral presentations, role playing, and other methods; prepared lesson plans, projects, reports, and assignments.
- Composed and prepared a variety of written materials, including the course syllabus, testing materials, etc. as well as preparing lecture material for verbal presentation.
- Evaluated individual performance through formal examination and personal observation; counseled and assisted students who were having difficulty with the course.

SCHOOL COUNSELOR INTERN. Kingsbury Elementary School, Richmond, VA (1998). Provided individual and group counseling to seventh and eighth grade students while completing a five-month internship at this local junior high school; interacted with students, parents, teachers, and administrators to facilitate the counseling process.
- Counseled troubled students on an individual basis, as well as coordinating and facilitating counseling groups; assisted with the Peer Leadership Training program.
- Designed course materials and implemented plans for classroom guidance lessons.

SCHOOL COUNSELOR INTERN. Scott Elementary School, Richmond, VA (1998). Counseled troubled students in kindergarten through sixth grade while completing a five-month internship at this local elementary school; wrote a successful grant to provide funding for a substance abuse prevention program.
- Created and developed classroom guidance lessons on conflict resolution for use with Alternative Education students.

M.S.W. INTERN. Sierra Veteran's Center, Richmond, VA (1996-1998). While completing my Master of Education, provided individual and group counseling during a 21-month internship at this local veteran's center; conducted research into Vicarious Traumatization.
- Counseled adolescents and adults who were facing issues related to physical, emotional, or psychological trauma, substance abuse, and grief management.

PERSONAL

Excellent personal and professional references are available upon request.

College Professor

Date

Exact Name of Person
Title or Position
Name of Company
Address (number and street)
Address (city, state, and zip)

College Professor

Dear Exact Name of Person: (or Sir or Madam if answering a blind ad.)

This individual is armed with the doctorate or "terminal degree" as it is often called in academic circles. Now he must circulate his resume widely to see where the opportunities are. Notice that he mentions his publishing credits and publishing activities, since this is what may differentiate him from other college professors.

I would appreciate an opportunity to talk with you soon about how I could contribute to your faculty and students through my exceptional writing, editing, and research skills, my creativity, and my thorough grasp of the English language. You will see from my resume that I hold a Ph.D. in Comparative Literature, an M.A. in Classics, and a B.A. in English. I have won formal recognition as a college teacher and have enjoyed considerable success in publishing. I have nearly completed a definitive work on Milton about which several publishing houses have expressed an interest.

You will see from my enclosed resume that I have been teaching at the college level since 1988. I thrive on research and have published numerous works of a comparative nature rather than limiting myself to one narrow area of specialization. My daily schedule includes reading in eight foreign languages, which allows me to constantly bring new material into my studies.

I offer wide-ranging experience in preparing manuscripts to be published, knowledge of eight foreign languages, and a reputation as a respected educator in several areas of the Humanities. I am widely considered to be an expert writer, proofreader, and editor as well as teacher.

I hope you will welcome my call soon to arrange a brief meeting to discuss your current and future needs and how I might serve them. Thank you for your time.

Sincerely,

Malcolm Smith

MALCOLM SMITH

1110½ Hay Street, Fayetteville, NC 28305 • preppub@aol.com • (910) 483-6611

OBJECTIVE   To engage in demanding, worthwhile challenges through my exceptional skills as a researcher, writer, and editor who possesses a thorough command of the English language and a versatile background including knowledge of eight foreign languages.

EDUCATION   **Ph.D., Comparative Literature,** The University of Vermont, Burlington, VT, 1988.
- Received a Graduate Fellowship awarded by faculty on the basis of academic merit.

M.A., Classics, University of Vermont, 1980.

B.A., English, University of Vermont, 1978.
- Was elected to Phi Beta Kappa on the basis of academic merit.

PUBLICATIONS   Am continuously in the process of researching, writing, editing, and preparing material for publication; works include novels, children's books, poems, and short stories as well as critical papers, book reviews, and dozens of scholarly publications and papers.

EXPERIENCE   **COLLEGE PROFESSOR.** *Have applied my analytical, research, speaking, and writing skills while broadening my areas of interest and study as a college professor:*

University of Vermont, Burlington, VT (1995-present). Respected for my analytical skills and in-depth knowledge, have played a key role on a subcommittee involved in revising the English curriculum while teaching composition and world literature as well as upper-division courses on Milton, Dante, and Chaucer.
- Successfully co-authored application for funding of summer stipends for research, and was among the first group of scholars to receive one of these grants.
- Completed the a grant-sponsored study of how the "electronic mentality" affects society resulting in a 50,000-word manuscript which addresses literary criticism.
- Organized annual creative writing workshops and provided guidance for writing efforts.

Shenandoah University, Winchester, VT (1992-95). In this private school with a diverse student population, built a reputation for my ability to earn the respect of the non-traditional (older adults attending night school classes) and foreign students.
- Advised students who typically were not Humanities majors.
- Taught composition, world literature, Great Books survey, and Milton classes.

Seton Hall University, South Orange, NJ (1991-92). Became interested in film studies and taught classes in the subject as well as in composition, world literature, and epic tradition.

Saint Michael's College, Winooski Part, VT (1990-91). Displayed a high level of versatility and the willingness to teach courses that others preferred not to take on and to make them interesting and informative; major subjects taught included upper-division courses in world literature, the Romantic Period, children's literature, and Latin.
- Developed the syllabus for the children's literature course.

COLLEGE INSTRUCTOR. Seattle University, Seattle, WA (1988-90). Gained insight into the special atmosphere and problems of a small college while teaching first and second year French and acting as an advisor.

LANGUAGES   Have experience teaching, reading, and writing in Latin and Ancient Greek, French, German, Italian, Spanish, Irish and Scots Gaelic, Medieval and modern Welsh.

College Professor

Date

Exact Name of Person
Exact Title
Exact Name of Company
Address
City, State, Zip

College Professor

This accomplished university professor is exploring opportunities at colleges or universities which can offer her the combination of administrative and teaching duties which she seeks. Although she does not communicate this fact, she is trying to attract the attention of federal policy makers so that one day she can work at the national level in some appointed position related to public health.

Dear Exact Name of Person (or Dear Sir or Madam if answering a blind ad):

With the enclosed resume, I would like to make you aware of my interest in joining your faculty in some administrative or teaching role.

As you will see from my resume, I have been a tenured faculty member with the College of William and Mary while also serving as Dean of Health Sciences. As a University Instructor, I lecture in several subjects which include Epidemiology, Public Health, Biochemistry, Pharmacology, Pharmaceutical Chemistry, and Environmental Health. I achieved tenured status in an unusually short time, and I enjoy a reputation as a popular teacher who can "translate" complex scientific and technical subjects into easily understood language and concepts.

As Dean of Health Sciences, I planned and implemented programs in Medicine, Environmental Health, Pharmacy, Radiography, and Medical Laboratory Technology. In addition to developing numerous budgets for the faculty, I coordinated the Accreditation Program for Registered Pharmacists including the establishment and supervision of the clinical rotations.

You will also see from my resume that my educational credentials are top notch. I received a scholarship to complete my Masters in Biochemistry at the College of William and Mary and then earned my Ph.D. in Public Health at the College of William and Mary.

I can provide outstanding personal and professional references at the appropriate time, and I would be delighted to make myself available for a personal interview at your convenience. Thank you in advance for your professional courtesies.

Sincerely,

Dyann F. Wirth

DYANN F. WIRTH

1110½ Hay Street, Fayetteville, NC 28305 • preppub@aol.com • (910) 483-6611

OBJECTIVE   To benefit an organization that can use a dedicated professional and distinguished scholar with experience in university teaching along with knowledge related to public health, environmental health, scientific and pharmaceutical research, and medical laboratory technology.

EDUCATION   **Ph.D. in Public Health,** College of William and Mary, Williamsburg, VA, 1989.
Master of Science, Biochemistry (on scholarship), College of William and Mary, 1983.
Bachelor of Science, Biology/Chemistry, University of North Carolina at Chapel Hill, 1980.

EXPERIENCE   **Excelled in this track record of accomplishment with the College of William and Mary, College of William and Mary, Williamsburg, VA:**
UNIVERSITY INSTRUCTOR & DEAN OF HEALTH SCIENCES. (1995-present). As a University Instructor who became a tenured faculty member, develop curriculum and lecture in several subjects which include Epidemiology, Public Health, Biochemistry, Pharmacology, Pharmaceutical Chemistry, and Environmental Health; as **Dean of Health Sciences,** planned and implemented programs in Medicine, Environmental Health, Pharmacy, Radiography, and Medical Laboratory Technology.
- Coordinated the Accreditation Program for Registered Pharmacists to include establishing and supervising clinical field rotations; developed and managed budgets for the faculty.
- Was a member of the National Planning Team for programs funded by the Future American Health Organization; was a member of the Appointments Board responsible for professional recruitment.
- Held responsibility for Student Affairs; served as External Examiner for the Faculty.

SENIOR INSTRUCTOR. (1989-95). For the Faculty of Natural Science, administered laboratory programs for students; coordinated and directed research experiments including research related to indigenous plants for pharmaceutical properties; also procured laboratory materials and equipment and maintained effective control of inventory.
- Became respected by hospital department heads as well as manufacturing companies and private pharmacies for my outstanding intellect and strong consulting skills.
- Through extensive consulting with major pharmaceuticals, played a major role in developing a new skin care product which successfully underwent FDA approval.

Other experience:
RESEARCH ASSISTANT. Virginia Science Council, Williamsburg, VA (1982-89). As a graduate student and Ph.D. candidate, was responsible for field work and analysis in protein energy malnutrition project.

ADVANCED BIOLOGY MONITOR. University of North Carolina at Chapel Hill, Chapel Hill, NC (1980-81). Oversaw laboratory testing for graduate-level certifications in biology.

COMPUTERS   Highly proficient in computer applications.

PERSONAL   Outstanding personal and professional references on request. Well developed analytical, planning, organizational, and administrative skills. Excellent communication, consulting, and work management skills. Effective leadership, teamwork, creative problem-solving, and decision-making skills. Strong report preparation and excellent presentation skills.

Counselor

Exact Name of Person
Exact Title
Exact Name of Company
Address
City, State, Zip

Counselor

This educator specializes in the counseling area, and she is seeking positions which will give her an opportunity to utilize her skills in special education counseling. Notice how she shows the degree she is in the process of completing by giving her anticipated degree completion date.

Dear Exact Name of Person (or Dear Sir or Madam if answering a blind ad):

With the enclosed resume, I would like to introduce you to my credentials related to the counseling of students with special education needs. I am a compassionate and caring young professional with a reputation for strong communication skills.

I have built a reputation as an individual who is known for the ability to listen and remain nonjudgmental while providing counseling and assistance. My reputation has been established in jobs as a counselor and outreach worker for pregnant teenagers and in working with high-risk children experiencing delayed development. Completing a Master's degree in Special Education Counseling, I also hold a B.S. in Applied Science and an A.A.S. degree in Human Services Technology.

I am highly experienced in providing excellent listening skills while helping people who need assistance in coping with stressful, demanding, and life-changing circumstances. With exceptionally strong communication and interpersonal relations skills, I offer the ability to deal with a wide range of people who include educators as well as health care and social services professionals from other community agencies.

If you can use an enthusiastic and caring young professional who offers proven ability to address the needs of special populations, I hope you will contact me to suggest a time when we might discuss your needs. I can provide excellent professional and personal references at the appropriate time, and I can assure you that I could quickly become a valuable part of your efforts to provide compassionate counseling services to special needs students.

Sincerely,

Gladys Tamkun

GLADYS TAMKUN

1110½ Hay Street, Fayetteville, NC 28305 • preppub@aol.com • (910) 483-6611

OBJECTIVE
I want to contribute to a school that can use an experienced young professional with a proven ability to provide results-oriented guidance and counseling designed to help others shape their goals and modify their lives in positive ways.

EDUCATION
Completing **Master's degree in Special Education Counseling,** Alverno College, Milwaukee, WI; degree expected 2001.
Earned **Bachelor of Science degree in Applied Science,** Alverno College, Milwaukee, WI, 1996.
Completed **Associate in Applied Science degree in Human Services Technology**, Alverno College, Milwaukee, WI, 1991.
Human Services Internships:
- **Department of Social Services**, Milwaukee, WI; 100 hours; administrative work.
- **Field Counselor**, Alverno College, Milwaukee, WI; 66 hours; internship emphasized planning, organizing, and counseling skills.
- **Drug and Alcohol Abuse Counselor,** Field Placement, 66 hours.
- **Practicum and Observation,** Vocational Institute; 30 hours.

EXPERIENCE
MASTER'S DEGREE STUDENT. Alverno College, Milwaukee, WI (2000-present). Completing Master's degree in Special Education Counseling.

SPECIAL EDUCATION COUNSELOR. Fegan School, Milwaukee, WI (1998-2000). As a Support Mother for pregnant teenagers, assisted young women with goal setting and encouraged them to stay in school while interacting with other agencies and sources of support.
- Planned workshops and monthly support group meetings.
- Maintained accurate records on clients; made home visits and established cordial relationships with the families and significant others in the women's lives.
- Decided that I wished to continue my education in special education counseling at the Master's degree level.

MATERNAL OUTREACH WORKER. Girls Group Home, Milwaukee, WI (1995-98). In this job while earning my Bachelor's degree, counseled pregnant women and with goal setting.
- Taught parenting classes and was involved in community outreach.
- Provided support to families of pregnant teenagers.
- Facilitated the use of external resources provided by other agencies and community service organizations; made appropriate referrals to agencies.
- Provided follow-up and served as client advocate.

CHILD SERVICE COORDINATOR. Leader's Day Care Service, Milwaukee, WI (1992-94). Worked with 22 high-risk children experiencing developmental delay; also worked with and counseled families; assessed parent child interaction.
- Performed service planning and worked as part of a team to accomplish multi-faceted goals on behalf of the children.
- Acted as a lay person of a local consortium which determined eligibility for the infant toddler program in coordination with six agencies and parents.
- Provided support to families and facilitated usage of health and community services.
- Maintained accurate records on clients; made home visits.

PERSONAL
Can provide strong personal and professional references.

Counselor

Date

Exact Name of Person
Exact Title
Exact Name of Company
Address
City, State, Zip

Counselor

Compare the resume and cover letter of this young counselor to the one on the previous page. This counselor is seeking her first full-time job in a public school system. This young person is untested as a school counselor but she has had related experiences which demonstrate her commitment to her field.

Dear Exact Name of Person: (or Dear Sir or Madam if answering a blind ad):

With the enclosed resume, I would like to make you aware of my desire to explore employment opportunities with your organization. I have recently completed my Bachelor's degree in Counseling and offer strong communication and counseling skills.

As you will see from my resume, I have excelled in counseling positions in a camp environment, in a home for displaced children, and at the YMCA. While working as a Counselor at an orphanage, I became known for my creativity and program development skills. On my own initiative, I organized a store at the orphanage so that youth aged 9-19 could learn money-handling and budgeting skills. I was commended for my efforts which resulted in building self-esteem and a feeling of self worth.

In a job as a Case Manager at the YMCA, I worked as an intern with the Big Brothers/Big Sisters of Forest City. In that capacity, I organized an after-school program at Forest City Middle School designed to build self-esteem in children. The program I developed began with 10 children and grew to serve 40 children, and after my internship the program received formal funding so that it can continue. For my efforts and initiative, I received a certificate of appreciation.

As a teenager, I discovered my orientation toward the social work field while working as a Camp Counselor with children aged 6-13. I also volunteered as Office Manager and Receptionist at the local women's shelter, where I developed a book of essays written by the homeless clients of this nonprofit organization.

If you can use a caring and enthusiastic young professional with a true desire to make a difference in the lives of others, I hope you will contact me to suggest a time when we might meet to discuss your needs. I can provide excellent references.

Sincerely,

Brownie Sullivan

BROWNIE SULLIVAN

1110½ Hay Street, Fayetteville, NC 28305   •   preppub@aol.com   •   (910) 483-6611

OBJECTIVE   I want to contribute to an organization that can use an outgoing young professional who offers strong communication skills and proven management potential along with a desire to serve the public and work with others in achieving top-quality results.

EDUCATION   **Bachelor of Science degree in Counseling,** Waldorf College, Forest City, IA, 2000.
- Activities included Resident Advisor, Resident Hall Association, Spencer Hall Council **President,** Ki Alpha Phi **President,** Counseling Club, Social Work Club, Omega Chi Delta Historian, Waldorf Playmakers, Puppetry Association.

Training: Professional training included Teaching Parent Model and PC Essentials.

COMPUTERS   Windows operating system and Microsoft Word, Works, Excel, WordPerfect, SPSS, Internet

EXPERIENCE   **RESIDENT COUNSELOR.** Baptist Home for Children, Forest City, IA (5/99-present). As a volunteer at this orphanage, provide training related to life skills for youth aged 9-19 while also implementing parent training; developed programs for each child which resulted in building self-esteem and a feeling of self worth.
- **Program Development:** On my own initiative, organized a store at the Baptist Home for Children so that children could earn money and learn skills in handling money and budgeting for their expenses; designed and managed the store's policies and procedures.

CASE MANAGER. YMCA, Forest City, IA (Spring 1999). As an Intern with the Big Brothers/ Big Sisters of Forest City, interviewed and placed prospective mentors and worked as the trusted "right arm" to the program manager.
- **Program Development:** Organized an after-school program designed to build self-esteem in children and worked closely with children making failing grades; the program at Forest City Middle School was widely praised and considered a success and I was praised for my creativity and professionalism. Began with 10 students and grew the program to 40 students. The program received funding after its pilot year and is being continued.
- **Award:** Received Certificate of Appreciation from the PTA.

HISTORIAN. Saint Simons Catholic Church, Forest City, IA (9/98-12/98). Developed a scrapbook which provided the school's first permanent record of its after-school program; planned photographic events and arranged photo opportunities with children, tutors, and staff.

OFFICE MANAGER & RECEPTIONIST. Women's Shelter of Forest City, Forest City, IA (1/98-5/98). While working as a volunteer, applied my creativity in developing a book of essays by the clients of this nonprofit organization serving battered women.
- **Social worker responsibilities:** Routinely handled duties of a social worker and counselor; processed intakes, made referrals to other agencies, supplied clients with clothing.

CAMP COUNSELOR. Carthage Summer Fun Camp, Carthage County, IA (6/95-7/97). Found many opportunities to express my creativity and resourcefulness while scheduling events, planning educational programs, and working with children aged 6-13.
- **Programming:** Planned a talent show for the children and nurtured their creativity.

SALES REPRESENTATIVE. Hecht's Department, Duluth, IA (12/91-2/95). Began working at the age of 13 and worked for four years part-time; was commended for bringing a youthful outlook into the department. Decorated windows, assisted customers, and handled money.

Curriculum Vitae for a Social Studies Teacher Aspiring to Assistant Principal

Date

Teachers often wonder what a curriculum vitae looks like. In the next few pages, you will see examples of curriculum vitae (CVs) which are the equivalent of resumes. Usually CVs are lengthier than resumes, which are often one page. CVs are usually two pages or longer.

Dear Principal:

With the enclosed curriculum vitae, I would like to make you aware of my credentials as well as my interest in becoming an Assistant Principal at your school. I am qualified to serve as an Assistant Principal at a school from K-12.

As you will see from my resume, I hold a B.A. in Elementary Education and am completing a Master's Degree in Administration which I expect to complete in May 2001. As part of my degree requirements, I am working as an Assistant Principal Intern at Roman Elementary School where I perform teacher assessments and am involved in activities ranging from planning bus routes, to training new personnel, to developing partnerships within the community to support learning "beyond the textbook."

I am an accomplished teacher, and I have won numerous teaching honors. I was named Social Studies Teacher of the Year for the State of VA in 1999, received the Innovating Teacher Award for Junior Quiz Bowl in 1999, and won Innovative Teaching Awards for Excellence in 1995, 1996, 1997, 1998, and 1999. I have also been named Teacher of the Year at two separate schools. I have become skilled at writing grants, and I have authored publications which have been aired on television and published in newspapers.

I believe my greatest strengths lie in the area of program development, curriculum development, and new technology development. With a reputation as a creative and resourceful individual, I have been successful in establishing partnerships with community leaders, training new teachers to implement computer learning in the classroom, and developing hands-on learning activities such as Junior Quiz Bowl and The Stock Market Game. I was recognized as being the advisor for the Junior Quiz Bowl teams which took first place and second place honors in the state.

If you can use an enthusiastic and hard-working professional to become a valued member of your administrative staff, I hope you will contact me to suggest a time when we might discuss your needs in person. I am currently excelling as a Fifth Grade Teacher at Roman Elementary School, and I can provide excellent personal and professional references at the appropriate time. It would certainly be an honor to meet you in person, and I will look forward to hearing from you.

Yours sincerely,

Caitlin O. Gibbs

CAITLIN O. GIBBS

1110½ Hay Street,
Fayetteville, NC 28305
(910) 483-6611
preppub@aol.com

CURRICULUM VITAE

Objective

I want to contribute to an educational institution as an Assistant Principal through applying my strong communication, motivational, planning, organizational, and teaching skills.

Education

Master's Degree in Administration, Shenandoah University, Holden, VA; degree anticipated 2001.
B.A. in Elementary Education, Shenandoah University, Holden, VA, 1989.

Special Awards and Honors

Social Studies Teacher of the Year for the State of VA, Feb. 1999; recognized for accomplishments related to the Social Studies curriculum.
Innovating Teacher Award for Junior Quiz Bowl, 1999; recognized for integrating economics and the Junior Quiz Bowl into the curriculum.
Advisor for 1st and 2nd Place Teams in Junior Quiz Bowl for State of VA, 1999; recognized as advisor of winning state teams.
Innovative Teaching Awards for Excellence, 1995, 1996, 1997, 1998, and 1999; recognized for accomplishments related to integrating economics into the curriculum.
Nominee for the Unsung Hero Award, 2000 and 1999.
Teacher of the Year, 1996 and 1995.

Publications and Grants

Grants: Wrote and received grants from the Education Foundation, 1996, 1997, and 2000.
Publications: Published two magazine articles for my work on Junior Quiz Bowl, 1998 and 2000.
Television: Wrote a fifteen-minute story on Junior Quiz Bowl and the Stock Market Game with a CBS affiliate which was aired on television; am contributing to a textbook in this area.

Experience

ASSISTANT PRINCIPAL INTERN. Roman Elementary School, Holden County Schools, Holden, VA (July 1999-June 2001). As an intern in my Master's Degree program leading to a Master's in Education, am gaining hands-on field experience as a principal.
- Perform teacher observations; have gained TPAI experiences.
- Have been involved in activities including curriculum development, problem solving related to student discipline, bus transportation planning and route management, personnel training, the implementation of new programs, as well as Initial Licensure Teacher Training, and the portfolio process.
- Contributed to the development of after-school program to raise End of Grade (EOG) tests: developed a budget, designed classes, and arranged transportation.
- Implemented innovative programs and training that enhanced the vitality of the curriculum.

- Developed partnerships within the community in order to support curriculum programs.

FIFTH GRADE TEACHER. Roman Elementary School, Holden County Schools, Holden, VA (1995-present). Provide a stimulating and creative educational environment for fifth grade students while focusing on teaching and learning objectives.

- Planned and orchestrated theatrical productions and other after-school activities.
- Instilled climate of positive discipline in the classroom which emphasized assessment of growth and individual needs.
- Was named **Social Studies Teacher of the Year for the State of VA.**
- Developed and implemented programs to enhance curriculum effectiveness.
- Was selected as the **Presenter** for new curriculum programs and trained teachers for new programs.
- Initiated Partnerships in Education.
- Integrated computer technology into the curriculum and the classroom.

FIFTH GRADE TEACHER, SECOND GRADE TEACHER, AND KINDERGARTEN TEACHER. Cavin Elementary School, Holden County Schools, VA (1991-95). Provided educational opportunities for fifth grade, second grade, and kindergarten students while focusing on teaching and learning objectives, emphasizing discipline as a positive force in the learning environment, and providing assessment of growth and individual needs.

- Selected as **Presenter** for Holden County Schools beginning teachers.
- Was recognized for programs implemented into curriculum.
- Wrote and received grants which were used to enhance the curriculum.

Professional Training

Completed the following training sponsored by Holden County Schools, 1990-present:

Total Quality Management Training	Learned Centered Supervision
Beginning Teacher Support Training	Individual Growth Plans
Literacy Based Assessment	Mind Maps
Computer Lab Assessment	Initial Teachers Licensure
Marco Polo Internet	4th Grade Writing
Stock Market Game	Computer Technology Specialist
Multiple Intelligence	Math Manipulations
Character Education	Junior Quiz Bowl
Cooperative Discipline	Experience Based Education
Discipline	Critical Thinking
Writing Integration Into Curriculum	Four Mat
Instructional Theory Into Practice	Instructional Alignment
Elements of Instruction	Mastery Learning
Classroom Management	Tesa
IBM Network	Open Court Reading and Writing
Breaking the Code	Calculators in the Classroom
Lions Quest	Mastery Learning
Intermediate Cooperative Learning	Mini Society
Place Called School	VA State Social Studies
CCC Lab Training	PowerPoint Training

Cooperative Learning Elementary and Intermediate Calculators in the Classroom
Principal Leadership: Budgeting, Laws, Interviewing, and Culture Differences

Special Skills and Competencies

Program Development: Have excelled in developing and implementing hands-on learning activities which can expand children's knowledge beyond their textbooks.

- When I was named **Social Studies Teacher of the Year for the State of VA,** was commended on my resourcefulness and creativity in implementing hands-on learning activities such as "Kids Vote," Junior Quiz Bowl, the Stock Market Game, and Economics Based Education.

Computer Technology Specialist: Have been trained by Holden County Schools in test assessment, CCC, ILS, PowerPoint, and IBM Network.

- Have been responsible for training 52 teachers to implement computer skills database, spreadsheets, Microsoft, computer terminology in the curriculum.
- Prepared more than 1,000 students for the 6th grade computer test.

Curriculum Development: Won numerous teaching excellence awards because of my ability to enhance curriculum, design learning "beyond the textbook," and create hands-on experience based educational opportunities.

- Developed Partnerships and brought in community leaders to support education.
- Established pilot programs for Junior Quiz Bowl and Economics is Fun programs.

Curriculum Vitae

Curriculum Vitae for an Aspiring Assistant Principal

This young professional has worked hard to obtain the credentials which will allow her to advance to assistant principal and to principal.

Dear Principal:

With the enclosed curriculum vitae, I would like to make you aware of my credentials as well as my interest in becoming an Assistant Principal at your school. I am qualified to serve as an Assistant Principal at a school from K-12.

As you will see from my resume, I hold a B.S. in Music Education and a Master's in Music Education, and I am completing a Master's Degree in Administration in May 2001. I feel that one of my special qualities is my true enthusiasm for education, and I thrive on the challenge of helping other teachers enrich their classroom environments. With a reputation as a "teacher's mentor," I have earned the respect of other teachers in this county as well as statewide because of my ability to help teachers develop a multi-disciplinary approach to learning which facilitates the transference of learning across multiple functional areas. In addition to my extensive responsibilities at Laferty School, I have been selected as East Coast Music Representative, and I counsel other teachers in McCleary and surrounding counties regarding teaching methods, issues related to aligning state standards with federal standards, and other matters.

In addition to my responsibilities as a Music Teacher at Laferty Elementary School, I have served as School Improvement Chairperson for five years and as Southern Association Chairperson for three years. In those administrative and planning roles, I have made significant contributions in the areas of program development and implementation. I joined Laferty Elementary School as a Music Teacher when this 1,100-student school was in a start-up phase, and I authored the school's School Improvement Plan bylaws and remediation plan; I edit the School Improvement Plan annually. Highly technology-oriented, I have applied my knowledge of Accelerated Reader (AR), Teaching and Learning with Computers (TLC), California Computer Curriculum (CCC), and Test Magic. I won Teacher of the Year awards at both Laferty Elementary School and Merlin Elementary School.

With a reputation as a popular and enthusiastic teacher who is always willing to share my knowledge and creativity with other educators in order to maximize learning for our children, I can provide excellent references. I respectfully request that you consider me for assignment as an Assistant Principal at a school that can use a bright, resourceful, and congenial professional who could contribute significantly to the teaching and learning process as well as to the development and implementation of new programs.

Yours sincerely,

Anne K. Dickinson

Anne K. Dickinson

1110½ Hay Street,
Fayetteville, NC 28305
(910) 483-6611
preppub@aol.com

CURRICULUM VITAE

Objective

I want to contribute to an educational institution as an Assistant Principal through applying my proven ability to work effectively with other teachers in developing multi-disciplinary approaches to teaching and learning while applying my strong communication, motivational, planning, organizational, and teaching skills.

Education

Master's Degree in Administration, Hendrix College, Conway, AR; degree anticipated May, 2001.
Master's Degree in Music Education, Hendrix College, Conway, AR, 1991
B.S. in Music Education, Hendrix College, Conway, AR, 1982.

Special Awards and Honors

Exceptional Idea Grant, 2000, for $1,000 by implementing a pilot program with music and language arts in third grade.
Teacher of the Year award, 1998-99, Laferty Elementary School; **District Winner** for Western Heights, 1998-99.
Teacher of the Year award, 1994, Merlin.
Certified as a **Cognitive Coach in Learning Supervision,** state of Arkansas, Spring 1998, and certified as a **state mentor**, summer 1999.
Was named **Tornado Pride Educator** by the PTA for Laferty Elementary School.
Southern Association Chairperson (SACS) for five years; **School Improvement Chairperson** for five years.

Experience

ADMINISTRATIVE INTERN. Laferty Elementary School, McCleary County Schools, Laferty, AR (1995-present). Began with this school when it started as a new pilot school, and have played a key role in developing the systems, policies, procedures, and operations manuals for a school which now has 1,100 students K-5.
- Was the **Chairperson of the Accreditation Committee** which resulted in the accreditation of the school in 1999.
- As **Chairperson for the School Improvement Committee**, wrote Bylaws, Test Magic remediation plan, and co-wrote the School Improvement Plan; review and edit the plans annually. Wrote the School Improvement Plan for reading, writing, math, computer technology, parental involvement, and communications.
- Was **co-writer with the principal of the Remediation Plan**; after the first year of implementing the plan, 70% of students demonstrated Level III Mastery Level.
- After implementing a quality vision for Laferty students, improved student achievement through disaggregating student data including End of Grade, Test Magic Benchmarks, and California Curriculum.

Curriculum Vitae

- With the guidance counselor, am continually involved in analyzing trends, weaknesses, opportunities, and problems facing the school. Identify ethnic, gender, and socio-economic weaknesses and address those issues through the School Improvement Plan via staff development funding.
- **Program development:** Played a key role in facilitating programs including the Remediation Program, All-County Chorus, Honeycutt Chorus, Laferty Drama, "Kids Vote USA," Junior Quiz Bowl, and choral performances with partners-in-education.
- Am very involved in working with third grade End Of Grade (EOG) testing. Currently involved in administrative staff development of INTASC standards for beginning teachers, K-2 Literacy Assessments for students, K-2 Math Assessments for students, and "Total Quality" for the McCleary County School System.
- Am actively involved in **writing the teacher and student handbooks** and master scheduling for PE, Art, Music, Computer Technology, Lunchroom, and abbreviated early release schedules for 1,100 students.
- Have come to be regarded as a "teacher's teacher" because of my strong desire to help other teachers, and am highly respected for my ability to help other teachers implement a multi-disciplinary approach in the transference of learning.

MUSIC TEACHER. Merlin Elementary School, McCleary County Schools, McCleary, AR (1995-present). Provided a state workshop in the Fall of 2000 entitled "I've-Been-There-and-Done-That Teachers with Experience Helping Beginning Teachers."
- Taught two pilot classes with music and language arts in the third grade which resulted in a minimum mean class growth of nine points on the EOG state assessments for two years.
- Am currently providing brain research examples and effective strategies to other teachers in implementing multi-disciplinary approaches to learning.

MUSIC TEACHER. Laferty Elementary School, Laferty, AR (1988-95). Was actively involved in developing the school's vision after being elected **School Improvement Chairperson** for three years.
- Facilitated afterschool programs with All-County Chorus, Laferty Chorus, Laferty Drama, chorus was selected to perform at the Southern Association Banquet in the Fall of 1993.
- Served as enrichment chairperson, and served on textbook committees for music.
- Mentored beginning teachers and student interns from O.S.U. and Indiana University.

Highlights of Professional Training

Completed the following training sponsored, 1989-present:

1999-00	Administrative Leadership Institute training in the McCleary County School System
1999-00	Administrative Leadership training in Total Quality
1999-00	Administrative Leadership training in INTASC Standards
1999-00	Administrative Leadership training in Arkansas Individual Growth Plans for students
1999-00	Administrative Leadership training in Arkansas K-2 Literacy Assessments
1999-00	Administrative Leadership training in Arkansas K-2 Math Assessments

Curriculum Vitae

Here's some advice. If you do choose a CV format to show off your background and potential, be sure you put the "best stuff" on the first page. It's a little like writing a novel: you have to keep your CV fast paced and interesting so that your reader wants to read more!

1998-00	Computer Technology training in the areas of Accelerated Reader, Teaching, and Computers
1998	Administrative Leadership training in Arkansas ABC's Assessments of Student's Growth California Computer Curriculum Integration, and Test Magic
1998	Administrative Leadership training in Remediation Goals
1998	Certified as a state mentor, and state cognitive coach
1997	District Administrative staff development on bus transportation, and safety of students
1993-97	Administrative Leadership training in School Improvement Goals
1991	Multiple Intelligence Training workshops, extensive training

Special Skills and Competencies

Program development and implementation: Highly skilled through experience as a School Improvement Chairperson for eight years, at two different schools; also, Southern Association Chairperson for five years.
- Currently involved in McCleary County Administrative Leadership Programs for "Total Quality," and "INTASC standards for beginning teachers.

Outstanding communication skills and extensive curriculum development experience:
- Actively involved with K-5 students, parents, faculty, and staff.
- Provide inservice workshops for school improvement plans, southern association goals, individual and grade level growth plans of students.
- Facilitate state workshops for music curriculum, and INTASC standards for beginning teachers, and professional growth plans for teachers.

Reputation as a "teacher's mentor" because of my ability to train other teachers to implement a multi-disciplinary approach to transference of learning.
- Completed extensive graduate-level education related to Multiple Intelligence Training, and have utilized that knowledge to help other teachers develop multi-disciplinary approaches to learning.
- Develop professional growth plans for teachers.
- Skilled in analyzing strengths and weaknesses of students achievement.
- Proficient in incorporating a total quality vision that works for everyone.

Memberships and Affiliations

- M.E.N.C. – State Music Representative, 1997-present
- Selected by the State Music Department to represent my peers in McCleary, Sheridan, Upton, and Murphy Counties.
- Work on issued related to aligning state standards with federal standards, and am a resource for elementary and middle school teacher; counsel other teachers on auditioning standards, web page design, curriculum standards, and other matters. Am called on frequently for advice by teachers in several counties.
- M.E.N.C. – Member of the Music Educators National Conference since 1982
- N.C.A.E. – Member of the Arkansas Association of Educators since 1982
- P.T.A.   – Member of the Parent Teacher Association since 1982

Curriculum Vitae

Date

Exact Name
Exact title
University or School
Address
City, State

Dear Exact Name:

With the enclosed CV/resume, I would like to introduce my background and qualifications. Although I am highly regarded in my current situation and enjoy my colleagues and students very much, I am acquainted with the reputation of your institution and feel I could make a significant contribution to your teaching mission and/or administrative needs.

Administrative Expertise and a Creative Flair for Programming and Marketing. In my current position, I am excelling as Dean of the Evening and Weekend College Division at Castleton State College, where I have worked since 1985. When I joined the college in 1985, there were 15 students in the evening program and none in the weekend program. Now there are 250-300 in the evening program and 80 students in the weekend program. As Dean, I report directly to the College Vice-President, and I am widely regarded as the "father" of our evening and weekend programs. I feel I have been successful because of my creativity in developing new courses and programs tailored to student needs and also because of my ability to recruit and maintain an outstanding faculty who view me as highly responsive to their needs. You will see from my CV/resume that I have been successful at writing and implementing grants.

My First Love is Teaching. Although I have been successful as an administrator, my first love is teaching, and I would be thrilled at the opportunity to be in the classroom. My teaching experience includes statistics and algebra at Castleton State College; English, Sociology, and Black History at Butler University; Math and Accounting at Butler University; and Political Science at Butler University. While in a teaching role at Butler University, I received an Outstanding Instructor award, and I have earned a reputation among students as a caring and helpful professional. For example, in my current position, I work routinely with students in helping them solve numerous types of problems including researching which institution will accept the most transfer credits.

I Possess Outstanding Educational Credentials. With a Ph.D., M.A., and B.A., I am highly regarded by colleagues and truly enjoy an academic environment.

It would certainly be a pleasure to meet with you to discuss your needs and, although I could provide outstanding references at the appropriate time, I would appreciate your holding my interest in confidence until after we talk. Thank you in advance for your professional courtesies, and I look forward to talking with you.

Sincerely,

Dr. Nate Simpson

DR. NATE SIMPSON

Dean of the Evening and Weekend College Division

Castleton State College, Castleton, VT

1110½ Hay Street,
Fayetteville, NC 28305
(910) 483-6611
preppub@aol.com

CURRICULUM VITAE

Education

Ph.D., Education Administration	Butler University	1980
M.A., Political Science	Butler University	1974
B.A., Political Science	Butler University	1970

Professional Experience and Activities

<u>1985-present: Castleton College.</u> Have made significant contributions to this growing college while excelling in the following track record of promotion:

DEAN OF THE EVENING AND WEEKEND COLLEGE DIVISION. (1997-present). Am widely credited with being the "father" of the college's Evening and Weekend Division. When I joined Castleton State College in 1985 as Evening Director, there were 15 students in the evening program and 0 students in the weekend program. Now there are 250-300 in the evening program and 80 students in the weekend program, which represents 28% to 33% of the Full Time Enrollment (FTE). Report directly to the College Vice-President for Instruction.

Curriculum Development: For the weekend program, developed new courses in Criminal Justice, Cosmetology, Information Systems Technology, as well as College Transfer Courses ranging from history to microbiology.

- Am respected for my creative programming skills and my aggressive desire to tailor curricula to student needs and schedules.
- In 1985, there were no College Transfer Courses; now there are 25 College Transfer Courses.
- After initiating the college's computer courses "from scratch," have developed them into three full programs which are: (1) a two-year degree program in Information Systems Programming with a Programming Concentration; (2) a two-year degree program in Information Systems (Non-Programming Concentration); and (3) Business Administration.

Grants:

- Wrote successful grant proposals which resulted in grants from the Vermont Humanities Council and the Kaiser Foundation; used the grant money to sponsor the first-ever Native American Literature and Writers Conference in 1997, which has been held three times since then.

Teaching and Faculty Supervision & Development:

- Have taught algebra and statistics; additionally, have tutored students in advanced math through calculus, 1989-present.
- Through my strong recruiting skills and retention ability, have been successful in attracting adjunct faculty to the Evening and Weekend College, and am regarded as a fair and popular administrator who goes out of my way to be supportive and responsive to faculty needs.
- Supervise and evaluate 40 part-time and full-time faculty members recruited for evening and weekend instruction.

Student Recruiting:

- Believe that the most effective method of recruiting students is by designing curricula that meet their course and schedule needs.

Curriculum Vitae

- Am a naturally outgoing individual who thoroughly enjoys working with students; apply my strong problem-solving skills and customer service orientation to help students in numerous ways, including finding the college that accepts the most transfer credits.
- Have established a reputation as a popular and effective dean who makes a genuine effort to help students.

Budgeting & Payroll:
- Develop annual budget of $370,000 for the Evening and Weekend College; am known for my resourceful style of optimizing the dollars we spend.
- Prepare contracts and time sheets for the Evening and Weekend payroll.

EVENING DIRECTOR. (1985-98). Was promoted to Dean of the Evening and Weekend College Division in 1998 based on my effectiveness in this job. Supervised the counseling and registration of 400 students while developing the quarter and semester schedules for evening and weekend classes; functioned as Director of the Evening/Weekend Planning Unit; prepared the quarter million dollar budget for the Evening/Weekend Division.

1980-1985: Butler University, Indianapolis, IN.
ACADEMIC DEAN. Made significant contributions to this college in the following ways:

Curriculum Development: Managed and developed diverse curricula for the traditional minority private school student body. Transformed the college into a respected show-case of curricula tailored to this traditional minority private school student body.

Grants: Administered a grant from the "Fund for the Improvement of Post-Secondary Education" for implementing the Mastery Learning Program; administered $108,000 over two years.
- Through guiding faculty in their interaction with a consultant from Columbus Community College, developed new techniques to improve learning among the disadvantaged enrollment (95% of the total enrollment, or 300 students, were African-American, Asian, or other ethnic minorities).
- By writing academic proposals, was responsible for securing Title III funds for academic budget and the administration of related payroll responsibility; administered funds of $350,000.

Accreditation: Provided leadership for the college during its Association accreditation process.

Teaching: Taught Algebra, English, Literature, Sociology, Black History, and Marketing.

1978-1980: Butler University, Indianapolis, IN.
DEAN OF THE COLLEGE. Directed the operation of the college in the absence of the President who was a consultant for many institutions and away from town 50% of the time. Was responsible for Registrar's office and library in a private, profit-making school.

Accreditation: Led all the licensing and accreditation efforts which were successful in securing the College's first accreditation as a junior college and first licensure to grant Associate Degrees by the Board of Governors of the University of North Carolina.
- Led the school in the Veterans Approval process through the State of Indiana and for the VA Administration relations and inspection visits.

Phenomenal Growth of the Student Body: Instrumental in building enrollment.

College Administrator and Teacher

This talented administrator is excelling in his management responsibilities, but he yearns to be back in the classroom.

Teaching: Taught Business Math, Accounting, and English.
Faculty Instruction: Employed, supervised, and evaluated 45 faculty members as well as a counselor in day and evening business programs.

1976-78: Butler University, Indianapolis, IN.
POLITICAL SCIENCE INSTRUCTOR.
Teaching: Instructed 12 different political science courses on a rotating basis, day and evening.
Research: Conducted political research and participated in a national conference.
Consulting: Campaign consultant for congressional candidate Kevin James. Also participated as a member of Congressman Mary Jenkins Congressional Advisory Committee. Acted as a paid consultant for political surveys, polling, and voting pattern studies.
Bookstore Sales: Managed and built up the volume of business at the Butler University Bookstore which served up to 2000 students per academic year.

Honors and Affiliations

Received a 1999 honor in the form of a Residency from the Crayton Foundation because of my writing skills.
Belong to **Top 1% Society,** a Mensa-like organization.
Evaluated as **Outstanding Instructor (top 10%),** Butler University.
Member, Organization for Community College Administrators
Member, Board of Trustees of IN Writers Network.
Member, IN Writers Network
Included in *Marquis Who's Who in the North and Northeast,* Twenty-Third Edition

Highlights of Research and Publications

"Phone Poll," *Campaign Insight,* Castleton, VT.
"Reply to John Smith's 'No Such Thing as Cultural Disadvantaged,'" *Instructor.*
"Two Ways: Pulse and Publicity," *Campaign Insight.*
"The Two-Year Business School in the United States," *Journal of Business Education.*
"The Vermont Business School's Markets and Competition in the 80s." Presentation before the Owners and Managers Meeting of the 1970 Annual Convention of the Vermont Association of Business Colleges.
"Mastery Learning at Butler University." Presentation at Indiana Department of Community College Workshop at Lee's College at Oneonta, Oneonta.
Ph.D. Dissertation, "Resources in Education," January, 1982. ED 191 514, SUNY, Oneonta, NY.
"The Mastery Learning Program at Butler University: Final Report," *Resources in Education,* ED 188 723, SUNY, Oneonta, NY.
"Journeys," *Indiana Observer.*
"A Tippicanoe Summer," "*Indiana Observer*
"The Soul Is Within Each of Us," *Indiana Observer.*
"The Arrowmaker," *Indian Magazine,* Vol. 12-1, p. 20.
Numerous poems published in *Indiana Observer.*

Primary Interests and Strengths

Primary teaching interests: Mathematics, algebra, geometry, trigonometry, calculus, statistics, political science.
Primary strengths: Highly effective communicator who excels in pragmatic problem solving and in creative envisioning; excel in establishing and maintaining excellent working relationships with faculty and students. Offer an aggressive public relations and marketing orientation.

Elementary School Teacher

Date

Employers always wonder why you want to change jobs. This teacher states clearly in his cover letter that he is seeking to relocate to Florida so that he can work and live near his extended family.

Dear Sir or Madam:

I am writing to express my strong interest in obtaining a position as an Elementary School Teacher within the school system. With the enclosed resume, I would like to make you aware of my background as an enthusiastic educator and coach with exceptional leadership and motivational skills who offers a background in elementary school teaching as well as coaching high school track and college and high school football.

As you will see from my resume, I am currently excelling as an Elementary School Teacher, providing classroom instruction to fourth-grade students at Myron Watt Elementary in Muncie, IN, while also coaching Football and Track at Reiner Senior High School. I have been honored for my outstanding performance, by my selection as Lear County Schools Employee of the Month for May of 2001. Through collaboration with faculty members and administrators, I have gained valuable experience in a number of diverse teaching and classroom management techniques, and I have conducted research via the Internet to obtain innovative new lesson ideas.

In early Student Teaching and Practicum experience, I exhibited my natural leadership and communication skills, building a quick rapport with students, teachers, and parents in a variety of educational environments. My enthusiasm for teaching as well as the discipline and adaptability that I developed during my years as a student-athlete have served me well in challenging classroom situations where I was able to modify existing lesson plans and materials to fit the needs of my students.

Although I am highly regarded by my present employer and can provide excellent personal and professional references at the appropriate time, I am in the process of relocating to Florida to be nearer to my family, and I am interested in exploring career opportunities in area school systems.

If you can use an articulate young educator and coach with natural leadership ability and exceptional planning and motivational skills, I hope you will write or call me soon to suggest a time when we might meet to discuss your needs and goals and how my background might serve them. I can provide outstanding references at the appropriate time.

Sincerely,

Alan M. Peaceman

ALAN M. PEACEMAN

1110½ Hay Street, Fayetteville, NC 28305 • preppub@aol.com • (910) 483-6611

OBJECTIVE   To benefit an organization that can use an enthusiastic young educator with exceptional leadership, planning, and organizational skills who offers a background of excellence in classroom management, lesson planning, teaching, and coaching.

EDUCATION   **Bachelor of Science** in **Elementary Education**, Ball State University, Muncie, IN, 1997.
- Excelled in college athletics, lettering as a member of the Ball State University Football Team; attended college on a partial athletic scholarship.

CERTIFICATIONS   Awarded the Indiana Instructional Certificate I in Elementary Education.
Passed the National Teacher's Exam—General, Professional, and Specialty Knowledge.

EXPERIENCE   **ELEMENTARY SCHOOL TEACHER.** Myron Watt Elementary School, Muncie, IN (1998-present). Excel in this position providing daily instruction to a diverse population of up to 27 fourth graders; structure diverse lessons ranging from hands-on learning to reporting, building confidence, trust, and enthusiasm in each child by allowing them to experience success.
- Develop a rapport with parents maintaining open lines of communication to encourage student motivation and classroom performance.
- Design and implement lesson plans that exceed the standards of the state of Indiana, resulting in increased student scores on annual End-Of-Grade (EOG) tests.
- Collaborate with faculty members and administration, gaining diverse teaching and classroom management techniques; conduct Internet research to obtain lesson ideas.
- Achieved a high average score of level three in state-wide End-Of-Grade (EOG) testing for students in my class, despite this being my first exposure to state testing.

FOOTBALL and **TRACK COACH.** Reiner Senior High School, Muncie, IN (1998-present). Contribute my playing experience, discipline, and college coaching experience, planning and executing daily practice sessions for high school student-athletes; provide positive feedback, ensuring athlete's optimum mental and physical condition for each football game or track meet.

STUDENT TEACHER. Gregg Elementary School, Muncie, IN (1998). Developed and implemented lesson plans in Mathematics, Reading, Health, and Language Arts, teaching as many as 25 third grade students in this local elementary school.

STUDENT TEACHER. Lobos Elementary School, Muncie, IN (1998). Instructed as many as 22 fourth grade students in Mathematics, Social Studies, Reading, and Spelling, creating and implementing a variety of interactive teaching methods.
- Organized hands-on group learning experiences to promote cooperative learning.

FOOTBALL COACH. Ball State University, Muncie, IN (1997). Provided leadership and experience as a Coach for the University football team, planning and executing drills for daily practices; utilized game film to analyze opponent's performance; monitored the study table for all freshman athletes, ensuring that they retained eligibility.

PRACTICUMS   Excelled in various elementary school practicum teaching positions, including:
- **Lakecrest Elementary** – First Grade, Spring 1997.
- **Lobos Elementary School** – Second Grade, Fall 1997.
- **St. Michael's** — Kindergarten, Spring 1996

PERSONAL   Excellent personal and professional references are available upon request.

Elementary School Teacher

Date

Exact Name of Person
Exact Title
Exact Name of Company
Address
City, State, Zip

Elementary School Teacher

This young professional feels that her strengths lie in her strong written communication skills which have resulted in successful grant writing.

Dear Exact Name of Person (or Dear Sir or Madam if answering a blind ad):

With this letter and the enclosed resume, I would like to introduce you to a dedicated and motivated young educator who offers exceptional communication and organizational skills.

As you will see from the resume, I have quickly become known for my excellent abilities in the areas of classroom management, lesson planning and implementation, and teaching. With a B.S. in elementary education which I earned with honors, I have been awarded the Minnesota Instructional Certificate I in Elementary Education and have passed the National Teacher's Exam of General, Professional, and Specialty Knowledge.

Presently a first grade teacher for 31 students, I am excelling in a school with a diverse student population. I create and implement lesson plans which are designed to foster individual learning styles and promote student mastery of English, Language Arts, Social Studies, and Science. Among my accomplishments since becoming a member of this school's faculty in 1998, has been assisting in writing a grant which resulted in the implementation of a new reading program (Success For All) which grouped students by reading levels rather than strictly by age and grade.

Earlier as a Student Teacher and Substitute Teacher, I worked with first graders in one school and six graders at a second school while learning effective classroom management techniques and methods of tailoring instruction programs to individual learning styles. The learning experience as a student teacher allowed me to gain exposure to the realities of teaching elementary age students and verify that as the career path I desire to follow. I truly love the challenge of being a role model for these impressionable children and helping guide them as they learn and grow.

If you can use a dedicated educator who offers exceptional organizational and planning skills along with a creative and innovative style, I hope you will call me soon for a brief discussion of how I could contribute to your school and its continued success. I will provide excellent professional and personal references at the appropriate time.

Sincerely,

Juanita Jackson

JUANITA JACKSON

1110½ Hay Street, Fayetteville, NC 28305 • preppub@aol.com • (910) 483-6611

OBJECTIVE
To benefit an organization that can use a motivated young educator with exceptional communication and organizational skills who offers a solid background of excellence in classroom management, lesson planning and implementation, and teaching.

EDUCATION
Bachelor of Science in **Elementary Education**, Macalester College, St. Paul, MN, 1997.
- Maintained a **3.63 GPA** in my major, 3.24 overall; named to **Dean's List** three semesters.
Completed continuing education courses which included the **Lindamood LIPS**
- Developing phonological awareness for decoding and spelling.
- Courses in **Technology:**. Introduction to Office, Excel, PowerPoint, E-mail, Internet.
- **Mentor/Mentee** training: classroom management and effective teacher profiles.
- **Maximizing Student Potential**: meeting the needs of diverse student populations.

CERTIFICATIONS
Awarded the Minnesota Instructional Certificate I in Elementary Education.
Passed the National Teacher's Exam–General, Professional, and Specialty Knowledge.

HONORS
Selected as **Employee of the Month** for E.E.Platt Nesbit Elementary and Public Schools of Platt County, March 1999.

AFFILIATIONS
Appointed Vice-President of the Student Minnesota Education Association; attended the SPSEA National Conference, as well as child abuse and classroom discipline workshops sponsored by the Association.

EXPERIENCE
ELEMENTARY SCHOOL TEACHER. E.E. Platt Elementary School, St. Paul, MN (1998-present). Excelling in this position providing daily instruction to a diverse population of up to 31 first graders; create and implement lesson plans designed to foster individual learning styles and promote student mastery of English, Language Arts, Social Studies, and Science.
- Set high expectations for student behavior and maintain those standards through classroom management techniques and positive reinforcement.
- Assumed additional responsibility, tutoring fourth-grade students in Writing, Reading, and Arithmetic in order to improve End Of Grade (EOG) testing scores.
- Assisted in writing a grant that allowed the school to implement Success For All, a new reading program grouping students from different grades according to reading levels.

STUDENT TEACHER. Mankin Elementary School, St. Paul, MN (1998). Taught Language Arts, Reading, and Mathematics to classes of up to 25 first-graders in this local elementary school, tailoring lessons to the individual learning styles of my students.

PRACTICUMS
Excelled in various elementary school practicums/teaching positions including:
- **Dean Lufkin Elementary**, Spring 1997 – taught Math and Language Arts lessons to first grade students; used positive reinforcement for behavior management.
- **Hall Day School**, Fall 1996 – taught Language Arts and Math lessons which encouraged cultural diversity; developed a thematic unit and an interactive bulletin board.
- **Children's Museum**, Spring 1996 – assisted children with a variety of hands-on learning experiences; created art boxes for the craft center.
- **McCall Center**, Fall 1995 – while teaching kindergarten classes, provided opportunities for very young students to learn and practice on an individual basis.

PERSONAL
Excellent personal and professional references are available upon request.

Elementary School Teacher (First Grade)

Date

**Elementary School Teacher
(First Grade)**

A cover letter is
sometimes called a
"letter of interest" or
"broadcast letter."
Perhaps that is because
you broadcast your
intentions and career
interests in such a letter.

Dear Sir or Madam:

With the enclosed resume, I would like to make you aware of my interest in teaching in a school system that can use an industrious and creative young teaching professional with a proven ability to teach, motivate, and instill a love of learning in others.

As you will see from my resume, I have taught in both wealthy school districts as well as in a rural, poor district. In most recent positions in California, I taught kindergarten and first grade in the public schools of Damron County. I also played a key role in implementing changes recommended by a state-appointed Assistance Team that transformed elementary school student scores from low-performing to within two percent of "exemplary." In 1998-99, I was honored by selection as Teacher of the Year at Frieder Elementary School, where I have served as both a Kindergarten and First Grade Teacher.

In previous teaching assignments after earning my B.S. in Education in 1994, I worked as a Homebound Teacher and Substitute Teacher in California. My experience as a substitute teacher was valuable, because I learned the importance of planning classroom activities far in advance so that student learning is not interrupted when the regular classroom teacher is absent. I am certified to teach in California and New Mexico.

If you can use a enthusiastic young educator who thrives on the challenges and complexities of teaching, I hope you will contact me to suggest a time when we might meet to discuss your needs. I can assure you in advance that I could rapidly become an asset to your organization.

Sincerely,

Dorothy Middleton

DOROTHY MIDDLETON

1110½ Hay Street, Fayetteville, NC 28305 • preppub@aol.com • (910) 483-6611

OBJECTIVE   To contribute to a school that can use a hard-working young teacher with excellent communication, organizational, and planning skills who is known for exceptional creativity and resourcefulness as well as an ability to inspire children to excel.

EDUCATION   **B.S. in Education,** University of San Diego, San Diego, CA, 1994; named to Dean's List.

CERTIFICATIONS   Certified to teach in California and New Mexico.
& AFFILIATION   Member, National Education Association.
Member, California Association of Educators.
Member, Damron Association of Educators.

COMPUTERS   Familiar with Windows, MS Word, Excel, WordPerfect, MacWrite, and numerous proprietary programs specific to education.

EXPERIENCE   **FIRST GRADE TEACHER.** Public Schools of Damron County, Frieder Elementary School, San Diego, CA (1997-present). For two years, have excelled as a First Grade Teacher; have become known as a polished communicator who excels in working with children, parents, other educators, and administrators.
- Develop interesting lessons plans which stimulate initiative and curiosity in children.
- Served on the staff that earned a top-notch evaluation from the state-appointed Assistance Team; this staff made changes that transformed student scores in this very poor, rural county from low-performing to within 2 percent of a point of "exemplary."
- Served on the staff that passed the Southern States Accreditation, and was praised for my intelligent and resourceful suggestions.
- Was honored by selection as **" Teacher of the Year"** 2000 at Frieder Elementary School; this was a special honor to me because my fellow teachers voted.

KINDERGARTEN TEACHER. Public Schools of Damron County, Frieder Elementary School, San Diego, CA (1996-97). Performed all duties of a classroom kindergarten teacher while earning a reputation as a vibrant and creative teaching professional.
- Assured that all lessons planned met or exceeded the curriculum standards.
- Organized materials in such a way that students would find the presentation of skill-building lessons fun to do and non-threatening.
- Communicated with teaching professionals, administrators, parents, and care givers.

WAITRESS (Part-Time). Fragrant Garden, San Diego and Los Angeles, CA (1996-present). In a "second job" in addition to my full-time teaching responsibilities, have excelled as a waitress with this popular family steakhouse; was named **Most Valuable Player** in 1998.
- Although this is a part-time job, I enjoy it and take it seriously and have worked for the restaurant for more than four years. Worked on a staff that set record sales.

SUBSTITUTE TEACHER. Lopez School District and Hinslowe School District, Wide River and Fulton, CA (1994-95). As a substitute teacher, learned the importance of preparing detailed lesson plans days in advance so that classroom activities will not be interrupted because of a teacher's unexpected absence.
- Learned to prepare a "backup" plan when taking over a classroom in case the regular teacher did not plan far in advance, thus ensuring that student learning could occur.

PERSONAL   Can provide excellent personal and professional references.

Elementary School Teacher (First Grade)

Date

Elementary School Teacher (First Grade)

This newly minted college graduate is seeking her first "real" teaching position after internships. She stresses her dedication to her field in her cover letter.

Dear Sir or Madam:

With the enclosed resume, I would like to make you aware of my strong desire to become a part of your elementary teaching staff.

As you will see from my resume, I have recently earned my Bachelor of Science in Education (B.S.E.) degree at the South Carolina State University in Orangeburg. Since it has always been my childhood dream to become a teacher, my college graduation was an especially meaningful event in my life.

As you will see from my resume, I recently completed a teaching assignment as a First Grade Student Teacher, and I successfully assumed all the duties of a first grade teacher. During those two months, I wrote and completed my own professional growth and development plan, and I also planned and implemented a classroom and behavior management program.

In my previous two-month assignment as a Kindergarten Student Teacher, I performed with distinction in planning and implementing creative lessons, communicating with teaching professionals and parents, and working with the children, whom I truly loved.

You will notice from my resume that I have expressed my true love for children through my summer and part-time jobs while in college. For four years, I was a nanny for a professional family and in that capacity I cared for three triplet newborns as well as two older children. It is an understatement to say that I refined my time management skills in that part-time job! I have also worked in a day care environment where I worked with children from infant to 12 years while learning to work effectively with people from all backgrounds.

If you can use a highly motivated young professional with unlimited personal initiative as well as strong personal qualities of dependability and trustworthiness, I hope you will contact me to suggest a time when we might meet to discuss your needs. I can provide excellent personal and professional references, and I am eager to apply my strong teaching skills and true love for children in an academic institution which emphasizes hard work and a commitment to the highest learning goals.

Sincerely,

Gertrude Marlowe

GERTRUDE MARLOWE

1110½ Hay Street, Fayetteville, NC 28305 • preppub@aol.com • (910) 483-6611

OBJECTIVE

To contribute to an elementary school that can use a caring and well educated young teacher who offers a proven ability to instill a love of learning in children while stimulating their imaginations with creative tasks and activities that lead to the development of solid skills.

EDUCATION

Bachelor of Science in Education (B.S.E.), South Carolina State University, Orangeburg, SC, 2001.
- Elected Vice President, Sigma Sigma Sorority; chapter members elected me because of my ability to perform the job and also because of my reputation as a strong leader with exemplary character.
- Becoming a teacher has always been my dream since childhood, so completion of this degree was an extremely meaningful experience.

AFFILIATIONS

Member of Southern Early Childhood Association
Member of Fleming County Early Childhood Association

EXPERIENCE

FIRST GRADE STUDENT TEACHER. Fleming Public Schools, Orangeburg, SC (Spring 2001). In my second teaching internship, effectively assumed all duties of a first grade teacher and was commended for my skill in carrying out all my professional responsibilities.
- Wrote and successfully completed my own professional growth and development plan.
- Planned and implemented a classroom and behavior management program.

KINDERGARTEN STUDENT TEACHER. Fleming Public Schools, Orangeburg, SC (Fall 2000). Performed all duties of a classroom kindergarten teacher while working with a vibrant and enthusiastic teaching professional from whom I learned a great deal.
- Played a key role in planning and implementing lessons; was entrusted with planning and implementing my own unit of study; worked with a team of educators in planning.
- Assured that all lessons planned met or exceeded the curriculum standards.
- Organized materials in such a way that students would find the presentation of skill-building lessons fun to do and non-threatening.
- Communicated with teaching professionals, administrators, parents, and care givers.
- Evaluated student progress and communicated progress to students and parents.
- Because of my strong desire to become the best teacher I can be, maintained a log of personal growth to reflect on my own performance.

Summer and part-time jobs:
DAY CARE WORKER. (Summer 1999). Moss Daycare, Charleston, SC. Supervised children of all ages, from infant to 12 years old, at this respected facility which cared for 50 children.
- Planned daily activities; chaperoned field trips; communicated with parents.
- Gained experience working with children of varied ages and family backgrounds.

NANNY. (1998). In this part-time job with the Edward Brown family in Orangeburg, SC, handled the responsibility for newborn triplets and two older children.

CHILD CARE PROVIDER. Beatrice Smith family, Orangeburg, SC (1997). Was responsible for the daily supervision of a one year old boy which included managing the schedule for feeding, changing, napping, playing, nurturing, and entertaining.

PERSONAL

While in high school, worked during my junior and senior years.

Elementary School Teacher (Kindergarten)

Date

Elementary School Teacher (Kindergarten)

This young professional makes it known right away that she has recently moved to be with her husband and intends to resume her teaching career.

Dear Sir or Madam,

I have recently married a local businessman and am now making Sheboygan my permanent home after moving from St. Paul, MN. I am eager to resume teaching. In January of this year I completed my Effective Teacher's Training at Lakeland College. I am available for substitute teaching as a way of gaining familiarity with the Kobak County school system. My goal is to ultimately receive a lateral entry position at the K-6 grade level or in Special Needs Education.

I am a teacher who strongly believes in personal and professional growth related directly to student achievement and self-esteem. Teaching is a changing profession and through education and experience, I will change with it. For this reason, I have applied to Lakeland College in order to obtain my Wisconsin Elementary Education Certification. I believe through professional growth and teaching experience, I will provide the children with the best possible education.

I am a teacher who believes that all children can learn. Fairness, compassion and respect permeate my classroom. Communication among children, their peers, and myself are essential components in my classroom. All children are individuals with their own needs, ideas and values. I support and respect each child. I highly value ongoing and positive communication with parents to help each child in his/her growth.

I will provide the children with activities that will challenge and strengthen them based on their needs. I will provide a stimulating and motivating learning atmosphere that will enable children to develop, grow and reach their maximum potential. I believe in a cooperative learning environment and a child-centered program delivered through a variety of teaching strategies. I enjoy and value working cooperatively with other staff members and parents to involve them in the children's academic and social development.

I am also interested in becoming involved in extracurricular activities which include parent-teacher committees, school committees, sports, homework and after-school clubs.

I look forward to discussing my candidacy with you in greater detail.

Yours truly,

Amy Elizabeth Hadley

AMY ELIZABETH HADLEY

1110½ Hay Street, Fayetteville, NC 28305   •   preppub@aol.com   •   (910) 483-6611

OBJECTIVE   I wish to contribute to a school system that can use an effective teacher with excellent communication and organizational skills along with a proven ability to motivate students to excel and to forge a partnership between home and school to emphasize learning mastery.

EDUCATION   Completing **Elementary Education Certification**, Lakeland College, Sheboygan, WI, January 1999-August 2000; am pursuing this certification in the evenings.
Bachelor of Arts with Psychology major, Northwestern College, St. Paul, MN, 1997.
Earned **Associate's Degree in Early Childhood Education, with honors**, Macalester College, St. Paul, MN, 1993.

EXPERIENCE   **KINDERGARTEN TEACHER.** Lasalle School, Appleton, WI (1998-present). Am excelling in my job teaching all subjects to kindergartners in this respected private school.

PRE-KINDERGARTEN TEACHER. Morse Preschool, St. Paul, MN (1996-97). Used the team teaching plan with and in support of the pre-kindergarten staff, and provided curriculum ideas, lesson modifications, and strategies for all children in various classrooms.
* Promoted self-help skills, confidence, self-esteem, and the development of strong social skills.
* Administered informal testing to continually modify students' programming.
* Assisted in modification and implementation of **Parent Curriculum Night, Community Open House, report cards, field trips, and holiday festivals**.
* Taught individual children, small groups, and whole class experiences.

KINDERGARTEN TEACHER. Levet School, St. Paul, MN (1994-95). Planned and reorganized an existing classroom to develop and implement an effective learning environment for kindergarten children.
* Planned and implemented lessons from all curriculum areas including activity-based mathematics, whole language development, emergent literacy, and science concepts.
* Was responsible for organizing and presenting a **parent orientation evening, meet the teachers day, parent-teacher interviews, report cards, and an annual Community Open House.**
* Planned, assessed, and evaluated children based on the Common Curriculum Outcomes.
* Assisted and helped organize field trips, holiday pageants, and class participation in **Earth Day activities and the Toronto Garden Club Quilt Show.**

PRE-KINDERGARTEN TEACHER. Fulton Learning Centre, St. Paul, MN (1993-94). Was responsible for planning and providing a balanced program conducive to the emotional, physical, social, cognitive, and creative development of each individual child.
* Assessed and evaluated children's progress in accordance with their IEPs.
* Participated in an early morning breakfast program and the center's summer program.
* Provided support and feedback to fellow teachers, assistants, and co-op students.
* Worked with intervention professionals from the Children's Aid Society and hospitals.

Volunteer experience: Since making my permanent home in Sheboygan with my husband, have joined the **Junior League** and serve on the Great Ideas in Teaching Committee.

PERSONAL   Enjoy helping others. Polished communicator. Am a highly motivated teacher who truly believes in the power of education and teaching to enrich people's lives.

Group Home Teacher and Special Education Teacher

Dear Principal:

With the enclosed resume, I would like to make you aware of my interest in serving as an English or special education teacher in your school.

As you will see from my resume, I have held special education positions in several cities. Working with EMH, LD, and BEH students, I found the challenge to be refreshing after a quiet beginning in my teaching career. I became certified in special education during the "trial and error" period when all "special" students were estranged from the "normal" students. I have learned through the system's and my own mistakes and have developed a style of teaching that will reach "special" students.

Through my love of the special education field, I recently decided to establish a half-way house for substance abusers. A break in teaching helped me to realize my passion for special education. My residents in our half-way house had been in special classes during their school career and my heart bled for them.

I began my career as an English teacher, teaching students who were reading well above their grade levels. Slowly, I met the challenge of dealing with students because of cultural variations and slow learning ability at Junction City and Niagra Falls.

With a reputation as a popular and enthusiastic teacher who is always willing to share my knowledge and creativity to maximize learning for our children, I can provide excellent references. I respectfully request that you consider me for an English or special education position. I am a professional who could contribute significantly to the teaching and learning process as well as to the development of young minds.

Yours sincerely,

Penelope Howard

PENELOPE HOWARD

1110 1/2 Hay Street, Fayetteville, NC 28305 • (910) 483-6611 • preppub@aol.com

OBJECTIVE I want to contribute to a school system that can use an experienced teacher of English and special education who possesses excellent analytical, motivational, and organizational skills which will benefit children in a secondary education setting.

EDUCATION **Teacher Certification,** Brighton State University, Brighton, AZ.
Bachelor of Arts degree in English, Talford University, Talford SC.

CERTIFICATION Certified to teach special education, grades 6-12.

EXPERIENCE *Have established myself as a dedicated and hard-working teacher with a passion for setting a strong personal example while helping each student develop to his/her fullest potential:*
GROUP HOME MANAGER. Howard's House, Brighton, AZ (1998-present). With my knowledge of the special education area, established and manage a half-way house for substance abusers.
- Am entrusted with the responsibility of making decisions which effect the freedom and well-being of up to 12 individuals at a time.
- Have become widely respected for my unusually high success rate in working with troubled individuals.
- Provide career consulting and counseling on financial and personal problems; provide leadership in the development of educational goals.

SPECIAL EDUCATION TEACHER. Cambridge Hills High School, Cambridge Schools, Cambridge, MA (1996-98). Worked with LD and BEH students.
- Managed students in a self-contained classroom.
- Taught four periods of English, one period of math and social studies.

SPECIAL EDUCATION TEACHER. Davidson Middle Schools, Davidson City Schools, Davidson, TN (1994-96). Taught EMH students in an open middle school setting which created many distractions. Was successful due to innovative teaching methods and materials used.

SPECIAL EDUCATION TEACHER. Pilgrim Junior High School, Valley Forge, VA (1990-94). Constructed a learning lab for students of all disabilities in an open setting while teaching EMH in a self-contained classroom..

READING/ENGLISH TEACHER. Viagra Junior High School, Viagra Falls, NY (1988-90). Taught English to students one-on-one who required extra help while working in an extremely small setting.

READING TEACHER. Union Junior High School, Union City, IA (1986-88). Expanded my insight and knowledge in dealing with students by teaching children with various cultural backgrounds.

PERSONAL I am an educator who is willing to put forth extra effort and care to better the lives of the children in our school systems. Excellent personal and professional references.

High School Teacher

Date

Exact Name of Person
Exact Title
Exact Name of Company
Address
City, State, Zip

High School Teacher

Dear Exact Name of Person (or Dear Sir or Madam if answering a blind ad):

Probably this young teacher will find a new situation in a public or private school, although he accentuates that he has taught on a part-time basis in college. You will see that he shows his part-time business interests, too. You need to think carefully about revealing everything on your resume. Employers sometimes don't want to employ people who have too many outside profit-making activities which might compromise the time needed to do a good job in their main position.

I would like to take the opportunity to introduce you to a respected young educator who combines practical business experience and an education in business administration along with experience in teaching at the high school and college level.

As you will see from the enclosed resume, I am a well-educated and self-motivated professional with a versatile background as a small business owner and retail manager/supervisor. Simultaneously working as a Business and Marketing Teacher at the high school level, I also am refining time management, planning, and organizational skills in simultaneous jobs overseeing all aspects of rental property management and teaching business subjects as an Instructor at the University of Iowa.

Selected as Teacher of the Month at the county level, I have written a series of "business problems" which integrated the studies of business and math and which were published throughout the region. I excel at motivating students and in encouraging them to compete in Marketing Research events up to the state and national levels while introducing business concepts to high school students. As Business Instructor at the university level on a part-time basis, I teach a variety of subjects while motivating and encouraging students to participate in discussions and maintain a lively, informative, and stimulating environment in which to learn.

A member of the Iowa Marketing Education Association, I earned master's and bachelor's degrees in Business Administration as well as attending workshops and seminars in entrepreneurial methods and ideas and managerial techniques.

If you can use an articulate and dedicated teacher who is known for creativity as well as managerial abilities, I hope you will call me soon for a brief discussion of how I could contribute to your organization. I will provide excellent professional and personal references at the appropriate time.

Sincerely,

Arthur S. Lezin

ARTHUR STANFORD LEZIN

1110½ Hay Street, Fayetteville, NC 28305 · preppub@aol.com · (910) 483-6611

OBJECTIVE   To offer my extensive teaching experience and strong communication skills to a school system that can benefit from a creative individual who has the ability to ignite classrooms with enthusiasm through applying my background in business management and marketing.

EDUCATION   **Master's degree in Business Administration,** University of Iowa, Des Moines, IA 1989.
Bachelor of Science degree in Business Administration, Scott College, Bettendorf, IA, 1983.
Attended a ten-day entrepreneurial workshop through REAL (Rural Entrepreneurship through Action Learning) of Des Moines, IA.
Completed a ten-day Management and Training Seminar offered to senior management personnel of Rent & Sell Furniture, Storm Lake, IA.

EXPERIENCE   **BUSINESS & MARKETING TEACHER.** Perry County High School, Des Moines, IA (1994-present). Develop and implement lesson plans, maintaining classroom discipline and insuring the intellectual growth of the students.
  * Introduce business concepts such as Entrepreneurship, Marketing Management, Financial Management, and Principles of Business to high school students.
  * Motivate students to compete in Marketing Research events on the state and national levels, and to pursue District and State officer positions in vocational organizations.
  * Was one of the teachers selected for the Economics At Work pilot program.
  * Business problems that I wrote were published through the Regional Education Board, promoting integration of business and math.
  * Selected as Perry County Teacher of the Month.

BUSINESS OWNER. Your Own Property, Des Moines, IA (1990-present). Own a number of rental properties and handle all aspects of owning a small business to include arranging financing, maintaining tax records, accounts receivable, accounts payable, advertising, coordinating repairs, and maintenance of rental properties.

BUSINESS INSTRUCTOR. University of Iowa, Des Moines, IA (1990-present). On a part-time basis in the weekend college, teach a variety of business-related subjects.
  * Motivate students by encouraging them to express their thoughts and opinions through participation in classroom discussions.

MANAGER. Rent & Sell Furniture (the largest furniture rental company in the United States), Des Moines, IA (1981-1994). Supervised six office and warehouse personnel.
  * Motivated employees to insure that everyone contributed to the success and profitability of the organization.
  * Carried out safety checks to assure a safe work environment.
  * Conducted sales meetings to increase revenues and insure growth.

AFFILIATIONS   Member, Iowa Marketing Education Association.

PERSONAL   Excellent personal and professional references are available upon request.

High School Teacher

Exact Name of Person
Title or Position
Name of Company
Address (no., street)
Address (city, state, zip)

High School Teacher

Dear Exact Name of Person: (or Dear Sir or Madam if answering a blind ad.)

This enthusiastic teacher begins her cover letter with a question. Would any principal want to refuse such an intriguing and vivacious individual?

Can you use a dynamic, hard-working teacher who offers a well-organized and highly creative style that stimulates learning through a "hands-on" approach which involves students in exciting applications and unusual activities?

Since graduating from the University of Montana in Missoula with a B.A. in English, I have excelled as a Secondary English teacher responsible for teaching 11th grade American literature, 10th grade world literature (honors and regular), and 9th grade literature. I am proud that I have helped literature "jump off the page" for students through guiding them in activities such as making movies, orally interpreting poetry, writing raps, and even participating in "human frog-jumping contests."

While earning a reputation as a popular and caring classroom teacher, I have also demonstrated my generosity in helping students outside the classroom. I have served as Varsity Cheerleading coach, sponsor/organizer for the Junior/Senior Prom, Journalism advisor, as well as chaperone on the Senior class trip and other activities.

I can provide outstanding personal and professional references at your request, and I feel certain when you meet me in person that you will conclude that I could make a valuable addition to your school.

I hope you will call or write me to suggest a time when we might meet to discuss your needs and goals and how I might serve them. Thank you in advance for your time.

Sincerely yours,

Theresa D. Gonzales

THERESA D. GONZALES

1110½ Hay Street, Fayetteville, NC 28305 • preppub@aol.com • (910) 483-6611

OBJECTIVE To contribute to an organization that can use a resourceful teacher who offers a command of the English language, a creative approach to helping students grasp concepts and appreciate ideas, as well as an enthusiastic, hard-working style of shouldering responsibility.

EDUCATION **Bachelor of Arts (B.A.)** degree, English education, University of Montana, Missoula, MT, 1993.

TRAINING Completed professional training related to teaching Advanced Placement English, conducting drug prevention workshops, improving the writing of secondary students, and applying Integrade grading procedures.

EXPERIENCE **SECONDARY ENGLISH TEACHER**. Leason County Schools, Missoula, MT (1995-present). Teach 11th grade American literature, 10th grade world literature (honors and regular levels), and 9th grade literature while serving as Varsity Cheerleading coach, as a sponsor and organizer for the Junior/Senior Prom, and as the spokesperson for the English Department at events such as a technology workshop.
- Led my 11th grade American literature class in the highly creative activity of writing soap operas!
- On my own initiative, spearheaded a behind-the-scenes effort with the Booster Club that resulted in the cheerleaders getting new uniforms.
- Became aware of how important peer involvement is to student success.
- Became Journalism advisor in 1995 and, in so doing, essentially took on a "third job" (in addition to teacher and cheerleading coach); learned to cheerfully handle situations when deadlines and ballgames fell on the same day.
- Coached a cheerleading squad that became known as "the best ever seen" at the school while also directing the yearbook staff in producing an outstanding yearbook which exemplified professionalism in every respect.
- Have acted as a chaperone on the Senior class trip and to a Shakespeare Festival.
- Have become well respected by veteran teachers for my ability to stimulate learning and motivate students through a creative yet highly organized teaching method.

SECONDARY ENGLISH TEACHER. Leason County Schools, Missoula, MT (1993-95). Taught llth grade American literature, 10th grade world literature (honors level), and 9th grade literature.
- Was in charge of the flag team during marching season (football).
- Served as the Scholastic Aptitude Test (SAT) preparation coordinator.
- On my own initiative, organized a new pep club for the basketball season.
- Directed my 11th grade classes in making a video production of short stories.
- Prepared/tutored my 10th grade honors students for the national ECOT in writing, and led two students to earn two of the highest scores countywide.

PERSONAL STRENGTHS Believe these strengths would make me a valuable part of any educational institution:
Versatility and capacity for hard work: Have cheerfully accepted simultaneous assignments which included teaching several subjects with different preparations while acting as a sponsor, coach, advisor, and project manager.
Creativity: Can truly make literature "come alive" to students through helping them in creative activities like movie making, orally interpreting poetry, writing raps, dramatically interpreting ideas, and even participating in human frog-jumping contests.
Communication and motivational skills: Can establish positive working relationships with students, other educators, parents, and outside organizations.

High School and Middle School Teacher

High School and Middle School Teacher

Date

Exact Name of Person
Title or Position
Name of Company
Address (no., street)
Address (city, state, zip)

Again we see a professional who omits the dates in which she earned her degrees. She is trying to downplay her age.

Dear Exact Name of Person: (or Dear Sir or Madam if answering a blind ad.)

I would appreciate an opportunity to talk with you soon about how I could contribute to your organization through my experience and education as well as through my dedication to improving the quality of education in our public schools.

As you will see from my resume, I am an educator with a great deal of experience in curriculum development, program coordination, and administration. With a B.A. in English and History, I earned my master's degree in Educational Administration. Having spent approximately 20 years as an educator, I am known as a persuasive and informative speaker who offers outstanding leadership and motivational skills.

By always taking part in professional development opportunities that come my way, I am continuing to grow as a professional educator. As the School Advisory Council Chairman for two years at Griffin American High School (Germany), I was a respected moderator of numerous debates and I earned respect for my ability to focus and manage group activities.

Because my experience has covered elementary and secondary schools, while my students have ranged from the learning disabled to the talented and gifted, I am capable of success at the elementary or secondary school level.

I can bring creativity, maturity, talent, and experience which will enrich your school and help make it one where children grow, learn, and prosper. Through the years, I have taken particular pride in my ability to mentor junior teaching professionals, and I am known for my ability to develop warm and effective working relationships.

I hope you will welcome my call soon to arrange a brief meeting at your convenience to discuss your current and future needs and how I might serve them. Thank you in advance for your time.

Sincerely yours,

Melissa P. Debose

MELISSA P. DEBOSE

1110½ Hay Street, Fayetteville, NC 28305 • preppub@aol.com • (910) 483-6611

OBJECTIVE To offer my background of dedication to excellence and progress in education to a school system that can use a creative and flexible administrator known for outstanding communication, motivational, and leadership abilities.

EDUCATION **M.Ed., Educational Administration,** Emory University, Atlanta, GA.
B.A., English and History, Emory University, Atlanta, GA.

CERTIFICATIONS Hold certifications from the states of GA, AL, and FL in the following areas: Administration, junior college, academically gifted, reading, world history, social studies, language arts, and English.

EXPERIENCE **CLASSROOM INSTRUCTOR.** Fuster Junior High School, Atlanta, GA (1994-present). Motivate and instruct Advanced Placement (AP) reading classes as well as teaching regular seventh grade reading and social studies classes.
- Contributed leadership to the Cultural Awareness and Young Authors committees.
- Was nominated for membership in Phi Delta Kappa professional education fraternity.
- Selected for my effective communication skills, delivered a presentation on Schools at the Fourth National Conference on Creating the Quality School.

HIGH SCHOOL TEACHER. Griffin American High School, Griffin Air Force Base, Germany (1989-1994) As a mentor for several student activities and special programs, provided advice and guidance as well as classroom instruction in subjects including Honors English, world history, contemporary issues, and general English.
- Elected for two terms as School Advisory Council Chairman, earned the principal's respect for keeping meetings productive and discussions to the point.
- Coordinated the Young Authors and Sketches literary magazine programs and acted as faculty advisor for the writing club.
- Was selected to participate in professional programs including three courses at the Culpepper Institute, a writing workshop sponsored by the University of Michigan, and staff development programs on teaching and expectations.

LANGUAGE ARTS TEACHER. Henry Leonard Middle School, Atlanta, GA (1985-88). Applied my knowledge while developing special projects for the enrichment of the curricula and as a seventh grade teacher for approximately 120 students each day.
- Revised the language arts curricula in order to address district objectives and standards.

DEPARTMENT CHAIRPERSON and **EDUCATOR.** John Hill School, Atlanta, GA (1981-85). Honored as the 1984-85 "Teacher of the Year," supervised and motivated members of the Social Studies and English departments while involved in planning and conducting seventh and eighth grade language arts and social studies classes.
- Designed and then conducted in-service writing instruction for the faculty at two area junior high schools.
- Analyzed curricula and created courses which updated faculty effectiveness.

Highlights of earlier experience: Refined my motivational, instructional, administrative, and leadership abilities in positions including Learning Disabilities Teacher, Educational Consultant, and Middle School Classroom Teacher.

PERSONAL Hold memberships in the Education Association. A creative and dependable professional, I thrive on motivating others to exceed their expectations. Am very flexible and perceptive.

High School Mathematics and Language Teacher

Date

Exact Name of Person
Exact Title
Exact Name of Company
Address
City, State, Zip

**High School Mathematics and
Language Teacher**

It's good to be versatile
in any field, and this high
school teacher offers the
ability to teach a foreign
language as well as
mathematics.

Dear Exact Name of Person (or Dear Sir or Madam if answering a blind ad):

I would like to take the opportunity to introduce you to a respected educator who combines communication and language skills with an education in math, school administration, and teacher education.

As you will see from the enclosed resume, I am a well-educated and self-motivated professional with a versatile background and certifications as a teacher of advanced mathematics as well as languages. A native of Korea, I am fluent in the English and Korean languages as well as offering solid knowledge of written Chinese.

With excellent time management, planning, and organizational skills, I have held often-simultaneous jobs as a language instructor for adults and children as well as for U.S. Army language programs at major military installations.

I have displayed my versatility and adaptability while providing effective instruction in settings which have included elite military language schools, a weekend college, and an Adult Continuing Education program. I have developed Programs of Instruction (POI) for a pioneer language program and gained experience in administrative support actions which include maintaining records of student progress and status.

If you can use an articulate and dedicated teacher with a solid background and education, I hope you will call me soon for a brief discussion of how I could contribute to your organization. I will provide excellent professional and personal references at the appropriate time.

Sincerely,

Nguyen X. Luong

NGUYEN X. LUONG

1110½ Hay Street, Fayetteville, NC 28305 • preppub@aol.com • (910) 483-6611

OBJECTIVE

To obtain a position as a Math or Korean Language Teacher in a secondary school in order to utilize communication and language skills obtained during numerous government and private-based jobs.

EDUCATION

Bachelor of Science degree in Math and Education, 1989, from Seoul University, Seoul, Korea; this is considered Korea's most prestigious university; certified by Ministry of Education to teach advanced mathematics.

Completed graduate courses in Alternative Teacher Education, concentration in psychology and reading, 1991, Bradley University, Peoria, IL; obtained a 3.5 GPA and certification to teach in Illinois.

Completed 12 hours in graduate course work in School Administration, 1989-90, University of Maryland, Yong San, Korea; obtained a 3.7 GPA.

LICENSES & CERTIFICATIONS

<u>Math Teaching License,</u> State of Illinois, 98 Provisional, July 1994.
<u>Math Teaching Certification,</u> State of Texas, Type C, December 1991.
<u>Math Teaching Certification,</u> Republic of Korea, Class 2, February 1989.

LANGUAGE ABILITIES

Native speaker in **Korean** language; Fluent in the English Language
Solid knowledge of the **Chinese** written word.

EXPERIENCE

KOREAN LANGUAGE INSTRUCTOR. St. Mary's College, San Antonio, TX (1995-present). For the Adult Continuing Education program, am responsible for teaching Korean.
- Instruct, evaluate, and supervise Department of Defense personnel with various backgrounds and ability levels in the only language preparation program for U.S. soldiers and their family members being assigned overseas.

PRINCIPAL/INSTRUCTOR. Hoey Oey Korean School, San Antonio, TX (1995-present). Supervise up to 14 instructors and assistants while also teaching Korean to adults and children with various linguistic and cultural backgrounds.
- Administer general affairs of this weekend college and obtained accreditation rights from the Consulate General of the Republic of Korea.

Prior experience:
KOREAN LANGUAGE INSTRUCTOR. Richard Nixon Special Warfare Training Center, San Antonio, TX (1994). Taught Korean language, culture, and communication skills to the Army's elite Green Berets; evaluated progress; maintained records of achievement.

ENGLISH AS A SECOND LANGUAGE INSTRUCTOR. Camp Michael, Korea (1992-93). Taught English as a Second Language (ESL) to Korean Augmentees to the U.S. Army (KATUSAs).
- Administered program instructing 100 Korean soldiers in the English language.
- Taught, evaluated, and maintained records and reports of the installation's program.

Additional non-language teaching experience:
Math Teacher. 32st High School, San Antonio, TX (1997).
Math Teacher. Graham Lock Junior High School, San Antonio, TX (1994-95).
Math/Science Teacher. Irvin High School, San Antonio, TX (1990-91).

PERSONAL

Can provide outstanding personal and professional references upon request.

High School Teacher and Varsity Coach

Date

Exact Name of Person
Exact Title
Exact Name of Company
Address
City, State, Zip

High School Teacher and Varsity Coach

This experienced young teacher can point to outstanding results both in the classroom and on the field.

Dear Exact Name of Person (or Dear Sir or Madam if answering a blind ad):

With the enclosed resume, I would like to introduce you to a high-energy, dedicated teacher and coach known for possessing a gift for motivating students to excel both in the classroom and on the sports field.

As you will see, I have established myself as a dynamic, dedicated, and enthusiastic coach and teacher who serves as a role model and example for my students. I am respected for my motivational skills, both in the classroom and on the field. I truly enjoy helping each student develop to his or her full potential. As a high school teacher, I provide instruction in math, physical education, and other topics for students in the ninth through 12th grades, and I also coach both boys and girls varsity soccer as well as junior varsity basketball teams.

I am very proud of my effectiveness as a coach for athletic teams which have all improved their results under my leadership. And as a teacher, I have earned a reputation for my ability to always be well organized and well prepared in providing instruction while maintaining discipline.

Prior to my current teaching assignment, I completed a practicum with a fifth grade classroom for which I prepared and presented health and physical education lessons. In a variety of teaching activities as a student teacher, I was given the opportunity to work with every age level from kindergarten through high school.

If you can use an articulate, energetic, and enthusiastic young coach and teacher, I hope you will call me soon for a brief discussion of how I could contribute to your institution. I will provide excellent professional and personal references at the appropriate time.

Sincerely,

John E. Marlborough

JOHN E. MALBOROUGH

1110½ Hay Street, Fayetteville, NC 28305 • preppub@aol.com • (910) 483-6611

OBJECTIVE

I want to contribute to a school system that can use a high-energy, action-oriented teacher and coach with outstanding written and oral communication skills along with a gift for motivating students to excel both in the classroom and on the sports field.

EDUCATION

Bachelor of Science degree in Physical Education with emphasis in Sports Management, Hiram College, December, 1992.
- Member, Kappa Delta Psi National Fraternity and was Intramural Chairman.
- Played intramural sports and in summer softball and golf leagues.
- Played varsity soccer; was 1st team All Star as well as varsity basketball; was 1st team All Star on a team that finished 16th in the state my senior year; ran track and qualified for districts.

CERTIFICATION

Certified to teach K-12 in NY and OH.

EXPERIENCE

Have established myself as a dedicated and hard-working teacher as well as a dynamic and enthusiastic coach who is known for my style of setting a strong personal example while helping each player develop to his/her fullest potential:
TEACHER & VARSITY COACH. Heaton County School District, Jarrett, OH (1996-present). Teach special topics, math, and physical education to students in grades 9-12; act as Varsity Soccer Coach for the boys and girls' teams and Junior Varsity boy's Basketball Coach.
- Improved results of all teams I have coached; for example, the varsity soccer team improved from the previous year and made it to the second round in fall 1997.
- As a teacher, have earned a reputation as a well organized and well prepared instructor; strongly believe that well developed lesson plans are a key to quality classrooms.

STUDENT TEACHER. Jensen School District, Lesser, NY (Sept-Dec 1995). Was involved in a variety of teaching activities as a student teacher.
- **Kindergarten:** Designed health lessons and activities to encourage individual, group, and whole class instruction.
- **Kindergarten, First Grade, and Second Grade:** Designed and presented Physical Education lesson directed toward developmentally appropriate practices.
- **Seventh Grade and Eighth Grade**: Designed health lessons and activities to encourage hands-on learning; designed and presented basketball unit which incorporated psychomotor, cognitive, and affective domains.
- **Ninth and Tenth Grades:** Designed and presented flag football unit.
- **Eleventh Grade:** Designed and presented a unit on nutrition.

FIFTH-GRADE TEACHER (PRACTICUM): James Elementary School, Lesser, NY (1995). Taught 73 fifth grade students; prepared and presented physical education lessons.

Other experience (1992-95):
YMCA Instructor/Facility Supervisor (Intern): Instructed and refereed for YMCA youth soccer, basketball, and swim programs; taught preschool physical education, swim, and recreation classes; supervised evening youth dance events; selected and trained volunteer coaches; supervised an arts and crafts youth program.
Junior High Basketball Coach. Coached 40 junior high school boys in 1995-96 seasons in Brighton, NY (Brighton School District).

High School Teacher and Coach

Date

High School Teacher and Varsity Coach

Sometimes talented people need to move on to the next challenge in their career. That is true of this fine coach and teacher. He is seeking to take his motivational skills and teaching credentials into a college setting. Although he lacks the Ph.D. at this time, he could make progress toward the terminal degree if he were in an academic environment.

Dear

With the enclosed resume, I would like to make you aware of my strong desire to become a college coach at your institution. I offer 14 years of experience in coaching, teaching, and directing athletic programs which I could put to work for your program. I am held in the highest regard by my current employer, and I can provide outstanding references at the appropriate time.

Coaching success

Since 1989, I have excelled as a Head Football Coach. I have led many schools to the state playoffs. My peers have voted me **Coach of the Year** during the past two seasons. I have experience in all areas of football, including offensive and defensive coordination.

Teaching experience and educational credentials

In addition to being a winning coach, I am also an excellent Physical Education teacher, administrator, and communicator. I hold a Tennessee Teaching Certificate G-20 as well as my M.A.Ed degree and B.S. degree. I am proud of the fact that I have earned a reputation as a powerful communicator and motivator in the classroom as well as on the ball field.

I believe the next step in my career is to apply my outstanding motivational, leadership, and administrative skills in a college program such as yours. I hope you will call or write me soon to suggest a time convenient for us to meet and discuss your current and future needs and how I might serve them. Thank you in advance for your time.

Sincerely yours,

Craven McAlister

CRAVEN McALISTER

1110½ Hay Street, Fayetteville, NC 28305   •   preppub@aol.com   •   (910) 483-6611

OBJECTIVE   To offer my positive, results-oriented leadership style, along with my experience in building and coaching winning teams, to an ambitious high school or college that can use an enthusiastic, intelligent professional with a reputation for the highest work and personal ethics.

EXPERIENCE   *Offer a track record of more than 100 wins as a football head coach and assistant coach in a 14-year career as an athletic director and coach; have guided teams to the state playoffs for nine years:*

HEAD FOOTBALL COACH and **INSTRUCTOR.** Bristol High School, Bristol, TN (1996-present). Have successfully rebuilt a football program and transformed a group of average players into champions with strong competitive spirits and the will to win in the tough 4A conference; teach physical conditioning and other P.E. classes.

- Doubled the level of participation by both parents and players in four years.
- In 1999 and 2000, coached back-to-back playoff teams—the first time in 30 years this has happened at this school; coached three winning seasons in a row for the first time in 20 years at Bristol High School: 6-5 in 1998; 7-5 in 1999; and 9-3 in 2000 (the best since 1983).
- Was voted **"Coach of the Year, 2000 and 1999"** by my peers; led Bristol High to its first state playoff win since 1991.
- Increased football gate receipts from $18,000 in 1995 to $60,000 in 2000.

OFFENSIVE COORDINATOR and **PHYSICAL EDUCATION TEACHER.** Mayfield Senior High School, Mayfield, TN (1994-96). Was hired as offensive coordinator for a football team which built an impressive record of wins in a conference recognized as the toughest and most competitive in the state.

- Averaged 10 wins a year over two seasons while building teams that worked together under pressure.
- Contributed intelligence, leadership, and knowledge of the game of football as a member of a coaching staff which was effective in winning "the big games."
- In two years, guided the team to an impressive streak of scoring.

HEAD FOOTBALL COACH and **ATHLETIC DIRECTOR.** Valley Senior High School, Tidewater, TN (1991-93). Provided the management and guidance for a project in which three high schools were combined and then coached the football program and directed all other sports for the consolidated school.

HEAD FOOTBALL COACH and **INSTRUCTOR.** Smithfield High School, Smithfield, TN (1989-91). Joined this organization as the youngest 4A high school head coach in the state; led the team to break several school records; supervised and trained an eight-person staff.

EDUCATION   M.A.Ed. degree, East Tennessee University, Grayson, TN, 1991.
B.S., Physical Education, University of Tennessee, Chattanooga, TN, 1989.
Hold Tennessee Teaching Certificate G-20.

**FOOTBALL
COACHING
EXPERTISE**

In my coaching career, have gained experience in these areas:

offensive and defensive coordination	formulation of game plans
special team coordination	fundamentals in all positions

PERSONAL   Was "MVP" of my high school football team and won a Merit Scholarship to UT.

Middle School Communications Skills Teacher

Date

**Middle School
Communications Teacher**

This young person
made a lateral
transfer into teaching
after earning her
degree and working
briefly in journalism.
Now, after some
teaching experience,
she is intrigued by a
position she recently
saw advertised in the
newspaper which
involves coordinating
educational activities.

Dear:

I am writing to express my strong interest in the position of Education Coordinator, which was recently advertised in the newspaper. With the enclosed resume, I would like to make you aware of my background as an articulate young professional with exceptional communication and organizational skills who offers a track record of accomplishment in education.

In my present position, I teach seventh grade Language Arts and Special Education students in the Francisco County School system, where I have become known for my ability to motivate and guide young people through my positive attitude and enthusiasm. I have previously worked at *The San Francisco Times* as a Newsroom Associate Editor, where I learned the "nuts and bolts" of the newspaper publication process.

As you will see from my enclosed resume, I earned a Bachelor of Arts in English and Media Journalism from the University of San Francisco. I have a strong history of success in leadership roles and in environments where I have excelled in selling my ideas and concepts to others. Beginning with my days as student body president of my high school, on through college volunteer activities requiring negotiating and communication skills, I have always been highly effective in getting my views across to others in a persuasive and effective manner while still displaying tact and an understanding of their views.

If you can use a highly motivated young professional who can combines excellent teaching skills with a background in journalism, I hope you will contact me to suggest a time when we could discuss your needs in person. I can assure you in advance that I have an excellent reputation and could quickly become an asset in the position you advertised.

Sincerely yours,

Theresa Perrone

THERESA PERRONE

1110½ Hay Street, Fayetteville, NC 28305 • preppub@aol.com • (910) 483-6611

OBJECTIVE	To contribute to a school system through my creativity and intelligence as well as my strong communication and interpersonal relations skills.
EDUCATION	Earned a **Bachelor of Arts (B.A.) degree in English and Media Journalism,** University of San Francisco, 1995. • Excelled in specialized course work related to desktop publishing including PageMaker. • *Publications*: worked on a team which designed pamphlets and written materials used to attract quality faculty; created an exciting new "welcome packet" that "sold" San Francisco and the college itself (1995). • Was named to the Dean's List for my academic achievements.
EXPERIENCE	**COMMUNICATIONS SKILLS TEACHER.** Francisco County School System, San Francisco, CA (1996-present). Have become known for my ability to motivate and guide young people while teaching seventh grade language arts, reading, and social studies. • Encouraged students to understand the importance of improving their verbal and written communication skills and to apply them in group discussions on current events. • Contributed to the safety and beautification of the campus by serving on a committee with the goal of improving and enhancing the facility and grounds. **NEWSROOM ASSOCIATE EDITOR**. <u>San Francisco Times</u>, San Francisco, CA (1996). Learned the "nuts and bolts" of how information gets disseminated to the public while working for the newspaper with the second largest circulation in California. • Was often complimented for my excellent writing and editing skills as well as my ability to determine the most appealing visual display. • Consistently met strict deadlines while editing and proofing for various departments. *Refined my time management skills attending college full time while participating in numerous community service and volunteer activities:* **COMMITTEE MEMBER.** Delta Theta Sorority, Inc., San Francisco, CA (1995-present). Participate in activities designed to promote economic, educational, and political growth as well as international awareness and physical/mental health among community members. **"BIG SISTER" PROGRAM VOLUNTEER.** Project LIFE, E.K. Salmen Elementary School, San Francisco, CA (1994-95). Provided an 11-year-old girl with one-on-one attention and a positive role model by spending time with her, helping her learn better study habits and ways to build confidence, and impress on her the value of getting an education. **STUDENT GOVERNMENT MEMBER.** Student Government Association, California Central University, San Francisco, CA (1991-92). Represented the freshman class during activities including organizing fund raising events, social events, and class trips. **TEEN BOARD REPRESENTATIVE.** Lazarus, San Francisco, CA (1990-91). Demonstrated outstanding communication and planning abilities as a member of the store's first teen board; learned marketing techniques and how to target advertising to the teen consumer. • Assisted with promotions for merchandise including L.A. Gear footwear, Lee jeans, and Claire Burke perfume; modeled and served as master of ceremonies for fashion shows.
PERSONAL	Am a creative individual with a positive attitude. Offer a high level of energy.

Middle School/Junior High Physical Education Teacher

Middle School/Junior High Physical Education Teacher

This effective young teacher communicates that he wishes to relocate back to his home turf.

Dear Sir or Madam:

With the enclosed resume, I would like to initiate the process of being considered for employment as a teacher and coach.

Prior to attending college, I graduated from Break Neck High School, where I was a star athlete and student leader. From Georgia Southern University, I earned my B.S. degree magna cum laude in Physical Education with an emphasis in Sports Management.

Since 1996 I have excelled as a teacher and coach with the Norcross County School System in Atlanta, GA. While teaching students in grades 7-12, I have earned a reputation as a well organized teacher while also becoming known as a coach who is successful in developing teams known for their motivation and discipline. Although I am highly regarded in my current position, I have decided that I wish to return to my "home turf" of New York. I am single, have been certified to teach K-12, and can provide excellent personal and professional references.

You will notice that I served my country in the U.S. Air Force after graduating from high school. I believe this military experience would help me communicate effectively with young people considering military service or other types of employment after high school.

You would find me in person to be a congenial individual who prides myself on my high personal and professional standards. If you can make use of my strong teaching and coaching skills, please contact me to suggest a time when we might talk in person or by phone about your needs. Thank you in advance for your consideration.

Sincerely,

Kenward Elmslie

KENWARD ELMSLIE

1110½ Hay Street, Fayetteville, NC 28305   •   preppub@aol.com   •   (910) 483-6611

OBJECTIVE   Challenging position teaching Physical Education (K-12).

SUMMARY OF QUALIFICATIONS
- Ability to prepare and implement daily, weekly, unit, and yearly plans for physical education activities. Ensure that these activities promote physical, social, and emotional development within each of the student's lives.
- Ability to maintain a classroom environment in an orderly and disciplined manner.

EDUCATION   **B.S., Physical Education with emphasis in Sports Management**, Georgia Southern University, Atlanta, GA, 1996.
(Magna Cum Laude)
Class "A" Teaching Certification in Physical Education
Honors:
- NCPEHA (National Collegiate Physical Education & Health Award), 1995.
- USAA (All-American Scholar Collegiate Award), 1995.
- National Dean's List, 1995.
- Who's Who/American Colleges and Universities, 1993-94.
- Georgia Southern University Dean's List: 1992-93, 1995.

EXPERIENCE   **HEALTH/PHYSICAL EDUCATION TEACHER.** Schloss Senior High School, Atlanta, GA (1996-present). Prepare weekly lesson plans and developed daily physical education activities while teaching middle and high school students.
- Provide individualized instruction to students; maintained classroom order in accordance with school's policies and procedures.
- Ensure all required equipment was available, in place for class activities and that it was in a serviceable and safe condition.
- Serve as Assistant Coach on both the **Varsity Wrestling** and **Varsity Fast-Pitch Softball** Teams; served as Acting Head Coach when the wrestling coach was out due to surgery.

COLLEGE STUDENT. Georgia Southern University, Atlanta, GA (1992-96). After serving my country in the U.S. Army, went to college full-time on the GI Bill and earned my degree.

ICBM & GLCM MAINTENANCE MANAGER AND SUPERVISOR. United States Air Force, locations worldwide (1989-92).
- Supervised, trained, disciplined, and counseled team members.
- Developed and implemented work, training, and leave schedules.
- Supervised maintenance operations to ensure that the mission was accomplished in a timely and professional manner.
- Briefed maintenance personnel, supervision personnel, and staff members on the status of all maintenance activities and mission accomplishments.
- Refined hands-on technical skills while serving as a **Technician**.

ACTIVITIES
- Club Member (Physical Education Majors' Club, Georgia Southern University).
- Student Member/NCAE-NEA (Georgia Association of Educators-National Education Association).
- Student Alliance for Health, Physical Education, Recreation and Dance.
- Member of KAPPA DELTA PI (International Honor Society in Education).
- Member of NFHS (National Federation of State High School Associations).
- Member of NFICA (National Federation of Interscholastic Coaches Association).

Middle School Science and Math Teacher

Date

Exact Name of Person
Exact Title
Exact Name of Company
Address
City, State, Zip

Middle School Science and Math Teacher

Beginning your cover letter with a question can get your reader on your "wave length" quickly. What principal wouldn't want such an individual on his or her teaching faculty?

Dear Exact Name of Person (or Dear Sir or Madam if answering a blind ad):

Can you use an articulate, enthusiastic, and self-motivated young professional with strong teaching skills who possesses a naturally outgoing personality as well as a proven ability to inspire and motivate others?

As you will see from my enclosed resume, I earned my B.S. in Biology from Centre College (Danville, KY) and maintained a 3.5 GPA. During my senior year I worked as many as 50 hours a week as a Research Assistant in the college's chemistry lab. I conducted research which resulted in a manual that was distributed at a national conference.

In my most recent job as a middle school science and math teacher, I refined communication, organizational, and time management skills while involved in numerous projects. I planned the school's first science fair as well as a Christmas play and a musical. My greatest accomplishment during this period was in taking a student who was working two grade levels below his classmates and developing an individualized plan to use while tutoring him. I spent four months working closely with him and brought him up to his proper grade level.

I want you to know that I more or less discovered teaching "by accident" and now feel that it is my life's work. I obtained a teaching position in the Republic of China when my husband was assigned there as part of the diplomatic corps, and I discovered that I wish to make teaching my career. Earlier while serving for four years in the U.S. Army, I earned both an Army Commendation Medal and an Achievement Medal for my performance as a supervisor, dental office administrator, and assistant during dental surgery procedures.

I am confident that I could become a valuable member of your teaching staff, and I hope you will contact me to suggest a time when we might meet to discuss your needs.

Sincerely,

Ruth M. Howland

RUTH M. HOWLAND

1110½ Hay Street, Fayetteville, NC 28305   •   preppub@aol.com   •   (910) 483-6611

OBJECTIVE
To offer excellent communication and teaching skills to a school system that can benefit from my enthusiasm, self-motivation, and initiative as well as from my strong desire to assist young people in gaining the skills needed for future careers related to math and science.

EDUCATION
Earned a **B.S. in Biology,** Centre College, Danville, KY, 1999.

SPECIAL SKILLS
Offer specialized knowledge and experience in areas which include:
computers/typing: type 45 wpm; basic computer skills include knowledge of MS Word
languages: speak, read, and write Spanish
medical office equipment: operate dental X-ray and instrument sterilization equipment

EXPERIENCE
SCIENCE AND MATH TEACHER. The People's Academy, The Republic of China (1999-2001). Refined communication, organizational, and time management skills as a classroom teacher for seventh grade natural science and eight grade algebra classes.
- Assessed the status and needs of one student who was two years below his proper grade level: in only four months of tutoring, gave him the guidance and personal attention which allowed him to catch up with his peers and perform at the proper level.
- Applied my creativity to plan and organize the school's first annual science fair – overcame a lack of adequate funding and produced a successful event.
- Participated in weekly faculty sessions where everyone would work together to find solutions for students' problems.
- Administered tests and prepared quarterly evaluations of each student.
- Organized the school's Christmas play and a musical.

Refined organizational and time management skills while attending college full time and gaining practical experience in the following jobs, Danville, KY:
RESEARCH ASSISTANT. Centre College, Danville, KY (1996-99). Conducted library research and chemical laboratory experiments which were used to prepare written reports; prepared the purchase orders for lab and office supplies.
- Produced a manual which was distributed at a national conference during the week before final exams my senior year – worked up to 50 hours a week on my research project my entire senior year and maintained a 3.5 GPA.
- Learned the importance of patience and team work while working closely with some difficult co-workers in a stressful environment.

NURSE'S ASSISTANT and **OFFICE ASSISTANT.** Veteran's Administration Hospital (1995-96). Handled a variety of patient care, inventory control, and clerical responsibilities.

ASSISTANT SUPERVISOR/DENTAL ASSISTANT. U.S. Army, Ft. Bragg, NC (1990-95). Became the youngest supervisor in the dental services organization and learned to work in close cooperation with people from varying backgrounds and skill levels while supervising nine people, assisting an oral surgeon in the operating room one day each week, and overseeing the logistics division of the hospital oral surgery office.
- Earned an Army Commendation Medal for my performance in a managerial and supervisory role and especially for my accomplishments in producing well-trained specialists in oral surgery assistance, X-ray, and clerical duties.

PERSONAL
Am an adaptable quick learner. Have an aptitude for developing mutual respect with co-workers and peers and for being able to deal with difficult people professionally.

Military Science Instructor

Date

Exact Name of Person
Exact Title
Exact Name of Company
Address
City, State, Zip

Military Science Instructor

This individual is seeking another position teaching in a military sciences department.

Dear Exact Name of Person (or Dear Sir or Madam if answering a blind ad):

With this letter and enclosed resume, I would like to express my interest in offering exceptional communication and leadership abilities to an institution in need of an experienced instructor who offers a background of accomplishments as a military officer.

As you will see from the enclosed resume, I am a well-organized and detail-oriented management professional who is completing a Master of Science degree in Management while also excelling as an Assistant Professor of Military Science at the university level. I earned a B.S. in Aviation Management and completed advanced training for military officers in the maintenance and logistics management fields as well as courses for aviators.

Handpicked for a prestigious teaching position in the Military Science department of Lock Haven University in Pennsylvania, I provide instruction for Army ROTC cadets. Subjects I instruct include leadership and tactics as well as physical training. My ability to communicate with others effectively extends beyond the classroom and training site as I oversee the screening and recruiting process for four schools in order to locate and enroll the best qualified young adults who will be groomed as the military's future leaders.

My prior military assignments were mainly in the operations, logistics, and aviation fields and called for strong abilities in managing human, material, and fiscal resources. I have consistently been evaluated as a gifted writer, briefer, and speaker with a strong ability to develop and present well-thought-out, persuasive, and informative written and oral materials.

If you can use an articulate and accomplished young professional who enjoys the challenge of passing knowledge on to others and seeing them learn and grow, I hope you will call me soon for a brief discussion of how I could contribute to your organization. I will provide excellent professional and personal references at the appropriate time.

Sincerely,

Kathy Sullivan

KATHY SULLIVAN

1110½ Hay Street, Fayetteville, NC 28305 • preppub@aol.com • (910) 483-6611

OBJECTIVE	To benefit an organization that can use an articulate, accomplished young professional with exceptional leadership, communication, and organizational skills who offers experience in managing human, fiscal, and material resources in aviation and logistics environments.
EDUCATION	Completing **M.S. in Management**, Lock Haven University of Pennsylvania, Lock Haven, PA; will graduate in August, 2001. **B.S. in Aviation Management,** Pennsylvania Institute of Technology, 1990.
COMPUTERS	Proficient in the operation of many popular computer operating systems and software applications, including Windows, Microsoft Word, Excel, and PowerPoint.
EXPERIENCE	*Rated in top 10% of officers and selected for leadership roles, U.S. Army, 1991-present:* *1999-present:* **ASSISTANT PROFESSOR.** Lock Haven University, Lock Haven, PA. Hand-picked for this prestigious position in the Military Science department, instruct Army Cadets in leadership and tactics, as well as overseeing their physical training.

- As Recruiting Operations Officer for four schools and more than 125 cadets, manage screening and selection of future Army leaders; oversee certification and contracting of new recruits.
- Manage all recruiting and cadet retention efforts for the Military Science program, to include developing marketing programs.

1998-99: **ASSISTANT OPERATIONS MANAGER.** Wills AFB, CA. Oversaw budget development, human resources management, purchasing and installation of equipment, and contracting issues related to civilian employees while assisting the Director of a Secretary of Defense-sponsored Joint Combat Search and Rescue Test and Evaluation program.

- Reviewed, negotiated, tracked, coordinated, and budgeted the civilian employee contract for this project; managed over $1.5 million in contract issues over a nine-month period.
- Managed personnel administration activities, from preparation of performance appraisals and awards, to overseeing matters related to security clearances and visit requests.
- Described as "an exceptionally gifted officer" and "articulate writer and orator," was credited with laying the groundwork for future multi-service integration efforts.

1996-98: **LOGISTICS PROGRAM MANAGER.** Willis AFB, CA. Directed logistics operations for a major test and evaluation program involving 36 aircraft from 12 aviation units and more than 800 personnel from all branches of military service; managed an operational budget in excess of $2 million while planning, coordinating, and executing logistical support for the project.

- Personally oversaw coordination of local construction, aircraft maintenance support, housing and dining facilities, environmental concerns, and transportation for the project.

1994-96: **OPERATIONS MANAGER** and **PRODUCTION SUPERVISOR.** Ft. Bragg, NC and England. Managed operations in the absence of the General Manager; supervised and trained up to 309 personnel, coordinating Aviation Intermediate Maintenance (AVIM) for 128 rotary-wing aircraft; supervised maintenance of 143 vehicles and support equipment valued at more than $15 million.

PERSONAL	Honored with many prestigious awards, including a Joint Service and two Army Commendation Medals as well as a Joint Service and an Army Achievement Medal. Excellent references.

Military Science Instructor

Date

Exact Name of Person
Exact Title
Exact Name of Company
Address
City, State, Zip

Military Science Instructor

Do you put Education
or Experience first on
your resume? It's a
judgement call, and
sometimes doing it one
way is as good as doing
it another way.
Generally you put first
the one which you feel
is your stronger suit.

Dear Exact Name of Person (or Dear Sir or Madam if answering a blind ad):

I would like to take the opportunity to introduce you to an adaptable and innovative individual who offers a reputation as a highly effective instructor who excels in motivating, managing, and setting an example of professionalism for others to follow.

Presently a Professor of Military Science at Indiana University in Bloomington, I supervise a staff of six military executive and junior manager while managing a 60-student ROTC (Reserve Officer Training Corps) program. Handpicked for this prestigious teaching and management position, I have been credited with developing an aggressive marketing plan which resulted in a six-fold increase in the number of students receiving scholarships.

In an earlier teaching assignment, I received the "Excellence in Teaching Award" for 1997 from the Department History at The United States Military Academy at West Point in recognition of my effectiveness as a classroom teacher and mentor. I was handpicked from a pool of 200 highly qualified executive for one of only 20 instructor positions and went on to build a reputation as one of the best and most effective of the academy's team of instructors.

Additional military assignments were mainly in the operations and logistics fields and called for strong abilities in managing human, material, and fiscal resources. I have been evaluated as a gifted writer, briefer, and speaker with a strong ability to develop and present well thought out, persuasive, and informative written and oral materials.

If you can use my experience and background, I hope you will call me soon for a brief discussion of how I could contribute to your organization. I will provide excellent professional and personal references at the appropriate time.

Sincerely,

Bernard T. Brennan

BERNARD THOMAS BRENNAN

1110½ Hay Street, Fayetteville, NC 28305   •   preppub@aol.com   •   (910) 483-6611

OBJECTIVE

To benefit an organization that can use an adaptable, articulate, and innovative individual who has consistently excelled through superior planning, communication, and leadership abilities.

EXPERIENCE

COLLEGE INSTRUCTOR. Indiana University, Bloomington, IN (1997-present). As a Professor of Military Science, supervise six military executives and junior managers while commanding an Army Reserve Officer Training Corps (ROTC) organization consisting of 60 students.

- Oversee planning and implementation of recruitment, training, administrative, and supply activities as well as controlling the fiscal, human, and material resources.
- Evaluated the university's ROTC program and developed an aggressive marketing plan that resulted in a six-fold increase in the number of ROTC cadets receiving scholarships.
- Established "from scratch" the ROTC alumni association, initiating the creation of newsletters and marketing tools to increase public awareness.

ASSISTANT PROFESSOR. U.S. Army, The United States Military Academy at West Point, West Point, NY (1990-97). Handpicked from a pool of 200 highly qualified executives for one of only 20 instructor positions, was recognized with the Department of History's 1997 "Excellence in Teaching Award" for my effectiveness as a classroom instructor and mentor.

- Singled out as a course director, directed 19 instructors teaching 935 cadets.

GRADUATE STUDENT. Indiana University, Bloomington, IN (1988-90). Refined in-depth research and investigative skills as an advisor for students in the university's ROTC program; earned a master's degree and developed a thesis praised in scholarly history circles.

Highlights of earlier experience:
GENERAL MANAGER. (1987-88). Provided outstanding leadership and guidance for 155 personnel working in a highly stressful environment, which called for constant alertness.

- Applied my communication/diplomatic skills dealing regularly with French and British allies.
- Was singled out as the "General Douglas MacArthur Leadership Award" winner.
- In a previous job as an Operations Manager, was cited as the area's best resource manager for my effectiveness in controlling the organization's $2.5 million annual ammunition budget.

EDUCATION & TRAINING

M.A., History, Indiana University, Bloomington, IN, 1990.
B.S., Social Sciences, Indiana University, Bloomington, IN, 1985; maintained a 3.74 GPA. Completed in excess of 3,000 hours of advanced management and staff development programs as well as special course work in effective teaching and counseling techniques.

SPECIAL SKILLS

Computer literate; familiar with popular computer operating systems and software including Microsoft Word, WordPerfect, E-mail, and Internet.
Offer special knowledge of research libraries, archives, museums, and data collection facilities.

PERSONAL

Known for my loyalty and honesty, was entrusted with a Top Secret security clearance. Am very adaptable and able to handle stress and changing circumstances. Will relocate.

Military Science Instructor

Exact Name of Person
Exact Title
Exact Name of Company
Address
City, State, Zip

Military Science Instructor

This military science instructor is proud of the accomplishments he had while teaching ROTC.

Dear Exact Name of Person: (or Dear Sir or Madam if answering a blind ad):

With the enclosed resume, I would like to take the opportunity to introduce you to a dynamic teacher who has excelled in a distinguished career as a U.S. Marine Corps officer.

After retiring from the Marine Corps in 1996, I took on the challenge of building, from the ground up, a Junior ROTC program for the oldest high school in the state of Nebraska. In this capacity I was effective in recruiting, mentoring, instructing, and guiding young people who took great pride in their individual and group accomplishments. This program has already produced five young people who have earned full four-year ROTC scholarships.

Earlier in a dual role as administrator and senior instructor for a university ROTC program, I provided managerial oversight for a program which enjoyed a reduction in the drop-out rate to less than 10% from a previous 58%. Enrollment rates nearly doubled and the number of full scholarships available increased fourfold from six to 25 a year.

My versatility in maximizing often-scarce resources and producing results in any situation was demonstrated in prior line and staff positions which included developing policy and strategy at the national defense level, serving as the USMC liaison to the FAA, as a flight officer, and as a City Manager for a large military community in Korea. The recipient of numerous medals and awards, I have consistently been cited for my integrity and well-documented interest and involvement in the personal growth and development of my students and subordinates.

If you can use a mature, intelligent, and dedicated teacher with a history of producing results and exceeding standards, I hope you will welcome my call soon when I try to arrange a brief meeting to discuss your goals and how my background might serve your needs. I can provide outstanding references.

Sincerely,

Maurice Torrey

MAURICE TORREY

1110½ Hay Street, Fayetteville, NC 28305 · preppub@aol.com · (910) 483-6611

OBJECTIVE   To benefit an organization that can use a dynamic administrator and executive with a distinguished history of achieving exceptional results in developing and managing programs, instructing and communicating, and ensuring others are guided to expend their best efforts.

EDUCATION   **M.A.,** National Security and Public Policy, Naval War University, Salem, MA, 1991.
M.S., Management and Public Policy, Salem State College, Salem, MA, 1985.
B.A., Economics, University of Nebraska-Lincoln, 1976.
A.A., Electronics, University of Nebraska-Lincoln, 1966.

EXECUTIVE   Was selected to receive in excess of 3,765 hours of training which included the naval aviator
TRAINING   program as well as courses in managing aviation supply, logistics, and maintenance.

EXPERIENCE   **PROGRAM DIRECTOR** and **SENIOR INSTRUCTOR.** Marie High School, Lincoln, NE (1996-present). Built from the ground up and managed a unique Marine Corps Junior ROTC program for the state's oldest high school: this program quickly earned outstanding ratings in all aspects of its leadership and character-building programs.
- Directed all aspects of the program from fiscal and budget management, to logistics and supply, to forecasting future equipment and supply needs.
- Managed student development and academics as well as testing and grading; held regular conferences with the parents of each student.
- Excelled in recruiting well-qualified, talented young people into the program who were motivated to work together and take pride in personal and group accomplishments.
- Provided guidance for five students who went on to receive full four-year scholarships.
- Represented the military services to the community and built a strong base of parent and community support.
- Planned and conducted numerous orientation trips to area facilities which included a submarine base as well as training sites.
- Singled out for my excellence as an instructor and emphasis on providing outreach for minority students, was honored as **"Distinguished Minority Educator"** (1998-99).

Advanced to the rank of colonel in the U.S. Marine Corps while earning a reputation as a talented manager of large, complex, and multifunctional organizations:
ADMINISTRATOR and **MILITARY SCIENCE INSTRUCTOR.** University of Nebraska-Lincoln (1994-96). Handled dual roles of directing administrative, personnel, logistics, and financial support while serving as a Professor and the Chairman of the Department of Naval Science for this university as well as for nearby Nebraska State University and Lincoln Community College.
- Became highly experienced in motivating young adults and instilling discipline, pride, and esprit-de-corps; gained knowledge about how university-level systems work and what is needed to develop strong academic, physical training, and professional development programs.
- Was credited with providing leadership which resulted in reducing the drop-out rate to less than 10% from its previous high of 58% and for nearly doubling enrollment levels.
- Sold university officials on the success of the program and increased the number of full scholarships available from six to 25 a year.
- Worked closely with ROTC units from the other military services, booster organizations.

PERSONAL   Excellent references upon request.

Principal (Applicant)

Date

Principal

After "paying her dues" in various positions in education, this individual is ready to take over the leadership of a school as principal, and this cover letter and resume are designed to explore suitable opportunities.

Dear Dr.:

With the enclosed resume, I would like to make you aware of my extensive background as an experienced elementary school assistant principal and teacher whose highly developed supervisory, administrative, and organizational skills have been proven in a solid track record of twenty-seven years in education and instructional leadership.

As you will see from my resume, I have been in an instructional leadership position as an Assistant Principal, currently at Milligan Elementary and previously at Helen Elementary. At Milligan, I have worked very closely with the principal, overseeing the interviewing, hiring, observation, and coaching of the teaching staff, as well as organizing and coordinating special programs such as the HOPES grant to assist parents in working with children at home to improve learning skills, and the COMET remedial skills program to increase end-of-year test scores for grades 3-5. In both of these positions, I acted as textbook coordinator, and I have experience in curriculum development and evaluation.

In my prior position, I taught many different grades at the elementary level, so I am familiar with the needs and concerns not only of the elementary school faculty and staff, but also of their students and parents. My goals as a teacher and administrator have always been clearly defined: to provide a safe and orderly environment; a positive school climate with improved student achievement, increased expectations both of the staff and the students, and strong school-based management.

It is my mission to continue the process of school improvement where all have a voice and a responsibility to elevate our students so that they will be able to better compete in an increasingly global economy. I believe that when you expect success, you prepare for success. As educators, we must do whatever it takes to help *every* student succeed.

I assure you in advance that I have an excellent reputation as a hard-working and dedicated administrator, with a results-oriented approach to troubleshooting problems and quickly developing solutions. I possess the personal character, people skills, and potential for future change through empowering and enabling faculty, staff, and students. As a principal, I will build a relationship of trust and collaboration within the school and the community. If my considerable education, experience, and skills interest you, please contact me during the day at (000) 555-0000, or in the evenings at (000) 555-0000.

Sincerely,

Jessica Lynn Goldman

JESSICA LYNN GOLDMAN

1110½ Hay Street, Fayetteville, NC 28305 • preppub@aol.com • (910) 483-6611

OBJECTIVE To serve as an elementary school principal with an organization that can benefit from my extensive training and experience in education and administration, as well as my skills in the coaching, observation, and supervision of education professionals, solid track record of advancement, and dedication to providing excellence in education.

EDUCATION **Principal's Certification**, Georgia State University, 1993.
Instructional Specialist Certification, Georgia State University, 1990.
Master of Arts degree in Early Childhood Education, Georgia State University, 1988.
Certification in Early Childhood Education, Georgia Southern University, 1987.
Bachelor of Arts degree in Elementary Education, Macon State College, Macon, GA, 1985.

EXPERIENCE **ASSISTANT PRINCIPAL.** Milligan Elementary School, Niagra County School System, Macon, GA (1991-present). Provided instructional leadership to faculty and staff members and worked closely with the principal in all aspects of school operation.
- Responsible for interviewing, hiring, observation, and coaching of teachers.
- Coordinated scheduling for the school; supervised the budget and the Title I program.
- Wrote and supervised the HOPES grant (Helping Our Parents Educate Exceptional Students), providing training to help parents work with children to improve skills at home.
- Directed COMET (Creating Opportunities To Master End-of-grade Testing), our remediation program for students in grades 3-5, supervising a team of three teachers and six instructional assistants.
- Improved end-of-grade test scores in grades 3-5; coordinated a new discipline form during the 1997-98 school year.
- Served on the School Improvement Team, to identify problem areas and troubleshoot solutions in all areas of school operations.
- Interacted with students that were experiencing difficulty, to help them plan for and achieve a level of academic success; worked with students, parents, and community leaders to foster a nurturing school environment; served as Textbook Coordinator, responsible for improving instruction and curriculum; served as half-time Title I Kindergarten Language Arts Resource Teacher.

ASSISTANT PRINCIPAL and TEACHER (half-time). Helen Elementary School, Niagra County School System, Macon, GA (1989-1991). Provided instructional leadership to faculty and staff members.
- Was responsible for observation and evaluation of teachers, supervised buses, textbook coordinator, wrote Junior Service League grant for second graders.

TEACHER. Northland Elementary School, Niagra County School System, Macon, GA (1985-1989). During my service at William H. Owen, I taught kindergarten, TK-1, first, and second grades.
- Served on several different occasions as grade-level chairperson, coaching other teachers.
- Also served on the school-based committee, working to help all children succeed by identifying those students who would qualify for the Exceptional Children's Program.

CONFERENCES
- Technology Training (1998).
- Math Manipulatives Workshop (1997).
- Thinking Maps (1997).

- Non-Violent Crisis Intervention (1997).
- Multiple Intelligences (1997).
- A.I.M.S. (1997).

Principal

Date

Exact Name of Person
Title or Position
Name of Company
Address (number and street)
Address (city, state, and zip)

Principal

This executive has
excelled as a principal in
a school environment
throughout her career.
Now she is seeking the
challenge of a staff
development role.

Dear Exact Name of Person: (or Dear Sir or Madam if answering a blind ad.)

With the enclosed resume, I would like to indicate my interest in the position as Staff Development Coordinator.

As you will see from my enclosed resume, while handling my administrative responsibilities as a principal, I have excelled in training others as well as in "selling" ideas and concepts to people including public citizens, children, teaching professionals, and school board members. Although I have thrived on my responsibilities as a principal and have made many contributions to the effective management of our schools, I believe I could be most useful to our school system if I were in a position in which I could supervise the continuing professional development of teachers.

I am highly respected by teachers throughout this community for my fair style of dealing with others, and I am confident I could gain widespread respect and support if I were to become our school system's Staff Development Coordinator. Although many in my profession might view the job of Staff Development Coordinator as a "step down" from principal, I feel strongly that teacher training and teacher development hold the key to our success as a school district, and I want to provide strong leadership in the area of developing teachers and equipping them with the tools and techniques they need in order to create vibrant classrooms.

I hope you will contact me to suggest a convenient time when we might meet to discuss the position and how my background might serve our community's needs. Thank you in advance for your time.

Sincerely yours,

Myrna Macias

MYRNA MACIAS

1110½ Hay Street, Fayetteville, NC 28305 • preppub@aol.com • (910) 483-6611

OBJECTIVE	To offer a background of achievements in developing innovative and exciting new programs, providing a fair and confident leadership style, and displaying an enthusiastic and open personality to an organization that can use an articulate and talented administrator.
EXPERIENCE	**PRINCIPAL.** The Casey School, Lawton, OK (1997-present). For a 400-student pre-kindergarten through fourth grade facility, am implementing change in a school which had the same principal for 30 years.

- Provide strong leadership and keep the school operating smoothly despite the fact that half of the staff changes at the end of each school year due to redistricting issues, the opening of new schools, and the normal turnover in a military community.
- Quickly earned the respect and trust of community members in an environment where support was strong for change and progress.
- Have excelled in dealing with budget procedures including keeping within government guidelines for average daily members and per-pupil cost.

PRINCIPAL. Baker School, Milton, OK (1987-97). Developed a number of creative, fun, and interesting programs which helped the school earn a reputation for being "on the cutting edge" with a very real spirit of team work and growth as teachers and staff learned to work together.

- Used a variety of resources and materials to prepare and write programs for staff development activities while focusing on providing staff members with information and the opportunity to earn CEU (continuing education units) credit and to assist them in advancing toward highly original and progressive styles of teaching.
- Played a significant role in developing sources for additional funding by researching and writing grants which resulted in funds for computers, math and science programs, reading programs, and a writing center.

ASSISTANT PRINCIPAL. Findley School, Macon, OK (1982-87). Learned to be a catalyst for change and progress while supervising the kindergarten teachers and custodial staff in a school with approximately 650 students; took on additional responsibilities as a staff development planner, test coordinator, observer/evaluator, and co-administrator.

EDUCATION	Have completed 36 hours in an **Ed.D. degree program in Education Administration,** University of Oklahoma, adjunct campus in Lawton, OK. **Master's degree in Education Administration,** Southern Nazarene University, OK, 1987. **B.S. in Elementary Education,** Southern Nazarene University, Bethany, OK, 1981.
TRAINING	Continuously attend training programs, courses, and seminars such as the following:

Higher-level Thinking Skills Workshops	Creative Leadership Workshops
Junior Great Books Leadership Workshops	Hands-on Science Workshops
Technology in Schools Conferences	Science Conferences
National Elementary Principals' Conferences	Multi-age Teaching Seminars

PROGRAMMING EXPERTISE	Applied my creativity and implementational skills in developing a wide range of programs: *Wellness Program*—addressed all aspects of physical wellness from nutrition and food preparation, to skin care, to dancing and aerobics. *Publishing Center*—motivated students to write a book and publish it—wrote the grant and used funds from the Burlington Corporation to fund the program. *Reading Is Fundamental (RIF)*—received funds which allowed the program to distribute free books three times a year (funds were provided through grants from Hallmark and Nestle's).
PERSONAL	Have often been described as decisive, fair, energetic, and supportive. Have a talent for building teams of committed teaching professionals dedicated to helping and educating youth.

Superintendent

This gentleman has been asked to prepare a letter of interest for a position as superintendent of a school system. He isn't sure who will be reading the letter, but he imagines a board or a committee will be reviewing the letters and resumes of each applicant.

Dear Sir or Madam:

With the letter of interest and resume, I would like to express my interest in the position of Superintendent of Schools for Holden Public Schools.

As you will see, I offer a proven track record of innovative leadership, aggressive commitment to providing learning opportunities for all children, and vigorous team building and staff development within the schools systems where I have provided leadership. In my current position as Superintendent of Schools for the Fitzgerald County Schools in San Diego, I lead a system preschool-9 which has a budget of $30 million and a student population of 8,000. I am proud that one of this school system's elementary schools was chosen as a testbed site for President Gore's Presidential Technology Initiative (PTI). This school will combine with 18 other sites of the National Science Foundation and the Advanced Research Projects Agency which is evaluating educational reform strategies.

I am considered one of the nation's fiercest supporters of staff development, and I have assured that vigorous staff development has preceded, and will continue throughout, this pilot project. I take pride that I have been selected as Administrator at the San Diego site for this Presidential Technology Initiative, because I have long been in the forefront of educators committed to vigorous reform, strengthening, and revitalization of education at all grade levels. At San Diego schools, I have also implemented an early childhood program for all four year olds, developed an award-winning volunteer program, expanded the summer enrichment program, and enhanced educational opportunities for children with special needs.

In the area of technology, I am highly respected nationwide as a strong advocate for maximizing the use of technology in the classroom. In my previous job as Superintendent of Schools for the Foster School District in Foster, IN, I significantly increased the use of technology in all grades while leading a school system preschool-12 with a student population of 6,000 and a school budget of $42 million. Indeed, I secured a technology grant to expand technology use. I also developed a teacher mentor program, instituted the Middle States Accreditation Process (K-12), planned major capital improvement projects, and established an inter-agency early childhood program with a $250,000 grant from the Indiana Education Department.

I would try to instill in all students at Holden a passion for education and a thirst for lifelong education, and I hope I will have an opportunity to talk with you about the position.

Yours sincerely,

Karl T. Cooper

KARL T. COOPER

1110½ Hay Street, Fayetteville, NC 28305   •   preppub@aol.com   •   (910) 483-6611

OBJECTIVE   To offer my leadership to the Holden Public Schools; I am a strong administrator with a history of contributions to school systems along with a reputation as a visionary strategic thinker, persuasive communicator and powerful motivator, as well as an innovative and resourceful manager of human and material resources.

EDUCATION   **Ed.D.**, California State University, Chico, CA, 1984.

M.Ed., Golden Gate University, San Francisco, CA.

B.S., California State University, Chico, CA.

Highlights of other coursework and continuing education:

- Courses at Kendall College, Ohio University, Yale University, Ohio State University
- *Labor Relations Course:* The Judge Advocate General's School, UNC
- *Mediation Training:* Justice Center, Indianapolis, IN
- *Technology and the School Executive:* IBM, Peoria, IL
- *Strategic Planning:* National Academy of School Executives
- *Marketing the Good News about Schools:* Walt Disney World Seminars Productions

EXPERIENCE   **SUPERINTENDENT OF SCHOOLS.** Fitzgerald County Schools, San Diego, CA (1990-present). Lead a Preschool-9 school system which has a budget of $40 million and a student population of 8,000.

- Am proud that one of my school system's elementary schools was chosen as a testbed site for President Gore's Presidential Technology Initiative (PTI).
- Am considered a strong su...   ...ve encouraged vigorous staff development for all personnel.
- Enhanced and expanded educational opportunities for children with special needs.
- Implemented an early childhood program for all four year olds.
- Expanded summer enrichment programs for students.
- Established a breakfast program; developed an award-winning volunteer program.
- Instituted partnership programs with law enforcement agencies and the medical community; provided leadership in the development of the Bus Strategic Plan.
- Planned and opened an 8 million dollar elementary school (1996).

Community involvement:

- Board of Directors, Boy Scouts
- Board of Directors, Combined Campaign, San Diego
- Metrovisions Steering Committee, Fitzgerald County, CA
- Scholarship Committee Member, Fitzgerald County, CA

Highlights of honors and recognitions:

- Selected as Administrator, Fitzgerald County Schools, for President Gore's Presidential Technology Initiative (PTI); visited schools in Italy, 1997.
- Member, Advisory Council on Dependent Education; visited schools in Japan, 1996
- Recipient of Education Society Award, Golden Gate University, 1995
- Distinguished Service Committee Member, American Association of School Administrators, 1995
- Certificate of Recognition, Phi Beta Kappa, 1994
- Recipient of Human Relations Award, San Diego, 1991

Superintendent

SUPERINTENDENT OF SCHOOLS. San Diego City School District, San Diego, CA (1986-90). Led a Preschool-12 school system with a student population of 6,000 and a school budget of $42 million.

* Established an inter-agency early childhood program with a $250,000 grant from California State Education Department.
* Planned major capital improvement projects totaling 10 million dollars.
* Secured technology grant from SED, San Diego, CA, to expand technology use in the classroom; significantly increased the use of technology in all grades.
* Provided leadership in developing School & Business Alliance Project; awarded $135,000 special appropriation from California State Legislature.
* Instituted Middle States Accreditation Process (K-12).
* Developed teacher mentor program.

Community involvement:
* Board of Directors, Urban League, San Diego
* Board of Directors, San Diego Summer Music Festival: Program Committee and Education Committee
* Board of Directors, WSKG Public Broadcasting: Chairman, Personnel Committee
* Board of Directors, Mom's House, San Diego, CA
* Lions Club International; Vice President
* Broome County United Way Campaign; Education Chairman

Highlights of honors and recognitions:
* Volunteer Award, Fitzgerald County Urban League, 1990
* Outstanding Service Award, San Diego, CA, 1990
* Executive Educator of the Month, "The Executive Educator:" 1990
* Volunteer Award, Boy Scouts of America, San Diego, 1989

Other experience:
AREA SUPERINTENDENT. Queens County Public Schools, Queens, NY (1977-86). Student population - 24,000; K-12
SUPERINTENDENT OF SCHOOLS. Foster School District, Foster, IN (1973-77). Student population 6,000; budget $42 million.
ASSISTANT SUPERINTENDENT OF SCHOOLS. Cambridge School District, Cambridge, MA (1971-73).
ELEMENTARY PRINCIPAL, Matthews School (1968-71) and **TEACHING PRINCIPAL,** Cobalt Elementary School (1967-68); Elvin School District, Elvin WI (1966-67).
CLASSROOM TEACHER. Burton and Reynolds School Districts, WI (1962-66). Grades 1, 4, 5, and 6.

PUBLICATIONS & CONSULTING

Authored "Always a Cure," *School Board Journal*; Nov. 1990
Conducted a national survey of school board members in conjunction with the *American School Board Journal*; published Jan.1985.
Co-authored "A Standard Process for Evaluation of Education Programs,"

Superintendent

This superintendent hopes to be moving on to "bigger and better" things. He is working with the executive recruiter who is handling the search for the new superintendent of Holden Public Schools.

Queens County Board of Education, 1981.
Co-authored Wisconson State Social Studies Guide (Grades 4-6), 1966.
Consultant to State Department of Education, Social Studies Division, Elvin, WI.
Consultant to Cooper High School, Elvin, WI.

AFFILIATIONS   American Association of School Administrators
California Association of School Administrators
California State Superintendents Association
California Superintendents Association, Vice President
Wisconson Regional Education Center Advisory Council
Phi Delta Kappa
Century Club
Superintendent's Association, Vice President

PRESENTATIONS Keynote speaker at superintendents' conferences, leadership conferences, community forums, and other events.

PART FIVE: REAL-RESUMES FOR TEACHERS
GETTING OUT OF TEACHING

In this section you will find resumes and cover letters of teachers who are changing careers. The purpose of this section is to provide expert tools and advice so that you *can* manage your career and find not just a new job but the type of work you want to do.

Overview of this section

Every resume and cover letter in this book actually worked. And most of the resumes and cover letters have common features: all are one-page, all are in the chronological format, and all resumes are accompanied by a companion cover letter. The section is divided into three parts. In this section you will find some advice about job hunting. **Step One** begins with a discussion of why employers prefer the one-page, chronological resume. In **Step Two** you are introduced to the direct approach and to the proper format for a cover letter. In **Step Three** you learn the 14 main reasons why job hunters are not offered the jobs they want, and you learn the six key areas employers focus on when they interview you. **Step Four** gives nuts-and-bolts advice on how to handle the interview, send a follow-up letter after an interview, and negotiate your salary. At the end of Part One, you'll find advice about how to research and locate the companies and organizations to which you want to send your resume.

Since the cover letter plays such a critical role in a career change, you will see suggested language to use in particular career-change situations. It has been said that "A picture is worth a thousand words" and, for that reason, you will see numerous examples of effective cover letters used by teachers to change fields, functions, and industries.

Some of the resumes and cover letters are of teachers who knew they definitely wanted a career change but had no idea what they wanted to do next. Other resumes and cover letters show teachers who knew they wanted to change fields and had a pretty good idea of what they wanted to do next. Whatever your circumstances, you'll find resumes and cover letters that will "show you the ropes" in terms of successfully switching careers.

Before you proceed further, think about why you picked up this book.
- Why are you dissatisfied with the type of work you are now doing?
- Are you interested in education but not satisfied with your particular role?
- Do you want to transfer your skills to a new industry?
- Even if you have excelled in your field, have you "had enough?" Would you like the stimulation of a new challenge?
- Are you aware of the importance of a great cover letter but unsure of how to write one?
- Are you preparing to launch a second career after retirement?
- Do you need expert advice on how to plan and implement a job campaign that will open the maximum number of doors?
- Do you want to make sure you handle an interview to your maximum advantage?
- Would you like to master the techniques of negotiating salary and benefits?
- Do you want to learn the secrets and shortcuts of professional resume writers?

Getting Out of Teaching

Using the Direct Approach

As you consider the possibility of a job hunt or career change, you need to be aware that most people end up having at least three distinctly different careers in their working lifetimes, and often those careers are different from each other. Yet people usually stumble through each job campaign, unsure of what they should be doing. Whether you find yourself voluntarily or unexpectedly in a job hunt, the direct approach is the job hunting strategy most likely to yield a full-time permanent job. The direct approach is an active, take-the-initiative style of job hunting in which you choose your next employer rather than relying on responding to ads, using employment agencies, or depending on other methods of finding jobs. You will learn how to use the direct approach in this book, and you will see that an effective cover letter is a critical ingredient in using the direct approach.

The "direct approach" is the style of job hunting most likely to yield the maximum number of job interviews.

Lack of Industry Experience Not a Major Barrier to Entering New Field

"Lack of experience" is often the last reason people are not offered jobs, according to the companies who do the hiring. If you are changing careers, you will be glad to learn that experienced professionals often are selling "potential" rather than experience in a job hunt. Companies look for personal qualities that they know tend to be present in their most effective professionals, such as communication skills, initiative, persistence, organizational and time management skills, and creativity. Frequently companies are trying to discover "personality type," "talent," "ability," "aptitude," and "potential" rather than seeking actual hands-on experience, so your resume should be designed to aggressively present your accomplishments. Attitude, enthusiasm, personality, and a track record of achievements in any type of work are the primary "indicators of success" which employers are seeking, and you will see numerous examples in this book of resumes written in an all-purpose fashion so that the professional can approach various industries and companies.

The Art of Using References in a Job Hunt

Using references in a skillful fashion in your job hunt will inspire confidence in prospective employers and help you "close the sale" after interviews.

You probably already know that you need to provide references during a job hunt, but you may not be sure of how and when to use references for maximum advantage. You can use references very creatively during a job hunt to call attention to your strengths and make yourself "stand out." Your references will rarely get you a job, no matter how impressive the names, but the way you use references can boost the employer's confidence in you and lead to a job offer in the least time. You should ask from three to five people, including people who have supervised you, if you can use them as a reference during your job hunt. You may not be able to ask your current boss since your job hunt is probably confidential. A common question in resume preparation is: "Do I need to put my references on my resume?" No, you don't. And even if you create a page of references at the same time that you prepare your resume, you don't need to mail your references page with the resume and cover letter. The potential employer is not interested in your references until he meets and gets interested in you, so the earliest you need to have references ready is at the first interview. An excellent attention-getting technique is to take to the first interview not just a page of references (giving names, addresses, and telephone numbers) but an actual letter of reference written by someone who knows you well and who preferably has supervised or employed you. A professional way to close the first interview is to thank the interviewer, shake his or her hand, and then say you'd like to give him or her a copy of a letter of reference from a previous employer. Hopefully you already made a good impression during the interview, but you'll "close the sale" in a dynamic fashion if you leave a letter praising you and your accomplishments. For that reason, it's a good idea to ask employers during your final weeks in a job if they will provide you with a written letter of recommendation which you can use in future job hunts. Most employers will oblige, and you will have a letter that has a useful "shelf life" of many years. Such a letter often gives the prospective employer enough confidence in his opinion of you that he may forego checking out other references and decide to offer you the job in the next few days. Whom should you ask to serve as references? References should be people who have known or supervised you in a professional, academic, or work situation. References with big titles, like school superintendent or congressman, are fine, but remind busy people when you get to the interview stage that they may be contacted soon. Make sure the busy official recognizes your name and has instant positive recall of you! If you're asked to provide references on a formal company application, you can simply transcribe names from your references list. In summary, follow this rule in using references: If you've got them, flaunt them! If you've obtained well-written letters of reference, make sure you find a polite way to push those references under the nose of the interviewer so he or she can hear someone other than you describing your strengths. Your references probably won't ever get you a job, but glowing letters of reference can give you credibility and visibility that can make you stand out among candidates with similar credentials and potential!

With regard to references, it's best to provide the names and addresses of people who have supervised you or observed you in a work situation.

The approach taken by this section is to (1) help you master the proven best techniques of conducting a job hunt and (2) show you how to stand out in a job hunt through your resume, cover letter, interviewing skills, as well as the way in which you present your references and follow up on interviews. Now, the best way to "get in the mood" for writing your own resume and cover letter is to read every resume and cover letter in this section. If you wish to seek professional advice in preparing your resume, you may contact one of the professional writers at Professional Resume & Employment Publishing (PREP) for a brief free consultation by calling 1-910-483-6611.

Part One: Some Advice About Your Job Hunt

What if you don't know what you want to do?

Your job hunt will be more comfortable if you can figure out what type of work you want to do. But you are not alone if you have no idea what you want to do next! You may have knowledge and skills in certain areas but want to get into another type of work. What *The Wall Street Journal* has discovered in its research on careers is that most of us end up having at least three distinctly different careers in our working lives; it seems that, even if we really like a particular kind of activity, twenty years of doing it is enough for most of us and we want to move on to something else!

Figure out what interests you and you will hold the key to a successful job hunt and working career. (And be prepared for your interests to change over time!)

That's why we strongly believe that you need to spend some time figuring out **what interests you** rather than taking an inventory of the skills you have. You may have skills that you simply don't want to use, but if you can build your career on the things that interest you, you will be more likely to be happy and satisfied in your job. Realize, too, that interests can change over time; the activities that interest you now may not be the ones that interested you years ago. For example, some professionals may decide that they've had enough of teaching and want a job in marketing or public relations, because they have earned a reputation for being an excellent communicator. We strongly believe that interests rather than skills should be the determining factor in deciding what types of jobs you want to apply for and what directions you explore in your job hunt. Obviously one cannot be a lawyer without a law degree or a secretary without secretarial skills; but a professional can embark on a next career as a financial consultant, property manager, plant manager, production supervisor, retail manager, or other occupation if he/she has a strong interest in that type of work and can provide a resume that clearly demonstrates past excellent performance in *any* field and *potential* to excel in another field. As you will see later in this book, "lack of exact experience" is the last reason why people are turned down for the jobs they apply for.

"Lack of exact experience" is the last reason people are turned down for the jobs for which they apply.

How can you have a resume prepared if you don't know what you want to do?

You may be wondering how you can have a resume prepared if you don't know what you want to do next. The approach to resume writing which PREP, the country's oldest resume-preparation company, has used successfully for many years is to develop an "all-purpose" resume that translates your skills, experience, and accomplishments into language employers can understand. What most people need in a job hunt is a versatile resume that will allow them to apply for numerous types of jobs. For example, you may want to apply for a job in pharmaceutical sales but you may also want to have a resume that will be versatile enough for you to apply for jobs in numerous industries.

Based on 20 years of serving job hunters, we at PREP have found that **an all-purpose resume** and **specific cover letters tailored to specific fields** is often your best approach to job hunting rather than trying to create different resumes for different occupational areas. Usually, you will not even need more than one "all-purpose" cover letter, although the cover letter rather than the resume is the place to communicate your interest in a narrow or specific field. An all-purpose resume and cover letter that translate your experience and accomplishments into plain English are the tools that will maximize the number of doors which open for you while permitting you to "fish" in the widest range of job areas.

Your resume will provide the script for your job interview.

When you get down to it, your resume has a simple job to do: Its purpose is to blow as many doors open as possible and to make as many people as possible want to meet you. So a well-written resume that really "sells" you is a key that will create opportunities for you in a job hunt.

This statistic explains why: The typical newspaper advertisement for a job opening receives more than 245 replies. And normally only 10 or 12 will be invited to an interview.

But here's another purpose of the resume: it provides the "script" the employer uses when he interviews you. If your resume has been written in such a way that your strengths and achievements are revealed, that's what you'll end up talking about at the job interview. Since the resume will govern what you get asked about at your interviews, you can't overestimate the importance of making sure your resume makes you look and sound as good as you are.

So what is a "good" resume?

Very literally, your resume should motivate the person reading it to dial the phone number you have put on the resume. (If you are relocating, that's one reason you should think about putting a local phone contact number on your resume, if possible, when your contact address is several states away; employers are much more likely to dial a local telephone number than a long-distance number when they're looking for potential employees.)

If you have a resume already, look at it objectively. Is it a limp, colorless "laundry list" of your job titles and duties? Or does it "paint a picture" of your skills, abilities, and accomplishments in a way that would make someone want to meet you? Can people understand what you're saying?

How long should your resume be?

One page, maybe two. Usually only people in the academic community have a resume (which they usually call a *curriculum vitae*) longer than one or two pages. Remember that your resume is almost always accompanied by a cover letter, and a potential employer does not want to read more than two or three pages about a total stranger in order to decide if he wants to meet that person! Besides, don't forget that the more you tell someone about yourself, the more opportunity you are providing for the employer to screen you out at the "first-cut" stage. A resume should be concise and exciting and designed to make the reader want to meet you in person!

Should resumes be functional or chronological?

Employers almost always prefer a chronological resume; in other words, an employer will find a resume easier to read if it is immediately apparent what your current or most recent job is, what you did before that, and so forth, in reverse chronological order. A resume that goes back in detail for the last ten years of employment will generally satisfy the employer's curiosity about your background. Employment more than ten years old can be shown even more briefly in an "Other Experience" section at the end of your "Experience" section. Remember that your intention is not to tell everything you've done but to "hit the high points" and especially impress the employer with what you learned, contributed, or accomplished in each job you describe.

Your resume is the "script" for your job interviews. Make sure you put on your resume what you want to talk about or be asked about at the job interview.

The one-page resume in chronological format is the format preferred by most employers.

STEP TWO: Using Your Resume and Cover Letter

Once you get your resume, what do you do with it?
You will be using your resume to answer ads, as a tool to use in talking with friends and relatives about your job search, and, most importantly, in using the "direct approach" described in this book.

When you mail your resume, always send a "cover letter."
A "cover letter," sometimes called a "resume letter" or "letter of interest," is a letter that accompanies and introduces your resume. Your cover letter is a way of personalizing the resume by sending it to the specific person you think you might want to work for at each company. Your cover letter should contain a few highlights from your resume—just enough to make someone want to meet you. Cover letters should always be typed or word processed on a computer—never handwritten.

1. Learn the art of answering ads.
There is an "art," part of which can be learned, in using your "bestselling" resume to reply to advertisements.

Sometimes an exciting job lurks behind a boring ad that someone dictated in a hurry, so reply to any ad that interests you. Don't worry that you aren't "25 years old with an MBA" like the ad asks for. Employers will always make compromises in their requirements if they think you're the "best fit" overall.

What about ads that ask for "salary requirements?"
What if the ad you're answering asks for "salary requirements?" The first rule is to avoid committing yourself in writing at that point to a specific salary. You don't want to "lock yourself in."

There are two ways to handle the ad that asks for "salary requirements."
First, you can ignore that part of the ad and accompany your resume with a cover letter that focuses on "selling" you, your abilities, and even some of your philosophy about work or your field. You may include a sentence in your cover letter like this: "I can provide excellent personal and professional references at your request, and I would be delighted to share the private details of my salary history with you in person." *Second,* you could give a range. If you feel you must give some kind of number, just state a range in your cover letter that includes your medical, dental, other benefits, and bonuses. You might state, for example, "my previous compensation, including benefits and bonuses, was in the range of $35,000-40,000." But, again, it's usually not in your best interest to communicate your salary history before you have a chance to meet the potential employer.

Analyze the ad and "tailor" yourself to it.
When you're replying to ads, a finely-tailored cover letter is an important tool in getting your resume noticed and read. On the next page is a cover letter which has been "tailored to fit" a specific ad. Notice the "art" used by PREP writers of analyzing the ad's main requirements and then writing the letter so that the person's background, work habits, and interests seem "tailor-made" to the company's needs. Use this cover letter as a model when you prepare your own reply to ads.

Negotiating salary can be tricky when you're changing fields.

Date

Mr. Arthur Wise
Chamber of Commerce of the U.S.
9439 Goshen Lane
Burke, VA 22105

Dear Mr. Wise:

I would appreciate an opportunity to show you in person, soon, that I am the energetic, dynamic salesperson you are looking for as a Membership Sales Representative of the Chamber of Commerce.

As you will see from my enclosed resume, I am an experienced teacher seeking to transfer my strong communication skills into a marketing area, and I believe I would be highly effective in the role you described for the following reasons:

- *I myself am "sold" on the Chamber of Commerce* and have long been an admirer of its goal of forming a cohesive business organization to promote the well-being of communities and promote business vigor. As someone better known than I put it long ago, "the business of America is business." I wholeheartedly believe in the Chamber's efforts to unite, solidify, and mobilize American business. My father is an independent businessman and has been a Chamber member all his life, so I have grown up hearing about the Chamber and its honorable goals.

- *I am a proven salesperson* with a demonstrated ability to "prospect." Because of my natural sales ability, I was elected Membership Chairperson of my sorority and I led my organization in achieving the most successful membership drive in its history. I have been told that I "could sell a refrigerator to an Eskimo," and I am confident I could be highly effective in recruiting new members. As a classroom teacher, I was "selling" ideas and concepts on a daily basis, and I offer a natural marketing orientation.

- *I am single and enjoy traveling and am eager to assist in the growth of Virginia and vicinity.* I am fortunate to have the natural energy, industry, and enthusiasm required to put in the long hours necessary for effective sales performance.

You would find me to be a friendly, good-natured person whom you would be proud to call part of the Chamber's "team."

I hope you will call or write me soon to suggest a convenient time when we might meet to discuss your needs further and how I might serve them. Please allow me an opportunity to show you in person that I am the enthusiastic and hard-working individual you are seeking.

Yours sincerely,

Your Name

Employers are trying to identify the individual who wants the job they are filling. Don't be afraid to express your enthusiasm in the cover letter!

2. Talk to friends and relatives.

Don't be shy about telling your friends and relatives the kind of job you're looking for. Looking for the job you want involves using your network of contacts, so tell people what you're looking for. They may be able to make introductions and help set up interviews.

About 25% of all interviews are set up through "who you know," so don't ignore this approach.

3. Finally, and most importantly, use the "direct approach."

More than 50% of all job interviews are set up by the "direct approach." That means you actually send a resume and a cover letter to a company you think might be interested in employing your skills.

To whom do you write?

In general, you should write directly to the *exact name* of the person who would be hiring you: say, the vice-president of marketing or data processing. If you're in doubt about to whom to address the letter, address it to the president by name and he or she will make sure it gets forwarded to the right person within the company who has hiring authority in your area.

How do you find the names of potential employers?

You're not alone if you feel that the biggest problem in your job search is finding the right names at the companies you want to contact. But you can usually figure out the names of companies you want to approach by deciding first if your job hunt is primarily geography-driven or industry-driven.

In a **geography-driven job hunt,** you could select a list of, say, 50 companies you want to contact **by location** from the lists that the U.S. Chambers of Commerce publish yearly of their "major area employers." There are hundreds of local Chambers of Commerce across America, and most of them will have an 800 number which you can find through 1-800-555-1212. If you think Atlanta, Dallas, Ft. Lauderdale, and Virginia Beach might be nice places to live, for example, you could contact the Chamber of Commerce in those cities and ask how you can obtain a copy of their list of major employers. Your nearest library will have the book which lists the addresses of all chambers.

In an **industry-driven job hunt,** and if you are willing to relocate, you will be identifying the companies which you find most attractive in the industry in which you want to work. When you select a list of companies to contact **by industry,** you can find the right person to write and the address of firms by industrial category in *Standard and Poor's, Moody's,* and other excellent books in public libraries. Many web sites also provide contact information.

Many people feel it's a good investment to actually call the company to either find out or double-check the name of the person to whom they want to send a resume and cover letter. It's important to do as much as you feasibly can to assure that the letter gets to the right person in the company.

At the end of this section, you will find some advice about how to conduct library research and how to locate organizations to which you could send your resume.

What's the correct way to follow up on a resume you send?

There is a polite way to be aggressively interested in a company during your job hunt. It is ideal to end the cover letter accompanying your resume by saying, "I hope you'll welcome my call next week when I try to arrange a brief meeting at your convenience to discuss your current and future needs and how I might serve them." Keep it low key, and just ask for a "brief meeting," not an interview. Employers want people who show a determined interest in working with them, so don't be shy about following up on the resume and cover letter you've mailed.

STEP THREE: Preparing for Interviews

Research the company before you go to interviews.

But a resume and cover letter by themselves can't get you the job you want. You need to "prep" yourself before the interview. Step Three in your job campaign is "Preparing for Interviews." First, let's look at interviewing from the company's point of view.

What are the biggest "turnoffs" for companies?

One of the ways to help yourself perform well at an interview is to look at the main reasons why companies *don't* hire the people they interview, according to companies that do the interviewing.

Notice that "lack of appropriate background" (or lack of experience) is the *last* reason for not being offered the job.

The 14 Most Common Reasons Job Hunters Are Not Offered Jobs (*according to the companies who do the interviewing and hiring*):

Anticipate the questions you will be asked at the interview, and prepare your responses in advance.

1. Low level of accomplishment
2. Poor attitude, lack of self-confidence
3. Lack of goals/objectives
4. Lack of enthusiasm
5. Lack of interest in the company's business
6. Inability to sell or express yourself
7. Unrealistic salary demands
8. Poor appearance
9. Lack of maturity, no leadership potential
10. Lack of extracurricular activities
11. Lack of preparation for the interview, no knowledge about company
12. Objecting to travel
13. Excessive interest in security and benefits
14. Inappropriate background

Department of Labor studies since the 1950s have proven that smart, "prepared" job hunters can increase their beginning salary while getting a job in *half* the time it normally takes. (4½ months is the average national length of a job search.) Here are some questions that can prepare you to find a job faster.

Are you in the "right" frame of mind?

It seems unfair that we have to look for a job just when we're lowest in morale. Don't worry *too* much if you're nervous before interviews (top television personalities say they usually are, too). You're supposed to be a little nervous, especially if the job means a lot to you. But the best way to kill unnecessary fears about job hunting is through 1) making sure you have a great resume and cover letter and 2) preparing yourself for the interview. Here are three main areas to think about before each interview.

Do you know what the company does?
Don't walk into an interview giving the impression that, "If this is Tuesday, this must be General Motors."

Find out before the interview what the company's main product or service is. Where is the company heading? Is it in a "growth" or declining industry? (Answers to these questions may influence whether or not you want to work there!)

Information about what the company does is in annual reports as well as newspaper and magazine articles. Just visit your nearest library and ask the reference librarian to guide you to materials on the company. Internet searches will also yield valuable information. At the end of Part One you will find many suggestions about how to research companies.

Employers are seeking people with good attitudes whom they can train and coach to do things their way.

Do you know what you want to do for the company?
Before the interview, try to decide how you see yourself fitting into the company. Remember, "lack of exact background" the company wants is usually the *last* reason people are not offered jobs.

Understand before you go to each interview that the burden will be on you to "sell" the interviewer on why you're the best person for the job and the company.

How will you answer the critical interview questions?
Put yourself in the interviewer's position and think about the questions you're most likely to be asked. Here are some of the most commonly asked interview questions:

Q: *"What are your greatest strengths?"*
A: Don't say you've never thought about it! Go into an interview knowing the three main impressions you want to leave about yourself, such as "I'm hard-working, loyal, and an imaginative cost-cutter."

Q: *"What are your greatest weaknesses?"*
A: Don't confess that you're lazy or have trouble meeting deadlines! Confessing that you tend to be a "workaholic" or "tend to be a perfectionist and sometimes get frustrated when others don't share my high standards" will make your prospective employer see a "weakness" that he likes. Name a weakness that your interviewer will perceive as a strength.

Q: *"What are your long-range goals?"*
A: If you're interviewing with Microsoft, don't say you want to work for IBM in five years! Say your long-range goal is to be *with* the company, contributing to its goals and success.

Q: *"What motivates you to do your best work?"*
A: Don't get dollar signs in your eyes here! "A challenge" is not a bad answer, but it's a little cliched. Saying something like "troubleshooting" or "solving a tough problem" is more interesting and specific. Give an example if you can.

Q: "What do you know about this company?"

A: Don't say you never heard of it until they asked you to the interview! Name an interesting, positive thing you learned about the company recently from your research. Remember, company executives can sometimes feel rather "maternal" about the company they serve. Don't get onto a negative area of the company if you can think of positive facts you can bring up. Of course, if you learned in your research that the company's sales seem to be taking a nose-dive, or that the company president is being prosecuted for taking bribes, you might politely ask your interviewer to tell you something that could help you better understand what you've been reading. Those are the kinds of company facts that can help you determine whether you want to work there or not.

Go to an interview prepared to tell the company why it should hire you.

Q: "Why should I hire you?"

A: "I'm unemployed and available" is the wrong answer here! Get back to your strengths and say that you believe the organization could benefit by a loyal, hard-working cost-cutter like yourself.

In conclusion, you should decide in advance, before you go to the interview, how you will answer each of these commonly asked questions.

Have some practice interviews with a friend to role-play and build your confidence.

STEP FOUR: Handling the Interview and Negotiating Salary

A smile at an interview makes the employer perceive of you as intelligent!

Now you're ready for Step Four: actually handling the interview successfully and effectively. Remember, the purpose of an interview is to get a job offer.

Eight "do's" for the interview

According to leading U.S. companies, there are eight key areas in interviewing success. You can fail at an interview if you mishandle just one area.

1. *Do wear appropriate clothes.*
   You can never go wrong by wearing a suit to an interview.

2. *Do be well groomed.*
   Don't overlook the obvious things like having clean hair, clothes, and fingernails for the interview.

3. *Do give a firm handshake.*
   You'll have to shake hands twice in most interviews: first, before you sit down, and second, when you leave the interview. Limp handshakes turn most people off.

4. *Do smile and show a sense of humor.*
   Interviewers are looking for people who would be nice to work with, so don't be so somber that you don't smile. In fact, research shows that people who smile at interviews are perceived as more intelligent. So, smile!

Don't appear excessively interested in salary and benefits at the interview.

5. *Do be enthusiastic.*
   Employers say they are "turned off" by lifeless, unenthusiastic job hunters who show no special interest in that company. The best way to show some enthusiasm for the employer's operation is to find out about the business beforehand.

6. *Do show you are flexible and adaptable.*

   An employer is looking for someone who can contribute to his organization in a flexible, adaptable way. No matter what skills and training you have, employers know every new employee must go through initiation and training on the company's turf. Certainly show pride in your past accomplishments in a specific, factual way ("I saved my employer $50.00 a week in my summer job by a new cost-cutting procedure I developed"). But don't come across as though there's nothing about the job you couldn't easily handle.

7. *Do ask intelligent questions about the employer's business.*

   An employer is hiring someone because of certain business needs. Show interest in those needs. Asking questions to get a better idea of the employer's needs will help you "stand out" from other candidates interviewing for the job.

8. *Do "take charge" when the interviewer "falls down" on the job.*

   Go into every interview knowing the three or four points about yourself you want the interviewer to remember. And be prepared to take an active part in leading the discussion if the interviewer's "canned approach" does not permit you to display your "strong suit." You can't always depend on the interviewer's asking you the "right" questions so you can stress your strengths and accomplishments.

An important "don't"

Don't ask questions about salary or benefits at the first interview.

Employers don't take warmly to people who look at their organization as just a place to satisfy salary and benefit needs. Don't risk making a negative impression by appearing greedy or self-serving.

The place to discuss salary and benefits is normally at the second interview, and the employer will bring it up. Then you can ask any questions you like without appearing excessively interested in what the organization can do for you.

"Sell yourself" before talking salary

Make sure you've "sold" yourself before talking salary. First show you're the "best fit" for the employer and then you'll be in a stronger position from which to negotiate salary.

Interviewers sometimes throw out a salary figure at the first interview to see if you'll accept it. Don't commit yourself. You may be able to negotiate a better deal later on. Get back to finding out more about the job. This lets the interviewer know you're interested primarily in the job and not the salary.

Now…negotiating your salary

You must avoid stating a "salary requirement" in your initial cover letter, and you must avoid even appearing **interested** in salary before you are offered the job.

Never bring up the subject of salary yourself. Employers say there's no way you can avoid looking greedy if you bring up the issue of salary and benefits before the company has identified you as its "best fit."

When the company brings up salary, it may say something like this: "Well, Mary, we think you'd make a good candidate for this job. What kind of salary are we talking about?"

Never name a number here, either. Give the ball back to the interviewer. Act as though you hadn't given the subject of salary much thought and respond something like this: "Ah, Mr. Jones, salary. . .well, I wonder if you'd be kind enough to tell me what salary you had in mind when you advertised the job?" Or ... "What is the range you have in mind?"

Don't worry, if the interviewer names a figure that you think is too low, you can say so without turning down the job or locking yourself into a rigid position. The point here is to negotiate for yourself as well as you can. You might reply to a number named by the interviewer that you think is low by saying something like this: "Well, Mr. Lee, the job interests me very much, and I think I'd certainly enjoy working with you. But, frankly, I was thinking of something a little higher than that." That leaves the ball in your interviewer's court again, and you haven't turned down the job, either, in case it turns out that the interviewer can't increase the offer and you still want the job.

Salary negotiation can be tricky.

Last, send a follow-up letter

Finally, send a letter right after the interview telling your interviewer you enjoyed the meeting and are certain (if you are) you are the "best fit" for the job.

Again, employers have a certain maternal attitude toward their companies, and they are looking for people who want to work for *that* company in particular.

A follow-up letter can help the employer choose between you and another qualified candidate.

The follow-up letter you send might be just the deciding factor in your favor if the employer is trying to choose between you and someone else. A sample follow-up letter is show. Be sure to modify it according to your particular skills and interview situation.

Information about companies is widely available through the Internet. You can use all the search engines to help you in your search for company information and company website addresses. To avoid giving you information which would be hopelessly out of date by the time you read this book, we will simply suggest that you maintain your up-to-date resume on a disk and be prepared to e-mail it to companies when you visit their websites. If you go to the search engines, typing in words like "employment" and "jobs" and actual company names should help you begin your journey toward the latest information and most interesting sites on the worldwide Web.

Getting Out of Teaching

Date

Exact Name of Person
Exact Title
Exact Name of Company
Address
City, State, Zip

Teacher

Employers are *very* inquisitive about why you want to make a change. The way you present yourself on a resume will influence how the potential employer "sees" you. For that reason, this teacher says very little about teaching and emphasizes previous experience.

Dear Exact Name of Person: (or Dear Sir or Madam if answering a blind ad):

Can you use a dynamic young communicator and motivator who seeks to transfer strong communication skills and proven leadership ability from the teaching field?

Although I have recently excelled as an English teacher in Salt Lake City, you will see from my resume that I previously achieved success outside the teaching field through my exceptional sales ability. While simultaneously managing a prosperous business as a private instructor in music, language arts, and gymnastics, I planned, developed, coordinated, and marketed an innovative sports program. I created the promotional brochures which marketed the program, and I made sales calls to local child care center directors and recreation departments. As a result of my initiative and resourcefulness, the program is being implemented in more than a dozen child private day care centers and within the Salt Lake City Parks & Recreation Department. It was during that time that I began to realize that I offer unusually strong abilities related to sales and marketing, and I have decided to leave teaching and embark upon a career in which I can utilize my sales skills in a profit-making environment.

When we have the opportunity to meet in person, I think you will agree that my outgoing personality, strong bottom-line orientation, and energetic, "take charge" attitude would be well suited to a selling environment.

If you can use a motivated professional with exceptional problem solving skills and the proven ability to sell concepts and services, I hope you will welcome my call soon to arrange a brief meeting to discuss your goals and how my background would serve your needs. I am confident that my dedicated hard-working style will make me successful outside teaching. I can provide outstanding references at the appropriate time.

Sincerely,

Christine Vogt

CHRIS M. VOGT

1110½ Hay Street, Fayetteville, NC 28305   •   preppub@aol.com   •   (910) 483-6611

OBJECTIVE

To benefit an organization that can use an articulate, experienced professional with exceptional planning and organizational skills who offers skills related to .sales and marketing, public relations, and project management.

EDUCATION

Bachelor of Science in **Education**, with a major in Language Arts, Dixie College, St. George, UT, 1991.

EXPERIENCE

ENGLISH TEACHER and **VOLLEYBALL COACH.** Childs High School, Salt Lake City, UT (1998-present). Provided classroom instruction in English and American Literature as well as in grammar and composition to eleventh and twelfth grade students and served as coach for the volleyball team.

MUSIC and **PHYSICAL FITNESS & COORDINATION INSTRUCTOR.** Self-employed (1991-1998). Salt Lake City, UT. While marketing my skills as a private piano and language arts instructor, also developed, successfully marketed, and was contracted to implement a new sports program focused on developing athletic skills at child development centers as well as through the Salt Lake City Parks & Recreation Department.
- **Planning:** Designed, planned, and implemented a new sports program which has benefits for all age groups, ranging from senior citizens to pre-schoolers.
- **Marketing:** Developed and produced informational flyers and other marketing and promotional materials for the program.
- **Sales:** Succeeded in "selling" the program to child development centers and to the Salt Lake City Parks & Recreation Department, which implemented it at several Recreation Centers; made "cold calls" to local child care directors and civic officials to present the program.
- **Staff development:** Trained and directed the work of two teaching assistants in addition to coordinating curriculum development and class schedules.
- **Program development:** Devised a program using piano and gymnastics to assist children with visual perception problems or dyslexia in overcoming obstacles and understanding "how" to learn.
- **Communication skills:** Instructed high school students privately in English grammar and composition, with a special emphasis on the elements of effective essay writing.
- **"Word-of-mouth" reputation:** Expanded my business to the point that prospective students had to be placed on a waiting list, through advertising in newsletters of home schooling resources.

EDUCATIONAL SERVICES COORDINATOR. Cubby Hole, Salt Lake City, UT (1991). In this challenging temporary position, was recruited to serve as facilitator and coordinator for tours of up to 500 students attending this traveling exhibit of robotic dinosaurs.
- Tasked with resolving logistical problems and performing liaison between the exhibit's management and local tour organizers, successfully handled scheduling conflicts.

Highlights of earlier experience: Excelled in earlier positions as a **FREELANCE TECHNICAL WRITER** preparing proposals for an engineer, **VETERINARY ASSISTANT** at a local animal clinic, and **SOCCER COACH** for the Youth Soccer League.

PERSONAL

Former member of the Dixie College gymnastics team and Instructor for Dixie College Recreation Department. Known for leadership ability and exceptional problem-solving skills.

Getting Out of Teaching

Date

Exact Name of Person
Title or Position
Name of Company
Address (no., street)
Address (city, state, zip)

**In Transition
From Teaching**

It didn't take more than a brief experience in student teaching to convince this young professional that she wasn't well suited to a long career in teaching. She has many talents, however, and will seek to transfer her excellent communication skills and outgoing personality to another type of work.

Dear Exact Name of Person: (or Dear Sir or Madam if answering a blind ad.)

Can you use an energetic and enthusiastic young professional who offers strong communication skills along with a persuasive professional style and sales experience?

As you will see from my enclosed resume, I recently received my Bachelor's degree from College of Atlanta, Atlanta, GA. While attending college, I refined my time management skills and displayed my adaptability in part-time and seasonal jobs requiring strong sales, communication, and instructional skills.

My experience as a student teacher was challenging and rewarding. I developed lesson plans which motivated and instructed the children while making learning fun. Among my greatest strengths are my tact and listening skills—I am able to hear both sides of an issue and diplomatically present my views. You would find me to be an optimistic and creative individual with a talent for "selling" ideas and effectively communicating concepts.

Although I love children and enjoyed my student teaching, I have decided that I wish to use my strong communication, organizational, and management skills in a business environment. I am certain that I will be able to apply my outgoing personality and multiple talents in a way that will help to enrich an organization's bottom line.

I hope you will welcome my call soon to arrange a brief meeting at your convenience to discuss your current and future needs and how I might serve them. Thank you in advance for your time.

Sincerely yours,

Annabelle Vines

ANNABELLE VINES

1110½ Hay Street, Fayetteville, NC 28305   •   preppub@aol.com   •   (910) 483-6611

OBJECTIVE
To apply my sales and communication abilities to an organization in need of a mature young professional who offers a talent for training and teaching others as well as a reputation as a creative thinker and good listener with a high level of enthusiasm and energy.

EDUCATION
Bachelor's degree, Elementary Education, the College of Atlanta, Atlanta, GA, 2000.

EXPERIENCE
STUDENT TEACHER. Macon Elementary School, Macon, GA (2000). After spending a short period of time observing the teacher's interactions with a class of third graders, took over all classroom activities including planning and carrying out daily activities for the children.
- Became skilled in planning lessons which called for a variety of learning styles and were interesting enough to motivate the students.
- Created a classroom management plan challenging enough to meet the standards of a very exacting supervisory teacher.
- Applied my creativity, optimism, and enthusiasm in making learning fun for children.
- Learned the importance of being patient and listening to the children's concerns.

Learned to manage my time while juggling the demands of attending college full time and excelling in often simultaneous part-time and seasonal jobs requiring strengths in the areas of sales, public relations, and providing instruction:
STOCKER. Talbot's, Washington, DC (1999). Applied my attention to detail while seeing that new merchandise was properly ticketed and also helped with unloading shipments and tagging merchandise for sale.

SALES REPRESENTATIVE. The Post and Courier, Charleston, SC (1996-98). Learned to use my persuasiveness and sales abilities while calling customers on the phone and letting them know the cost of subscriptions.
- Gained valuable experience in applying persistence and thoroughness when trying to sell a service.

HOSTESS/WAITRESS. The Captain's Restaurant, Hilton Head, SC (summers 1993-96). Became known for my cheerful attitude and patience while greeting customers and managing a waiting list that often stretched to two to three hours at this popular restaurant.
- Displayed the ability to work hard and still remain diplomatic and positive even when things were very hectic.
- Helped with daily activities including answering phone inquiries, serving drinks, and assisting in supporting other staff members to provide quality customer service.

SALES REPRESENTATIVE. House of Puppets, Charleston, SC (1993). Refined my sales skills working independently by setting up a booth and making attractive displays and then demonstrating different puppets for sale.
- Displayed creative talents by finding interesting and new ways to make the puppets attractive to potential buyers.

COMPUTERS
Computer knowledge includes Word, Excel, Access, and PowerPoint.

PERSONAL
Offer proven ability to quickly grasp and apply new concepts. Excel in motivating others to learn and grow. Excellent references. Am known for my attention to detail in all matters.

Getting Out of Teaching

Exact Name of Person
Title or Position
Name of Company
Address (no., street)
Address (city, state, zip)

Teaching Background

Teachers generally do well in career change situations because they usually offer strong communication skills. Here you see an all-purpose resume and cover letter that will help this professional explore opportunities in numerous fields. She is also using this letter to reply to a specific ad she has noticed for an executive director of a nonprofit organization. The ad asked for salary history, and you can see how she handled her response to that question by reading the last paragraph in her cover letter.

Dear Exact Name of Person: (or Dear Sir or Madam if answering a blind ad.)

I would appreciate an opportunity to talk with you soon about how I could contribute to your organization through my outstanding management, communication, and organizational skills. I am responding to your advertisement in the newspaper for an Executive Director of a nonprofit organization.

While most of my experience is in education and I am a successful classroom teacher, I have been singled out on numerous occasions to develop and manage special projects, contribute to management teams, and solve problems. I have been chosen ahead of more experienced professionals to take over where others have been unsuccessful and correct problems when services were not being provided up to standards. As a teacher I have become known for creativity and resourcefulness. For example, I transformed the "Terrific Kids" program from an ineffective operation into a well-organized program. I am an excellent writer and have utilized my writing skills to prepare several successful grants which have helped school systems acquire new technology and new equipment.

You would find me in person to be an individual who is capable of dealing with the public tactfully and graciously while making sound decisions quickly. I offer a proven ability to bring out the best in others as a team leader or as a strong contributor to group efforts.

If you can use an articulate individual known for resourcefulness, initiative, and relentless follow-through when managing any task or activity, I hope you will contact me soon to arrange a brief meeting at your convenience to discuss your current and future needs and how I might serve them. I can provide outstanding references at the appropriate time, and I would be delighted to discuss the private details of my salary history with you in person.

Sincerely yours,

Margaret Frances Stieg

MARGARET FRANCES STIEG

1110½ Hay Street, Fayetteville, NC 28305 • preppub@aol.com • (910) 483-6611

OBJECTIVE   To contribute to an organization that can use a mature professional known for possessing a friendly and enthusiastic personality and being truly interested in other people as well as for resourcefulness, creativity, and the ability to handle pressure, stress, and emergencies.

EDUCATION   **B.S., Elementary Education,** Butler University, Indianapolis, IN, 1992.
- Completed additional course work in accounting, business law, and economics.
- Maintained a GPA of at least 3.65 in all elementary education courses.

EXPERIENCE   **PROGRAM DEVELOPMENT SPECIALIST** and **EDUCATOR**. Toole County Board of Education, Indianapolis, IN (1995-present). Was handpicked by the school's principal to participate in leadership roles and develop special programs designed to build morale and self confidence in students on the basis of my success as a first-grade teacher.
- Transformed the "Terrific Kids" program from complete disorganization and chaos to a respected, well-organized method of singling out children for their accomplishments.
- Coordinated the efforts of a committee which planned programs and assemblies honoring successful academic efforts, attendance records, and other achievements.
- Honed my organizational skills planning three assemblies each nine weeks period to include decorating, ordering and stocking supplies, and assigning responsibilities to teachers and staff members in order to achieve success.
- Designed a form for maintaining statistics which in turn made preparing reports easier and less time consuming and helped in prioritizing for better time management.
- Selected to receive special training in developmental education, applied my communication skills while presenting county-wide staff development courses.
- Wrote a grant which was approved and resulted in funds for purchasing microscopes for first grade classes.
- Contributed the "voice" for a video produced by the county which is currently available at school libraries and is recommended for people moving into Toole County.
- Coordinated an international dinner which represented ten countries.
- Contributed my time as a teacher for an after-school reading program for fourth graders.

TEACHER. Toole County Board of Education, Indianapolis, IN (1994-95). Was specially selected to step in after the school year had begun and provide continuity for reading and math classes for fourth-grade students.
- Provided guidance and supervision for two student teachers completing their internships by preparing lesson plans and gaining exposure in actual classroom settings.

CURRICULUM DESIGNER. Sandford County Schools, Indianapolis, IN (1993). Displayed my versatility working with students ranging from academically gifted to learning disabled.
- Was chosen to contribute to the development of a communication skills curriculum.

EDUCATOR. Mayer County Schools, Indianapolis, IN (1992). Learned how to work within the strict guidelines of a federal government sponsored program providing instruction concentrating on math and science curriculum.
- Completed workshops emphasizing techniques of computer-assisted and manipulative instruction and applied these techniques in a classroom with seven computers.

PERSONAL   In excellent health, am interested in physical fitness and hold certification in aerobics, creative floor work and conditioning, and choreography. Have demonstrated skills as a public speaker. Trained in first aid and have the ability to react quickly in emergencies.

Getting Out of Teaching

Date

Once you realize that the occupation or profession or career field isn't your "fit," you must take some action, even if it is simply exploring options. There is no reason to stay with a career field that you don't enjoy. This teaching professional is stressing management and problem-solving skills which should be transferable to most industries.

Dear Sir or Madam:

With the enclosed resume, I would like to express my interest in exploring employment opportunities with your organization and make you aware of my strong skills and abilities.

As you will see from my resume, I have earned a Bachelor of Science degree as well as a Master's degree, and I have applied my knowledge as a teacher. While I have thoroughly enjoyed the challenge of educating young minds and stimulating young children to excel academically, I have made the decision to change careers and transfer my skills into another arena. I have acquired a reputation as an outstanding communicator, problem solver, and organizer, and I can provide outstanding personal and professional references at the appropriate time.

During my leisure time, I have gravitated toward volunteer work in which I could contribute to the well being of others. With strong organizational skills as well as a high degree of intelligence, I have become skilled at managing projects which required me to make prudent decisions about the best use of scarce resources. I have been told numerous times during my life that I have a "natural" sales personality. Indeed, I believe much of what I did as a teacher was to "sell" concepts and ideas to both students and their families. While working on numerous school committees and task forces, I became known as a resourceful problem solver who could always be counted on to come up with fresh ideas about how to implement new programs.

If my considerable talents and skills interest you, I hope you will contact me to suggest a time when we might meet. I am sure that it would be an honor to learn more about your fine organization, and I hope I will have the pleasure of meeting you. Thank you in advance for your time and professional courtesies.

Yours sincerely,

Nancy Goguen

NANCY GOGUEN

1110 1/2 Hay Street, Fayetteville, NC 28305　•　preppub@aol.com　•　(910) 483-6611

OBJECTIVE	To benefit an organization that can use an articulate and outgoing professional with outstanding written and oral communication skills along with strong natural abilities in the areas of public relations, customer service, management, and sales.
EDUCATION	**Master's degree in Education,** Ohio State University, Columbus, OH, 1989.
	Bachelor of Science in Social Service, Ohio State University, Columbus, OH, 1984.
	Completed two years of course work toward Master's degree in Counseling, Ohio University, Athens, OH.
	Extensive training in arbitration, mediation, and conflict resolution techniques.
EXPERIENCE	**EDUCATOR.** Lockton Public Schools and Miller County Schools, Ohio (1997-00). Excelled in all aspects of this job teaching math, social studies, art, science, reading, and other subjects to second graders.

- Refined my management skills in training and supervising a Teacher's Assistant.
- Played a key role in developing programs to motivate students to excel while working as a member of the Motivational/Academic Committee.
- Served on the committee to develop intervention strategies for "at risk" students.
- Was well known for my nurturing and caring personality as well as for my ability to inspire and motivate students.

GRADUATE STUDENT. Ohio University, Athens, OH (1993-97). Worked part-time in customer service positions while also completing course work towards a Master's degree in Counseling.

- Learned how to counsel individuals experiencing marital, child rearing, spouse abuse, and employment problems.
- Gained knowledge related to administering the Strong-Campbell Interest Inventory and other tools designed to help job hunters figure out their best fit in the job market through determining their strongest interests.
- Completed a practicum in Career Counseling that included freshman orientation.

EDUCATOR. Ft. Goddard, OH (1987-93). At a military base, taught second and third grade.

- Became known as a highly creative problem solver and vibrant communicator while working with a population which was culturally diverse in nature.
- Because of my enthusiastic and outgoing nature, was appointed to numerous committees which developed new programs aimed at strengthening internal and external communication, motivating students to aim for excellence, and integrating new technology in the classroom.

Other experience: In my leisure time, have provided leadership to community organizations; was a popular counselor at the Women's Center in Athens.

COMPUTERS	Knowledgeable of computers and possess the ability to rapidly master new software and applications; familiar with Microsoft Word and conversant with Internet.
PERSONAL	Although I have loved teaching and excelled in educating young minds, I have decided that I wish to transfer my skills into a new arena in which I can contribute to an organization that can use a dynamic self-starter with unlimited personal initiative.

Getting Out of Teaching

Date

Exact Name of Person
Exact Title
Exact Name of Company
Address
City, State, Zip

Dear Exact Name of Person: (or Dear Sir or Madam if answering a blind ad):

With the enclosed resume, I would like to make you aware of my interest in applying my talent for effectively presenting ideas and my exceptional communication skills for the benefit of an organization that can use an articulate young professional. I have been interested in pharmaceutical sales for some time, and I have decided to explore career opportunities within that field.

As you will see from my resume, I am currently excelling as a teacher and have made significant contributions to my school's growing success. I have succeeded in every aspect of the teaching profession and have become an individual to whom other educators have turned in order to have their point of view expressed. For example, I was asked by the principal to serve as county representative to the Northern Association for Accreditation of Schools and Colleges. I have also been named grade-level chairperson because of my leadership ability and proven skills in team management. Although I have enjoyed the challenge of educating young minds and have been told that I am one of the "best and brightest" members of the teaching profession, I have decided that I wish to embark on a career that will make use of my sales, public relations, and marketing abilities.

I am hoping that you will give me an opportunity to meet with you briefly in person because I am confident that you would find me to be a vivacious, congenial, and enthusiastic professional who could become a valuable member of your organization. I hope you will call or write me soon to suggest a time when we might meet to discuss your goals and how my background might serve your needs. I thank you in advance for your time and professional courtesies.

Sincerely yours,

Beverly Patton

BEVERLY PATTON

1110½ Hay Street, Fayetteville, NC 28305　•　preppub@aol.com　•　(910) 483-6611

OBJECTIVE　　To benefit an organization that can use an articulate, enthusiastic young professional with an outgoing personality and exceptional communication skills who offers a background of excellence in education as well as in community and civic activities.

EDUCATION　　**Bachelor of Science**, Wright State University, Dayton, OH, 1988.
- Maintained a 3.2 GPA overall, 3.6 in my major.

Graduated from Dayton High School, Dayton, OH, 1984; was a finalist in the Miss Dayton Beauty Pageant and was named **Miss Congeniality.**

CERTIFICATIONS　　Earned Ohio Teacher Academy Certification, 1997; certified as a Mentor Teacher, 1997.

EXPERIENCE　　*With Butler County Schools, have built a reputation as a loyal, enthusiastic and gifted educator, 1988-present:*

TEACHER. Warf Elementary, Dayton, OH (1994-present). Currently excelling in this position providing daily instruction to a diverse population of kindergarten students; implement lesson plans designed to foster individual learning styles and promote student mastery of basic skills and concepts.
- As grade-level chairperson, meet weekly with teachers to distribute information and develop lesson plans for use in all kindergarten classes.
- Played a key role in the school's achieving status as an **exemplary school** for the 1997-1998 school year, and an **exemplary school of distinction** for the 1998-1999 school year.
- Utilize my exceptional interpersonal and communication skills while interacting successfully with administrators, teachers, and parents, as well as with my students.

TEACHER. Young Elementary, Dayton, OH (1988-1994). Excelled in this challenging position, providing motivation and effective instruction to children at a school in one of the most economically depressed areas of the county.
- Planned and executed instructional plans for the subjects which I taught, developing visual aides and other tools for use in the classroom.
- Served as **county representative** for the Northern Association for Accreditation of Schools and Colleges; accepted additional responsibility as a School Improvement Team Member and Grade Level Chairperson.
- **Selected as one of only three teachers** who were rehired after the entire staff was displaced for a special project; passed a rigorous interview process to remain at Young.
- Assisted the Superintendent and Principal as part of the interview committee that examined prospective staff members applying at the school.

ASSISTANT TEACHER. Theodore Peary Elementary, Dayton, OH (1988). Worked with the exceptional children's program, quickly mastering time management and planning skills necessary to prepare lesson materials and run an organized, efficient classroom; developed a strong rapport with parents and other teachers.

CHILD CARE PROVIDER. Baptist Church, Dayton, OH (1986-1988). While still attending college, excelled in this position providing educational activities to children from infants to adolescents at this local church day care center.

PERSONAL　　A native and permanent resident of the Dayton area, have developed an extensive network of personal and professional contacts throughout the community. In my spare time, have modeled in local fashion shows. Excellent references are available upon request.

Getting Out of Teaching

Exact Name of Person
Title or Position
Name of Company
Address (no., street)
Address (city, state, zip)

Aiming for Social Services

This teacher wants out of the classroom but wishes to continue a lifestyle of helping others in a nonprofit arena. Therefore, she is seeking to transfer her skills into a social services area or into nonprofit management.

Dear Exact Name of Person: (or Dear Sir or Madam if answering a blind ad.)

I would appreciate an opportunity to talk with you soon about how I could contribute to your organization through my experience and administrative skills related to the social services and mental health field.

As you will see from my resume, I have been involved since childhood in helping others as a role model and mentor. While earning my B.S. degree in Marketing and my A.A. in Business Administration, I worked with troubled youth and convinced many young people that hard work and a positive attitude combined with staying in school can overcome a bad start in life.

For the past two years after graduating from college, I have worked in classroom and camp environments with children who have varying disabilities including autism, mental retardation, cerebral palsy, and Down's Syndrome. As a teacher in a classroom of behaviorally disturbed children in Nebraska, I learned how to develop and implement effective lesson plans for disruptive students. As a teacher with the Perry County School System, I taught reading to autistic and mentally handicapped children and, on my own initiative, I learned sign language in order to help a child with Down's Syndrome learn to better communicate in his world. Most recently I was recruited by a classroom teacher for autistic students as one of seven staff members responsible for starting up a new summer program for autistic children and youth aged 4-20.

If we meet in person, you will see that I am an outgoing young professional with excellent communication skills and a very positive attitude. I truly believe that hard work and a positive attitude can help people overcome even the most disadvantaged childhood, and I take pride in the fact that I have helped many youth get off the wrong track and set high goals for themselves.

I hope you will write or call me soon to suggest a time when we might meet to discuss your goals and needs and how I might serve them. I feel certain that I could become a valuable and productive member of your team.

Sincerely yours,

Suzanne Justice

SUZANNE JUSTICE

1110½ Hay Street, Fayetteville, NC 28305 • preppub@aol.com • (910) 483-6611

OBJECTIVE

To benefit an organization that can use a dynamic and articulate young professional who sincerely enjoys helping others while utilizing my strong organizational skills, computer knowledge, and thoroughly positive attitude.

EDUCATION

Bachelor of Science degree in **Marketing**, University of Nebraska—Lincoln, 1994.
Associate of Arts degree in **Business Administration**, University of Nebraska—Lincoln, 1992.

EXPERIENCE

ASSISTANT TO THE DIRECTOR & TEACHER. Camp Cloud Autistic Camp, Lincoln, NE (1995-present). Was specially recruited by a classroom teacher for autistic students as one of seven staff members to assist in starting up and implementing a new summer camp for autistic children which was funded by Jessimine County Mental Health, grants, and donations.
- Planned and implemented activities for children and youth aged 4-20.
- As the youngest member of the teaching/administrative team, have won the respect of my peers for my creativity, reliability, and willingness to always "go the extra mile."
- Helped children learn behavior skills while involving them in activities that promoted their academic, physical, and social development.
- Strongly expressed and implemented my belief that autistic children, like all children, need to learn and use good manners.

SUBSTITUTE TEACHER. Perry County Schools, Lincoln, NE (1995-96). Began as a substitute teacher with the Perry County System and taught reading skills to elementary children aged five to 11 years.
- Earned widespread respect among teachers and administrators for my highly refined public speaking skills as well as my positive attitude.

SUBSTITUTE TEACHER. Muncie County Schools, Lincoln, NE (1995). For children aged kindergarten-grade 12, provided instruction based on daily lesson plans; learned to prepare and implement effective lesson plans for classrooms containing children with behavioral problems.
- Instilled in children the concept that hard work and a good attitude are the keys to success in life, and that you can overcome disadvantages in your background through initiative and attitude.

Other experience: While in college, worked as a mentor/counselor three days a week with troubled youth; taught them that one can overcome a poor beginning in life and that staying in school is essential to happiness and success.
- Believe I helped many youth discover hope and set new goals in life.
- Have a strong "helping instinct" which I have expressed through volunteer roles in programs including Feed the Homeless, Adopt a Family, All Sports Youth Program, and as Secretary and Teacher in my Sunday School program at Dragon Bay Missionary Baptist Church.

COMPUTERS

Excellent computer operations skills; utilize Windows and WordPerfect.

PERSONAL

Believe that my strong religious convictions are the foundation of my strong personal qualities which include determination to excel and persistence in achieving goals.

Getting Out of Teaching

Date

Exact Name of Person
Title or Position
Name of Company
Address (number and street)
Address (city, state, and ZIP)

Teaching Background

You can compare and
contrast the cover
letters and resumes of
the teachers who
appear consecutively in
this section to see how
these individuals
describe themselves.
This is a good resume
to show how to market
your volunteer
experience in order to
demonstrate your
abilities and interests
outside the field you
are trying to exit.

Dear Exact Name of Person: (or Dear Sir or Madam if answering a blind ad.)

Can you use an energetic, and intelligent young professional who offers a reputation as a talented and persuasive communicator who can effectively market concepts to others? I am known as a detail-oriented individual who is determined to excel, and I offer the proven organizational skills which are required to carry transform concepts into operating realities.

As you will see from my enclosed resume, I have been effective in teaching positions and volunteer roles which called for the ability to "sell" ideas and persuade others. With a keen eye for detail and strong time management abilities, I offer management and communication skills which would transfer to many other environments.

While attending Atlanta Metropolitan College in Atlanta where I was a Dean's List student, I refined my time management skills while strengthening my public relations, communications, and project management abilities. I served simultaneously as a junior high school math tutor, coordinator for freshmen orientation activities, and volunteer in the pediatric section of the Emory University Hospital.

From my resume you will gather the facts about my success as an educator but what may not be as obvious is the fact that I possess a strong interest in sales and marketing. The qualities that have made me effective as a teacher will, I am confident, help me become successful in a new field: my persuasive style of communication, my ability to make others at ease in a variety of situations, my sincere concern for the individuals I am trying to serve, and my persistent dedication to quality results.

I hope you will welcome my call soon to arrange a brief meeting at your convenience to discuss your current and future needs and how I might serve them. Thank you in advance for your time.

Sincerely yours,

Deirdre R. Hackett

Alternate last paragraph:
I hope you will call or write me soon to suggest a time convenient for us to meet and discuss your current and future needs and how I might serve them. Thank you in advance for your time.

DEIRDRE R. HACKETT

1110 ½ Hay Street, Fayetteville, NC 28305   (910) 483-6611

OBJECTIVE

To offer a reputation as a detail-oriented, well-organized professional with excellent written and verbal communication and sales skills to a business in need of a quick thinker who is known as a talented manager of human, material, and fiscal resources.

EXPERIENCE

ADMINISTRATIVE AND PLANNING SPECIALIST and **CLASSROOM TEACHER.** Kappel Primary School, Atlanta, GA (1995-present). As a fifth grade teacher, handle a wide variety of administrative, budgeting, public relations, and management activities in addition to preparing lessons and working with approximately 26 students on a daily basis.

- Helped prepare an annual operating budget: conducted research and prioritized needs resulting in $134,570 being allocated for personnel and $7,630 for maintenance.
- Wrote material which was used on local radio stations and excelled in selling my ideas on numerous subjects to others.
- Planned and organized lessons for integrated units and developed a discipline plan.
- Supervised and oversaw the performance of one assistant.
- Applied organizational skills and patience while coordinating various field trips.
- Conducted twice-weekly tutoring sessions for students with problems.
- Maintained open communication with parents of my students so that accomplishments and problem areas could be fully discussed and acted on.
- Applied my organizational skills planning and carrying out seasonal parties for 72 faculty and staff members as well as an awards banquet for 200 people.

PROJECT COORDINATOR. Jaycees, Atlanta, GA (1995-present). Enjoy giving my time to help in planning and carrying out various service projects ranging from organizing a Halloween haunted trail, to visiting an area boys home, to participating in sharing ideas with other chapters, to planning a Christmas party for 500 people.

Strengthened public relations, communications, and organizational abilities while learning to manage my time effectively in part-time and volunteer positions during college:

STUDENT TEACHER. Atlanta Metropolitan College, Atlanta, GA (1994). Learned how to manage activities for a 28-student fourth grade classroom at Kallin Elementary School.

- Gained a strong base of experience with Macintosh computers with CD-ROM as well as VCRs and camcorders used to make presentations and conduct classroom activities.

TUTOR. Liza Middle School, Atlanta, GA (1993). As a volunteer for seventh grade math classes, prepared lessons and worked with at-risk students to help them improve their skills and learn how to develop good study habits.

EDUCATION & TRAINING

B.A., Psychology and Education, Atlanta Metropolitan College, Atlanta, GA, 1994.

- Placed on the Dean's List with a GPA above 3.5 for three semesters.

Excelled in more than 300 hours of training in areas including conflict resolution as well as in special techniques for teaching both gifted and learning disabled students.

SKILLS

Operate standard office equipment including telephones, typewriters, copiers, and computers using WordPerfect, Windows, MECC, and Print Shop software; am familiar with audiovisual equipment such as projectors, laser disc panels, and camcorders.

PERSONAL

Have a working knowledge of the French language. Easily adapt to changing situations.

Getting Out of Teaching

Date

Exact Name of Person
Title or Position
Name of Company
Address (no., street)
Address (city, state, zip)

From Probation Services to Private Industry

There are a variety of situations and emotions that can spark the desire for a career change. In the case of Cynthia Willis, she found herself increasingly uncomfortable working in an environment in which she dealt with adult offenders in the criminal justice system. She used this cover letter and resume to attract potential employers in a variety of industries, and she finally accepted a job in the insurance industry as a claims adjuster.

Dear Exact Name of Person: (or Dear Sir or Madam if answering a blind ad.)

With the enclosed resume and this letter of introduction, I would like to begin the process of formally applying for the job you recently advertised as a program manager.

As I believe you will see from my resume, I offer the skills, experience, and personal qualities which you are seeking. Since graduating with my B.A. degree, I have excelled in what is generally considered one of the most high-stress jobs in the world: teaching caseload management techniques to law enforcement officials. While teaching caseworkers how to manage their caseloads and serve clients in the parole system, I assist caseworkers in locating proper sources of referrals for all types of problems: locating employment opportunities, obtaining help for substance abuse problems, and managing personal affairs and finances. I believe my positive and cheerful attitude has been the key to my excelling in a profession known for its high "burnout" and turnover rate.

I have become skilled in finding creative solutions for difficult problems, and I can provide strong personal and professional references describing my character and professional abilities. Computer literate, I offer a reputation as a tactful and diplomatic communicator with excellent writing skills. I have become adept at working with people at all levels, from judges to police officers, while also performing liaison with attorneys, prison administrators, business managers, and private sector employers.

You would find me to be a warm and enthusiastic professional who offers an exceptionally creative approach to problem solving and public relations.

I hope you will write or call me soon to arrange a brief meeting at your convenience to discuss your current and future needs and how I might serve them. I feel certain I could become a valuable asset to your organization, and I would enjoy an opportunity to show you in person that I am the qualified individual you are seeking.

Yours sincerely,

Cynthia Willis

CYNTHIA WILLIS

1110½ Hay Street, Fayetteville, NC 28305 • preppub@aol.com • (910) 483-6611

OBJECTIVE

To contribute to an organization that can use an experienced manager who offers proven decision-making and problem-solving skills along with a reputation as a resourceful, creative, well-organized professional with excellent written and oral communication skills.

EDUCATION

Bachelor of Arts in Sociology and **Business Administration**, the University of Nevada, Reno, NV, 1996; completed this degree while working full time.
Have excelled in numerous seminars and courses related to management.
Completed extensive training at the Nevada Justice Academy, Reno, NV.

EXPERIENCE

Have become known for my ability to communicate well with others and to assist others in developing realistic strategies for solving their life problems, finding suitable employment, developing career goals, and becoming productive members of society:
ADULT PAROLE SERVICES TRAINING MANAGER. Department of Corrections, Reno, NV (1998-present). Am extremely knowledgeable of how to network and "get things done" within the legal, law enforcement, business, and social services communities; apply that knowledge while teaching techniques in caseload management to law enforcement and social services officials; also manage a personal caseload.

- Train caseworkers to assist parolees in all aspects of life management including seeking help for substance abuse problems, prospecting for and obtaining suitable employment, managing personal finances as well as personal relationships, and generally finding a "focus" in life that is meaningful and motivating.
- Am known for my compassionate attitude as well as for my tough, creative, and practical approach to solving difficult problems.
- Work with law enforcement officials at all levels, from judges to police officers, while also performing liaison with attorneys, prison administrators, business managers and employers in the private sector, and federal assistance programs of every kind.
- Excel in a job which requires constant attention to detail as I teach caseworkers to supervise numerous conditions of parole including compliance with community service, debt and fee payment obligations, and other matters.
- Have acquired excellent "crisis management" skills while dealing routinely with incidents such as threatened suicides and other volatile, high-risk situations.

ADULT PROBATION SERVICES CASE MANAGER. Department of Corrections, Reno, NV (1994-98). Became skilled in the counseling and supervision of offenders placed on probation by the court system; enforced conditions of parole.

- Became known for my tact and diplomacy as well as for my excellent writing skills.
- Excelled in a profession generally regarded as very stressful and which has a very high turnover and "burnout" rate.
- Established an impressive track record of success in assisting dysfunctional people.

CERTIFICATIONS

Am Department of Corrections certified in unarmed self defense.
Am CPR certified; Certified in Arrest, Search, and Seizure.

SKILLS

Computer literate and experienced in working with various types of software.
Skilled in operating electronic house arrest equipment.

PERSONAL

Pride myself on my positive and cheerful attitude, and believe that a healthy mental attitude is the key to dealing with life's difficulties in a positive manner. Excellent references.

ABOUT THE EDITOR

Anne McKinney holds an MBA from the Harvard Business School and a BA in English from the University of North Carolina at Chapel Hill. A noted public speaker, writer, and teacher, she is the senior editor for PREP's business and career imprint, which bears her name. Early titles in the Anne McKinney Career Series (now called the Real-Resumes Series) published by PREP include: *Resumes and Cover Letters That Have Worked, Resumes and Cover Letters That Have Worked for Military Professionals, Government Job Applications and Federal Resumes, Cover Letters That Blow Doors Open,* and *Letters for Special Situations.* Her career titles and how-to resume-and-cover-letter books are based on the expertise she has acquired in 20 years of working with job hunters. Her valuable career insights have appeared in publications of the "Wall Street Journal" and other prominent newspapers and magazines.

Judeo-Christian Ethics Series

BACK IN TIME

Patty Sleem

Published in large print hardcover by Simon & Schuster's Thorndike Press as a Thorndike Christian Mystery in November 1998.
(306 pages)
"An engrossing look at the discrimination faced by female ministers." – *Library Journal*
Trade paperback 1-885288-03-4—$16.00

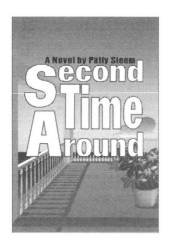

SECOND TIME AROUND

Patty Sleem

"Sleem explores the ugliness of suicide and murder, obsession and abuse, as well as Christian faith and values. An emotional and suspenseful read reflecting modern issues and concerns." – *Southern Book Trade*
(336 pages)
Foreign rights sold in Chinese.
Hardcover 1-885288-00-X—$25.00
Trade paperback 1-885288-05-0—$17.00

A GENTLE BREEZE FROM GOSSAMER WINGS

Gordon Beld

Pol Pot was the Khmer Rouge leader whose reign of terror caused the deaths of up to 2 million Cambodians in the mid-1970s. He masterminded an extreme, Maoist-inspired revolution in which those Cambodians died in mass executions, and from starvation and disease. This book of historical fiction shows the life of one refugee from this reign of genocide.
(320 pages)
"I'm pleased to recommend *A Gentle Breeze From Gossamer Wings*. Every Christian in America should read it. It's a story you won't want to miss – and it could change your life."
—Robert H. Schuller, Pastor, Crystal Cathedral
Trade paperback 1-885288-07-7—$18.00

BIBLE STORIES FROM THE OLD TESTAMENT

Katherine Whaley

Familiar and not-so-familiar Bible stories told by an engaging storyteller in a style guaranteed to delight and inform. Includes stories about Abraham, Cain and Abel, Jacob and David, Moses and the Exodus, Judges, Saul, David, and Solomon.
(272 pages)
"Whaley tells these tales in such a way that they will appeal to the young adult as well as the senior citizen."
– *Independent Publisher*
Trade paperback 1-885288-12-3—$18.00

WHAT THE BIBLE SAYS ABOUT... Words that can lead to success and happiness

Patty Sleem

A daily inspirational guide as well as a valuable reference when you want to see what the Bible says about Life and Living, Toil and Working, Problems and Suffering, Anger and Arguing, Self-Reliance and Peace of Mind, Justice and Wrong-Doing, Discipline and Self-Control, Wealth and Power, Knowledge and Wisdom, Pride and Honor, Gifts and Giving, Husbands and Wives, Friends and Neighbors, Children, Sinning and Repenting, Judgment and Mercy, Faith and Religion, and Love.
(192 pages)
Hardcover 1-885288-02-6—$20.00

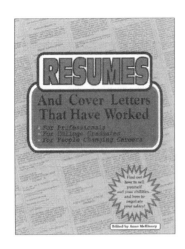

RESUMES AND COVER LETTERS THAT HAVE WORKED

Anne McKinney, Editor

More than 100 resumes and cover letters written by the world's oldest resume-writing company. Resumes shown helped real people not only change jobs but also transfer their skills and experience to other industries and fields. An indispensable tool in an era of downsizing when research shows that most of us have not one but three distinctly different careers in our working lifetime. (272 pages)

"Distinguished by its highly readable samples...essential for library collections." – *Library Journal*

Trade paperback 1-885288-04-2—$25.00

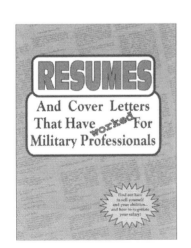

RESUMES AND COVER LETTERS THAT HAVE WORKED FOR MILITARY PROFESSIONALS

Anne McKinney, Editor

Military professionals from all branches of the service gain valuable experience while serving their country, but they need resumes and cover letters that translate their skills and background into "civilian language." This is a book showing more than 100 resumes and cover letters written by a resume-writing service in business for nearly 20 years which specializes in "military translation." (256 pages)

"A guide that significantly translates veterans' experience into viable repertoires of achievement." – *Booklist*

Trade paperback 1-885288-06-9—$25.00

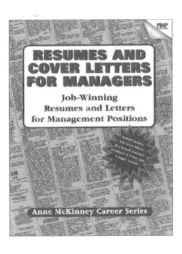

RESUMES AND COVER LETTERS FOR MANAGERS

Anne McKinney, Editor

Destined to become the bible for managers who want to make sure their resumes and cover letters open the maximum number of doors while helping them maximize in the salary negotiation process. From office manager to CEO, managers trying to relocate to or from these and other industries and fields will find helpful examples: Banking, Agriculture, School Systems, Human Resources, Restaurants, Manufacturing, Hospitality Industry, Automotive, Retail, Telecommunications, Police Force, Dentistry, Social Work, Academic Affairs, Non-Profit Organizations, Childcare, Sales, Sports, Municipalities, Rest Homes, Medicine and Healthcare, Business Operations, Landscaping, Customer Service, MIS, Quality Control, Teaching, the Arts, and Self-Employed. (288 pages)

Trade paperback 1-885288-10-7—$25.00

GOVERNMENT JOB APPLICATIONS AND FEDERAL RESUMES:
Federal Resumes, KSAs, Forms 171 and 612, and Postal Applications

Anne McKinney, Editor

Getting a government job can lead to job security and peace of mind. The problem is that getting a government job requires extensive and complex paperwork. Now, for the first time, this book reveals the secrets and shortcuts of professional writers in preparing job-winning government applications such as these:

The Standard Form 171 (SF 171) – several complete samples
The Optional Form 612 (OF 612) – several complete samples
KSAs – samples of KSAs tailored to jobs ranging from the GS-5 to GS-12
Ranking Factors – how-to samples
Postal Applications
Wage Grade paperwork
Federal Resumes – see the different formats required by various government agencies. (272 pages)

Trade paperback 1-885288-11-5—$25.00

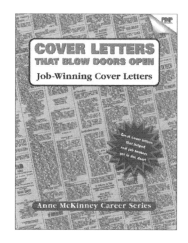

COVER LETTERS THAT BLOW DOORS OPEN
Anne McKinney, Editor
Although a resume is important, the cover letter is the first impression. This book is a compilation of great cover letters that helped real people get in the door for job interviews against stiff competition. Included are letters that show how to approach employers when you're moving to a new area, how to write a cover letter when you're changing fields or industries, and how to arouse the employer's interest in dialing your number first from a stack of resumes. (272 pages)
Trade paperback 1-885288-13-1—$25.00

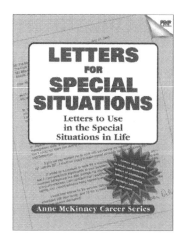

LETTERS FOR SPECIAL SITUATIONS
Anne McKinney, Editor
Sometimes it is necessary to write a special letter for a special situation in life. You will find great letters to use as models for business and personal reasons including: letters asking for a raise, letters of

resignation, letters of reference, letters notifying a vendor of a breach of contract, letter to a Congressman, letters of complaint, letters requesting reinstatement to an academic program, follow-up letters after an interview, letters requesting bill consolidation, letters of reprimand to marginal employees, letters requesting financial assistance or a grant, letters to professionals disputing their charges, collections letters, thank-you letters, and letters to accompany resumes in job-hunting. (256 pages)
Trade paperback 1-885288-09-3—$25.00

PREP Publishing Order Form

You may purchase any of our titles from your favorite bookseller! Or send a check or money order or your credit card number for the total amount*, plus $3.20 postage and handling, to PREP, Box 66, Fayetteville, NC 28302. If you have a question about any of our titles, feel free to e-mail us at preppub@aol.com and visit our website at http://www.prep-pub.com

Name: _____

Phone #: _____

Address: _____

_____

E-mail address: _____

Payment Type: ☐ Check/Money Order ☐ Visa ☐ MasterCard

Credit Card Number: _____ Expiration Date: _____

Check items you are ordering:

☐ $25.00—RESUMES AND COVER LETTERS THAT HAVE WORKED.

☐ $25.00—RESUMES AND COVER LETTERS THAT HAVE WORKED FOR MILITARY PROFESSIONALS.

☐ $25.00—RESUMES AND COVER LETTERS FOR MANAGERS.

☐ $25.00—GOVERNMENT JOB APPLICATIONS AND FEDERAL RESUMES: Federal Resumes, KSAs, Forms 171 and 612, and Postal Applications.

☐ $25.00—COVER LETTERS THAT BLOW DOORS OPEN.

☐ $25.00—LETTERS FOR SPECIAL SITUATIONS.

☐ $16.00—BACK IN TIME. Patty Sleem

☐ $17.00—(trade paperback) SECOND TIME AROUND. Patty Sleem

☐ $25.00—(hardcover) SECOND TIME AROUND. Patty Sleem

☐ $18.00—A GENTLE BREEZE FROM GOSSAMER WINGS. Gordon Beld

☐ $18.00—BIBLE STORIES FROM THE OLD TESTAMENT. Katherine Whaley

☐ $20.00—WHAT THE BIBLE SAYS ABOUT... *Words that can lead to success and happiness.* Patty Sleem

New titles!

☐ $16.95—REAL-RESUMES FOR SALES. Anne McKinney, Editor

☐ $16.95—REAL-RESUMES FOR TEACHERS. Anne McKinney, Editor

☐ $16.95—REAL-RESUMES FOR CAREER CHANGERS. Anne McKinney, Editor

☐ $16.95—REAL-RESUMES FOR STUDENTS. Anne McKinney, Editor

☐ $16.95—REAL ESSAYS FOR COLLEGE AND GRAD SCHOOL. Anne McKinney, Editor

☐ $10.95—KIJABE An African Historical Saga. Pally Dhillon

_____ **TOTAL ORDERED (add $3.20 for postage and handling)**

Volume discounts on large orders. (910) 483-6611 for more information.

THE MISSION OF PREP PUBLISHING IS TO PUBLISH BOOKS AND OTHER PRODUCTS WHICH ENRICH PEOPLE'S LIVES AND HELP THEM OPTIMIZE THE HUMAN EXPERIENCE. OUR STRONGEST LINES ARE OUR JUDEO-CHRISTIAN ETHICS SERIES AND OUR BUSINESS & CAREER SERIES.

Would you like to explore the possibility of having PREP's writing team create a resume for you similar to the ones in this book?

For a brief free consultation, call 910-483-6611
or send $4.00 to receive our Job Change Packet to
PREP, Department Teachers, Box 66, Fayetteville, NC 28302.

QUESTIONS OR COMMENTS? E-MAIL US AT PREPPUB@AOL.COM

Made in the USA
Lexington, KY
27 February 2014